THE CITY THAT WOULD NOT DIE

By RICHARD COLLIER

CAPTAIN OF THE QUEENS
  (with Capt. Harry Grattidge)

TEN THOUSAND EYES

THE CITY THAT WOULD NOT DIE
  The Bombing of London, May 10–11, 1941

THE CITY
That Would Not Die.

THE BOMBING OF LONDON
May 10 - 11, 1941

RICHARD COLLIER

New York

E P Dutton and Company Inc

1 9 6 0

FIRST PUBLISHED IN THE UNITED STATES 1960 BY E. P. DUTTON & CO., INC.
Copyright, ©, 1959 by RICHARD COLLIER
All rights reserved. Printed in the U.S.A.

FIRST EDITION

Library of Congress Catalog Card Number: 59-12579

To those
who wondered
what it was like
—and to those
who knew

The spirit of the English people enables it to carry through to victory any struggle that it once enters upon, no matter how long such a struggle may last or however great the sacrifice that may be necessary

—A<small>DOLF</small> H<small>ITLER</small>

The worst attack was the last

—W<small>INSTON</small> C<small>HURCHILL</small>

CONTENTS

ILLUSTRATIONS

MAP
Pages 10 and 11

THE CITY THAT WOULD NOT DIE

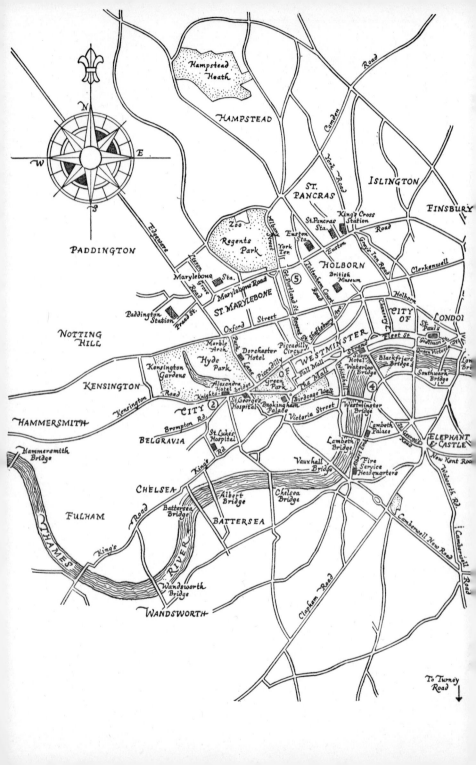

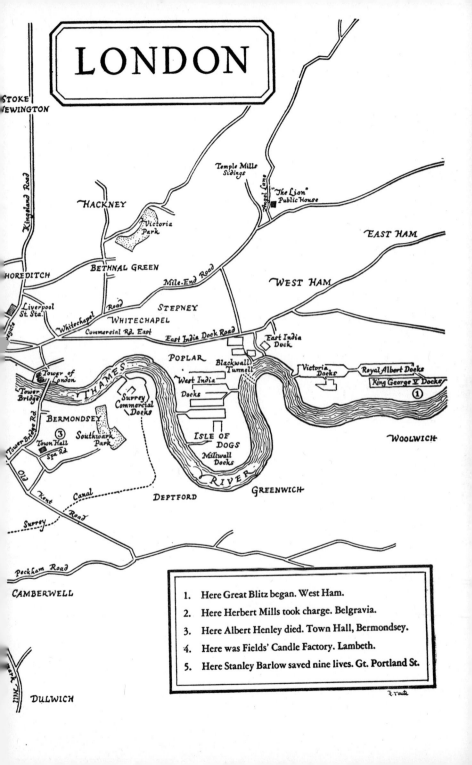

LONDON

STOKE NEWINGTON

Kingsland Road

HACKNEY

Victoria Park

Temple Mills Sidings

Angel Lane

"The Lion" Public House

EAST HAM

BETHNAL GREEN

HOREDITCH

Liverpool St. Sta.

Mile-End Road

WEST HAM

Whitechapel Road

STEPNEY

WHITECHAPEL

Commercial Rd. East

East India Dock Road

East India Dock

POPLAR

Blackwall Tunnell

Victoria Docks

Royal Albert Docks

King George V Docks

①

Tower of London

West India Docks

THAMES

Tower Bridge

Surrey Commercial Docks

BERMONDSEY

③

Town Hall Spa Rd.

Southwark Park

ISLE OF DOGS

Millwall Docks

WOOLWICH

Tower Bridge Rd.

Old

Kent

Canal

RIVER

GREENWICH

Surrey

Road

DEPTFORD

Peckham Road

CAMBERWELL

1. Here Great Blitz began. West Ham.
2. Here Herbert Mills took charge. Belgravia.
3. Here Albert Henley died. Town Hall, Bermondsey.
4. Here was Fields' Candle Factory. Lambeth.
5. Here Stanley Barlow saved nine lives. Gt. Portland St.

DULWICH

R. route

CHAPTER ONE

"Go Down to St. Paul's, Boy"

8 A.M.—12 noon

PALE morning sunlight flooded the back bedroom of No. 48 Turney Road, Dulwich, South London, and Marguerita Stahli awoke. It was 8.30 A.M. on a May morning, yet as she hurried to the kitchen to cook breakfast, Marguerita shivered. Overnight the wind had veered northeast; people said later they had never known a spring so cold.

As Marguerita spooned a soft-boiled egg she leafed through the morning papers propped against the teapot: a quick peep at *The Daily Telegraph*, a longer browse through *The Daily Sketch*—Aunt Maud called it "The Clean and Clever." This morning, though, the *Sketch's* headlines were routine—"RAF WIPE OUT IRAKI AIR FORCE." There was no food for thought in the dateline either—Saturday, May 10, 1941.

It was now thirty-five weeks since the all-out German air bombardment of London had begun, and already it was routine, too, that the City was in a state of siege. For nine months Marguerita and 6,000,000 other Londoners had eaten breakfast and worked and gone to bed each night under threat of invasion from the greatest army on earth, encamped across the English Channel less than a hundred miles from Buckingham Palace. Already, too, it was plain that Saturdays and Sundays were assuming a sinister significance in the calendar of Reichsmarschall Hermann Goering's Luftwaffe. Eighteen weeks tomorrow since Sunday, December 29, when the square mile of the

City of London burned like a haystack. Three weeks to the day since Saturday, April 19, the heaviest raid to date, when 400 bombers made the two-way trip.

Now the raids were spread more widely apart, each raid planned as a deathblow. And tonight the moon would be full for the first time since Good Friday.

But on this Saturday morning none of this mattered too much to Marguerita Stahli. Moonlight meant mostly what moonlight should mean to any twenty-five-year-old girl who is slim, dark, and lovely. It was the weekend, Aunt Maud, with whom she lived since the death of her father, a naturalized Swiss, was away until Monday, and she was in love. Tonight, with luck, her fiancé, Leading Aircraftman Windsor Neck, might arrive on special leave from the north, a precious forty-eight hours prised from the RAF.

Moreover, there was two days' freedom from the offices of the Church Missionary Society, where she worked as a short-hand-typist, shopping to be done, a fire to be lit. Rex, her black-and-white fox terrier, was pawing at the door, frantic for his walk. There was much to plan; a week's living to cram into two days.

So by 9.30 she had donned an old weatherproof and was pedaling to the shops on the Raleigh bicycle that Windsor had taught her to ride. At this hour the streets of the great gray capital were full of people. In long, gently-grumbling lines they queued interminably for fish, bread, sweets, a slender Sunday roast—even tomatoes at 1s. 6d each. After eighteen months of war, the keynote was a proud shabbiness. Men wore old fawn raincoats and suits that had gone unpressed for months. The women wore head scarves, fur-lined boots, and lisle stockings—like Marguerita they kept silk stockings for night and Sunday wear. And like Marguerita many wore their hair short—hairpins were hard to come by.

The streets, too, were shabby. You could not now walk more than a block without the war striking home: brick surface shelters, blasted windows, clocks without hands, mounds of yellow rubble. Moving from queue to queue along Herne Hill, Marguerita Stahli could even smell the bombing on the wind: a poisonous, always-present tang of damp plaster, coal gas, and blue London clay.

Already it seemed an old war. In the sprawling slumland of London's East End poppies and buttercups made bright splashes where the tiny yellow-brick houses had toppled in the winter's raids. Youngsters whooped through the ruins as cops-and-robbers or foraged for relics; twice that morning Bethnal Green's Town Clerk F. R. Bristow had to shoo off urchins with shrapnel to sell. Most London boroughs now held too many relics in perpetuity for owners who would never know—gold Alberts, dentists' drills, St. Christophers without number, forty ignition keys found in one man's pocket.

On this spring Saturday most people, like Marguerita Stahli, were planning nothing more complex than living another whole day. Over the hundred square miles of the County of London the mood was one of grim union, a union congealed by the blood of 18,000 Londoners who had died to date. Not many put this into words. But somehow on May 10, 1941, it was accepted that the street where you lived or worked was also the battlefield where you could die.

Most people, like true Britons, talked more of the weather and the spring flowers. In Kensington, Mrs. Isabel Penrose-Fitzgerald, a diplomat's wife, made up her diary for the Friday: "The chestnuts are just coming into bloom and Hyde Park is full of daffodils." Mrs. Olive Smith, a mobile canteen driver, thought the wind in Bayswater cut like a knife but the apple blossom was "a glorious cloud of shining whiteness." As after-thought Mrs. Penrose-Fitzgerald added: "There's very little news—the Germans *must* be preparing something."

Few were so curious. Down at Fields' Soap and Candle Factory, in the lee of Waterloo Station, the talk was all of that afternoon's Football Association Cup Final—Arsenal v. Preston North End at Wembley Stadium. Most, as Londoners, favored Arsenal's chances though no one was surprised when little

The City That Would Not Die

Jimmie Sexton, in the packing department, announced that he was working overtime instead. True, he was fire watching at the factory that night, but he would have stayed around anyway. After his flat had been bombed back in September, Sexton had sent his wife and son to the country near Cambridge. Now his camp bed was alongside his bench in the factory basement, his world reduced to a few square yards.

Sexton, a pink-cheeked leathery little Cockney from Lambeth Walk, with an explosive way of talking and gray twinkling eyes, was popular enough around the factory but a mystery man. He rarely mixed or took a pint with the lads—just worked endless hours of overtime in the hope of one day saving enough to furnish a new home. At the 11 A.M. canteen break he even took an old carrier bag, like any housewife, and set off for the street market called The Cut to do his weekend shopping—lamb chops, a pound of sausages, potatoes, spring cabbage, tinned apricots.

Now that the world had turned upside down, Jimmie Sexton was like many a Londoner—a man living on memories. They flooded back to him as he jostled through The Cut this Saturday morning—of how thirty years back he had shopped for Mum in this very market and of how different life had been then. A solid Cockney family of fifteen brought up by Dad on one golden sovereign a week; Mum's steaming bowls of giblet stew; wedding parties when aunts, cousins, and neighbors washed down plum cake with sweet port and fish and chips with nine-gallon casks of beer.

That family life had meant everything to Sexton so that tonight he was more than ready to mount guard on the factory roof within a hundred yards of Waterloo Station—a priority target if a raid came. The overtime would mean a few more shillings for *his* family.

Sexton, though, had less fears of a raid than of being bored; his young brother Bill, who lived in the basement with him and usually shared his fire-watching turn, was spending this weekend with his wife in Hertfordshire. In any case, the prospects of a raid seemed remote. The Germans must realize by this time that they could not reduce London by bombing.

Even lacking inside information, most Londoners shared this feeling. If there was more conscious courage, now the first exaltation had died, there was still a grim certainty of victory. When one Jeremiah in his repair crew that morning predicted ultimate defeat, Telephone Engineer Reg Matthews growled: "Go down to St. Paul's, boy—see them tombs and banners. We've never lost the last battle yet."

At Fighter Command Headquarters, Royal Air Force, twelve miles north on the Hertfordshire border, Air Marshal William Sholto Douglas, chief of fighter defenses, was in the same soberly confident mood. Today was one of odds and ends —a chat with Captain Riiser Larsen, chief of staff of the Norwegian Air Force, a matinee at the Haymarket Theatre—and the air chief's personal aide, Flying Officer Bob Wright, had hopes of finishing work earlier than the average 9 P.M.

As the chunky, forceful Douglas puffed at his pipe and rattled off dictation in the big pile-carpeted room overlooking the rose gardens, there seemed no reason why he shouldn't. If the Germans did plan a raid—and as yet there had been no advance warning—Douglas could call on only four night-fighter squadrons equipped with air-to-ground radar. But tonight, by 6.15 P.M., the moon would be at the full. Under those conditions, Douglas could throw twelve squadrons of day fighters, Spitfires, and Hurricanes Mark II into the battle. These might do a lot of damage on a calm, clear night with the moon well above the horizon.

As Douglas had put it to his chief administrative officer, Air Vice-Marshal Hazelton Nicholl: "For months the weather's been so foul it looked as if God was fighting on Hitler's side, but now it looks as if we've got the problem of the night bomber licked."

If the problem was licked, there were plenty remaining—as none knew better than Miss Mary Shearburn, secretary to Prime Minister Winston Churchill. Today The Old Man was

almost tractable—which always showed that things were worst
—and even growled less forcibly about the inevitable crackling
paper makes when inserted into a typewriter.

As always when the moon was full he was a long way from
London—at Ditchley Park, the eighteenth-century Oxfordshire
mansion of his friend Ronald Tree, the American-born social-
ite. Although Churchill himself scorned personal danger, those
close to him were taking no chances. On a moonlight night
both 10 Downing Street and Chequers, the official country residence of prime ministers, could prove too tempting a target.

Already Churchill had demolished an Englishman's breakfast—a man-sized sole, ham and eggs, a mountain of toast, and
jam. Now, elbows propped on a rubber pad, Cuban cigar going well, he was once more fighting the war—diving into the
special brown box reserved for top-secret papers, rumpling
through communiqués and dispatches, dictating to Mary Shearburn. An anniversary message to the Belgian premier; an
"Action This Day" memo on fighters for the Battle of Egypt;
a longer note to Roosevelt on training pilots in the United
States.

On the face of it, American Lend-Lease was the one star
shining on a dark horizon. Greece was already lost and the
bombers were pounding Alexandria. In North Africa Rommel
had forced the British back to Sollum. The lion-hearted Yugo-
slavs, on whom so many hopes had been pinned, had been forced
to give in. There was news from the Atlantic front and all of
it disastrous—almost two hundred merchantmen sunk in April,
more than double January's total and rising steadily.

It was a year to the day since the old warrior had taken office,
a year since he had promised his people nothing but blood and
toil, tears and sweat, and from a slogan this had become the
unvarnished truth.

This morning London was a city of slogans. Never for
twenty-five years had the people been so exhorted, cajoled.
Its streets were loud with hoardings and posters—"Don't Be a
Food Hog" ... "Careless Talk Costs Lives" ... "Give a Woman

"Go Down to St. Paul's, Boy"

Your Place in the Shelter." Minister of Home Security Herbert Morrison's slogan "Go To It!" flashed across at least one building in every block.

And lately a new slogan had won pride of place—"Britain Can Take It!" The City's seeming invincibility had more than just strategic significance now; if London died, a legend died with it. To Churchill and the War Cabinet the whole steady drift of American opinion toward more active involvement made it imperative to keep that legend alive.

To all this the average reaction was purest Cockney, a perverse refusal to dispense with a sense of humor. Novelty men in the Strand were selling buttons, "I've Got a Bomb Story, too!" The East London Tabernacle had a placard displayed: "If Your Knees Knock Together—Kneel on Them!" Only the incidents that had people excited showed how near the bone things were. For Barnes Businessman Jack Lippold it was a red-letter day—he'd managed to buy twenty Players' cigarettes and a bar of chocolate. In Hampstead Mrs. Monica Pitman thought a bath in five inches of tepid water worth a line in her diary.

Outsiders, too, felt a nip in the air that had no connection with the weather—a kind of tingle of expectancy. Lieutenant John Hodgkinson, a young army officer, was arriving in London for the first time since the raids began. Unconsciously, as he left Euston Station, he squared his shoulders: he was in the front line.

Dr. T. Mawby Cole, a businessman who dabbled in the occult, arriving from the north, felt it for different reasons. A month back he had predicted to an astrologers' conference that "something staggering" would happen on May 11. The last time the planets had been grouped like this, with the sun, Uranus, Saturn, Jupiter, Venus, and Mercury grouped in Taurus, directly opposite the moon in Scorpio, had ushered in an era of blood and slaughter: the onset of the Thirty Years' War and the persecution of the Huguenots.

Despite the inner tensions, old habits died hard. As always on a Saturday morning, for instance, Mrs. Margaret Daley was up early in her flat on Brighton Road, South Croydon, twelve miles from the City's center, polishing her parquet till it shone like plate glass. A motherly, carefully groomed woman in her forties, Mrs. Daley was tonight working an ambulance driving shift at the local St. Augustine's Depot—no sinecure if it came to a raid, for Croydon was a factory area. Yet the habit persisted, and Mrs. Daley was setting about her parquet just as the nuns in the Convent of the Sacred Heart of Jesus, at Mayfield, Sussex, had once taught her.

Blitz or no blitz, she wasn't easily satisfied; it would be noon before she was finished. But there was a real satisfaction in watching the soft glow steal through; it was the family cottage at Mayfield all over again, with her mother, a laundress, ladling the steaming soapy water into a zinc bath on the kitchen floor before scrubbing all nine children from head to foot. Then the ritual of Sunday best: white dresses, white calico drawers, starched white calico aprons trimmed with blue ribbon and hand-goffered frills. All her life cleanliness had come next to godliness, and Mrs. Daley was a woman close to God.

Eighteen months back she had been a waitress making good tips; now, she was an ambulance driver earning £2 a week, but something that she couldn't resist had impelled her to join. If it came to the risk, God would protect her—Mrs. Daley *knew* that—and she could no longer stomach serving expensive dinners to overfed people when she was needed more elsewhere.

Now that Bernadine, her fourteen-year-old daughter, was evacuated to the country, driving an ambulance helped her to feel right with the world—and helped her to forget the grief of a marriage that had ended in separation. Only one thing nagged gently at the back of Mrs. Daley's mind this Saturday morning: the indefinable feeling that she had yet to see the worst havoc a blitz could wreak. With one half of her she craved action—so much so that in the long, uneventful hours at St. Augustine's Depot she was the only one who never groused at Ambulance

"Go Down to St. Paul's, Boy"

Chief Harold Lock Kendell's habit of pressing the "Action Stations" buzzer to keep them on their toes.

Of course disappointment crept in when no action followed —but even scampering for the big converted Chrysler to show you were ready gave Mrs. Daley the sense of having something to do. She fretted to be busy, to be needed; on May 10, like millions of other Londoners, she had already plumbed the unglamorous truth—a blitz could be terrible, but it could be boring, too. Often for weeks on end there was only that mock summons to break the tedium. Mrs. Daley had seen routine casualties, but nothing that had been too much for her.

The paradox was that if the siren so much as sounded she was so terrified she could scarcely speak. The fear of being bombed and buried alive had paralyzed her ever since a strange wartime nightmare—when the walls of her bedroom seemed to close slowly in on her like a medieval torture chamber. Yet somehow she couldn't give up. The desire to be needed—just as her daughter had needed her, as Bernard her husband had needed her once—seemed to triumph over the fear.

Even if the blitz was over, many people felt this overriding impetus. Even in peacetime Albert George Henley, mayor of the dockland borough of Bermondsey, had been one to help others; now his whole life was a dedication. When the raids were on, he was without sleep for nights on end; working up to his knees in water, pulling away broken glass and wreckage until his bare hands streamed with blood; collapsing with sheer fatigue. He slept in the mayor's parlor at the Town Hall, often starting work still grimy from the night's raid; ate his Christmas dinner in the Control Room to remain on tap, then more work on his Air Raid Distress Fund until the siren drove him back to the street. Near to pneumonia he had even worked on from his hospital bed and was back at his desk in ten days flat.

A heavily-built, slow-spoken docker's son and a stanch trade unionist, Henley seemed to live for the smoky riverside borough where the air was always heavy with the smell of hops and salted hides.

The morning of May 10 was no exception: an hour's gardening before breakfast then back to the mayor's parlor, paying out money from his Distress Fund. Gladys, his wife, was out on welfare work this morning; usually she was always at his side to write out receipts and help fit out the homeless with clothes from the basement. It was painful work—a sad, shuffling queue of people who had lost everything, but Secretary Leonard Corder noted that everyone who went into the paneled parlor, gay with the carnations that the mayor loved, came out looking brighter. One old woman went in sobbing bitterly; she came out hooting with laughter, the mayor's arm around her shoulder.

And Henley had a busy afternoon ahead, too—a tea party followed by a long social evening at a local warden's post. Gladys hadn't seemed keen on going but Henley had promised to put in an appearance and he had never been known to break his word. Once, as mayor of the much-bombed borough, he had said: "I am the proudest man living." The kind of thing that mayors too often say, but coming from Henley it had rung true.

Meanwhile, the radio and the midday editions of the evening papers carried cheering news to all Londoners from Minister of Labor and National Service Ernest Bevin. "Night fighting," he opined, "becomes as expensive to Hitler as day fighting did a year ago." There seemed cause for jubilation, even a little complacency: in the first nine nights of May, 90 German bombers had been brought down over Britain.

A hundred miles away across the English Channel, at Vannes, in Brittany, Hauptmann Friedrich Karol Aschenbrenner was looking at the sky. He was squadron leader of *Kampfgeschwader* (Group) 100, nicknamed "The Fire Raisers," a task force of 20 German bombers whose crews, noted for their skill and daring, were all hand-picked officers. As pathfinders their function was to spotlight the target for the bombers of Air Fleets Two and Three with thousands of chandelier flares and incendiary bombs. Hence Aschenbrenner's study of the sky, for much depended on the weather. Despite the sparkling sunlight there was still plenty of low-flying cloud; the forecasters didn't put the visibility at much above six miles.

Until late afternoon, then, he must possess his soul in patience, although this wasn't easy. If the weather cleared, his orders for tonight were to set London on fire.

"You Don't Need Gloves Over England"
8 A.M.—12 noon

THE raid had been planned only ten hours before—and then almost as a whim. At midnight on the 9th a tea party was still in progress in the main salon of the Berghof, a white-painted chalet-style retreat perched on the Obersalzberg high in the Bavarian Alps. The twenty-odd guests, gathered in the darkened room around a leaping pine-log fire, were a mixed company: Generalfeldmarschall Wilhelm Keitel, head of the German Armed Forces High Command; Hans Baur, a former pilot of the Lufthansa airline; Fräulein Eva Braun; Dr. Otto Dietrich, press chief; Obergruppenfuehrer Julius Schaub; Minister of Labor Robert Ley and his wife.

Their host over the teacups: Fuehrer Adolf Hitler, Chancellor of the German Third Reich.

The tea parties had become almost routine now; the Fuehrer had suffered so long from insomnia that almost no one else in his close circle was allowed to get much rest. And tonight, in the cold, small hours of May 10, the pattern didn't vary. No smoking by order, but endless cups of tea and coffee served by S.S. men in white mess jackets; the Fuehrer continually leaping up to riddle the fire with a poker, toss on fresh logs, or fondle Blondi, his pet Alsatian bitch. The others slumped on wide, low-slung settees, grunting occasional agreement, but more often lost in private thought, watching the firelight play on the bronze bust of Wagner or glow delicately on the Botticelli nude above the mantelpiece.

"*You Don't Need Gloves Over England*"

The talk, as always, was a monologue. Already the Fuehrer had delivered homilies on religion, politics, vegetarianism, how to train dogs, Furtwängler's merits as a conductor.

Around 2 A.M., as he'd often done before, Martin Bormann, Hitler's bull-necked personal secretary, tried to liven up the proceedings. He said everything pointed to the British needing another sharp lesson. Obviously Air Marshal Sir Arthur Harris, chief of the English Bomber Command, now thought he could bomb German cities with impunity, and it was noticeable that Hermann Goering's Luftwaffe did little to prove him wrong. On the Thursday night the RAF had sent almost four hundred bombers, its largest force ever, to pound Hamburg, Bremen, Emden, and, above all, Berlin, at one and the same time. What, if anything, asked Bormann, did the Luftwaffe propose to do about it?

Then Baur, too, jumped in. For months now the policy had been reprisal—heavy raid for heavy raid. The City of London fire raid of December 29, to pay the British back for bombing Berlin over Christmas. The heavy raid of April 19 as an equalizer for the RAF's shock-punch attack on Berlin two days before. If these latest raids weren't followed up, too, the German High Command was going to look pretty small.

More logs on the fire, more cups of tea. Both Bormann and Baur could see that tonight Hitler was going to need some convincing. It wasn't that the Fuehrer didn't agree in principle—but to bomb London again in force seemed to fly in the face of his own decrees—the top-secret "Operation Barbarossa."

On June 22, one hundred and fifty divisions, German, Finnish, and Rumanian, supported by the massed bombers of Air Fleets Two and Three, were to launch a surprise all-out attack on Russia. So far as England was concerned, the order was to fly limited priority attacks—Channel convoys, industrial targets like the Rolls-Royce Aero-Engine Works at Hillington, Glasgow.

Now the interest quickened. Others in the circle—Colonel Schmundt, Hitler's chief A.D.C., Professor Morell, his doctor

—could see that tonight Bormann wasn't giving up. Just supposing the British had some inkling about "Operation Barbarossa"? Wouldn't a raid at this time serve as a powerful red herring, a suggestion that the blitz was continuing in full force? And Baur chimed in—a masterly piece of counter-strategy which only the Fuehrer could have conceived.

It wasn't that either of the two mischief-makers fully believed in the plot they were hatching. But Bormann particularly derived a tremendous kick from seeing the Fuehrer change his mind and knowing that he was the man who could bring it about. Moreover, it was nearly 3 A.M., everyone was tired and bored, yet nobody had leave to retire before the Fuehrer himself. And there was a certain amiable malice in indirectly proving to Goering (who lived nearby but was never invited except on business) that Bormann and Baur stood better with the Fuehrer than the chief of the Luftwaffe himself.

It was probably Baur, Hitler's personal pilot and rating high on the list of favorites, who swung the balance. He said, as he'd said before, that the Luftwaffe were reluctant to attack London because they were afraid. And if they failed to make the target and return without a night fighter shooting them down, that showed their lack of skill. Why, he himself would do the job—*and* pull it off—in an antiquated Junkers 52, the good old three-motor troop transport that was now obsolete as a bomber.

It was a tired old boast—and one that never failed. Hitler began to shake with anger. The failure of the Battle of Britain, the long-drawn-out blitz to make Britain sue for peace, these were attributable to Goering's incompetence and the cowardice of the Luftwaffe's pilots. Around dawn, when the tea party broke up, it looked to Bormann and Baur as if the reprisal raid was on.

It was indeed. At 8 A.M. that morning General Hans Jeschonnek, chief of staff to the Luftwaffe, had just reached his office in the Wolfsschanze (the Wolf's Redoubt), Hitler's highly fortified headquarters deep in a pine forest near Rostenburg, East Prussia. At once the telephone rang. It was the private line from the Berghof and Hitler was wasting no words: "There has been another attack on Berlin. We are staging a reprisal raid on London. What is the availability of aircraft?"

Jeschonnek called for the bulky file labeled *Schlacht gegen England* (the Battle against England) and had the answer within minutes: "Almost forty-three hundred, Fuehrer. Over twenty-three hundred of these are available for a large-scale attack."

Within an hour Jeschonnek had the machine clicking into action. First, a check with General von Seidel, the chief quartermaster, on the supply of aircraft—fuel and bomb tonnage. Next, a call to the chief of Air Fleet Three, Field Marshal Hugo Sperrle, at his Paris headquarters—the Hotel Luxembourg on the left bank. Jeschonnek said merely that the Fuehrer had ordered a raid on London and Sperrle would know what to do—reminding him that the bombers of Field Marshal Albert Kesselring's Air Fleet Two were also available to him. Kesselring and his Chief of Staff General Hans Seidemann were this morning already in Warsaw. But to keep the projected assault on Russia dark, not even Kesselring's corps commanders knew this. Nominally Kesselring remained in command of Air Fleet Two.

Jeschonnek hung up feeling that the staff work for the raid had been left in good hands. A monocled giant of a man, and a passionate devotee of the fleshpots, Field Marshal Sperrle knew most of what there was to be known about large-scale air attack. As commander of the famed "Condor Legion" in the Spanish Civil War, he had perfected the technique which until September 1940 was the pattern of all bombing—low-level saturation attacks which could reduce a city to a spawning mass of rubble in thirty minutes.

Since that date, though, Sperrle had been evolving a new technique: the creation of maximum chaos by a mingled non-stop rain of heavy high explosives and incendiaries. In the great City of London raid, the bulk of the explosives had been dropped at the tail end, primarily to hamper the Fire Service.

Sperrle now saw this as a mistake. It was probable that the heavy stuff when dropped late caused firebreaks as often as it impeded firemen.

The field marshal—whose motto was "Is there a foe that bombing cannot break?"—thought tonight was as good a time as any to put the new technique to the test.

His one regret was that Hitler, for reasons unknown, had contemptuously thrown out his scheme to make the blitz foolproof by first concentrating all-out attacks on the RAF's fighter fields. To Sperrle, this made no sense. If Sir Arthur Harris had concentrated all *his* bombers in hitting often enough and hard enough the twenty airfields from which the blitz was launched, Sperrle had a sneaking suspicion that the blitz might never have taken place.

Both Sperrle and his Chief of Staff General Karl Koller, viewed this morning's order with mixed feelings. It was small wonder. On the one hand, the standing orders for "Operation Barbarossa"—fly attacks but spare aircraft and crews as much as possible. This morning a complete turnabout: send all available aircraft.

And it wasn't the first time that it had happened by a long way. A few weeks back a meticulous plan for bombing Cardiff had been shelved at the eleventh hour—the Fuehrer wanted all available aircraft diverted to London. (Later, General Koller was to cite "Inconsistent and arbitrary orders by the High Command" as one of the prime reasons why the Luftwaffe's blitz failed.)

Sperrle and his chief of staff hashed it over. Plans for that night already included sorties against a number of coastal targets: Hartlepool, Middlesborough, Plymouth Docks and Weymouth, and one inland low-level mission, the Longbridge Steel Rolling Mills at Birmingham. But if the Fuehrer said all available aircraft, that meant using about a quarter of their total strength—say 500-plus.

The one factor that seemed ideal was the moonlight night. So far as Sperrle was concerned, indiscriminately plastering a target through low cloud was no way to bring a city to its knees. The answer was a full moon with Hauptmann Aschenbrenner's K.G.100 further lighting up the target to make London as bright as a circus arena. To Sperrle the primary consideration was always that the pilot should see his target; when a Nuremberg tribunal absolved him of terror bombing, the court broke into spontaneous applause. The fact that a night fighter might see the pilot at roughly the same time was a calculated risk. His crews knew him as "The Killer."

Allotting the targets came next—it took the field marshal and his aide no more than twenty minutes. Before the first heavy raid of September 7 the planning conferences had sometimes lasted hours but by now it was routine—at both the delivering and receiving ends. First, as usual, would go Hauptmann Aschenbrenner's K.G.100, to act as pathfinders—over the marshaling yards and docks of West Ham, to begin with, then, following the silver ribbon of the Thames, west beyond Tower Bridge. Each Kampfgeschwader (Group) had its own section of London, with targets allotted to its wings—some squadrons of No. 53 Wing to head for the Victoria Docks area, across the river from Woolwich—others to concentrate on Stepney, north and west of the U-bend that marked the Isle of Dogs; No. 55 to make for the same U-bend and then head due north to plaster Millwall Outer Docks and West India Docks; No. 28 Wing to set its sights on the tall chimneys of the Battersea Power Station, which supplied power enough for a city of 600,000 people.

So it went, until London was neatly divided into three—and the teleprinters at the Luxembourg Hotel began clacking out the basic operational orders to the commanding officers at twenty airfields in northern France and Holland: to Colonel Finck commanding K.G.2 at Cambrai; to Colonel Stahl, commanding K.G.53 at Lille; to Colonel Rath at Eindhoven, Holland, where K.G.4 was based.

It was a question of working fast. Heights had already been laid down—between 9,000 and 16,500 feet—but there were still a thousand details to settle: loading, take-off time, weather reports. Colonel Stahl, commanding K.G.53, directed one wing of 20 to take off from Vitry-en-Artois at 11.30 P.M., another wing of 20 at the same time leaving Lille. Colonel Rath, commanding K.G.4, decided that some of his planes, allotted to the area around King's Cross Station, should load up, as always on moonlight nights, with naval parachute mines.

Along with the urgency went a sense of fatalism. At the Castle Maria Kerke, near Ghent, an aide commented that moonlight made it tougher for the crews. "Ah, well," sighed General Paul Deichmann, chief of staff to No. Two Flying Corps, "You can't destroy a wasp's nest without getting into it."

At midday on the 10th the crews picked to fly had no more idea than Londoners that a mission was afoot; they, too, were more concerned with enjoying the sharp spring weather. At Vendeville, a small village near Lille where the air crews of No. 5 Wing, 53 Group, were quartered, Hauptmann Albert Hufenreuter used his connections with an army unit to borrow a horse. As the plans neared completion, Hufenreuter, oblivious, was cantering blissfully through the woods above the village, pleasantly lulled by bird song.

Not that the prospects of a raid displeased him. Aged twenty-five, tall and rugged, with the swarthy good looks of a man from the Harz Mountains, Hufenreuter was one of the Luftwaffe's best observers and wasn't unaware of the fact. A peacetime officer, he was equally a trained pilot though with less operational experience than some—for much of this war he had been flying a desk in the German Air Ministry until he begged for an operational transfer. Now, after 20 missions, Hufenreuter felt he knew most of the navigational answers. He had a kindly if patronizing contempt for most of the young conscript pilots that he'd worked with so far.

Leutnant the Baron Walther Von Siber was too busy to think far ahead. All this morning he was having the hundred-and-one afterthoughts of a man packing his bags: chasing his orderly to rescue some shirts from the laundry, writing out luggage labels for tomorrow, on the Sunday morning, the baron, a stocky twenty-five-year-old Austrian with sleek fair hair, was posted to Warsaw. The baron had no suspicions as to why; his group was due for transfer and he imagined he was being sent ahead because he had some knowledge of the terrain from the Polish campaign. He had permission to travel via Vienna, where his parents were living, and the prospect of a family reunion was good.

Once the thought of a mission did enter his mind, and the baron, who had flown 122 missions, decided privately that he would make three trips that night to complete the record number. He had picked his own target, too, whatever the briefing orders might be: Buckingham Palace. Whoever succeeded in flattening that was in line for a Knight's Cross from Goering himself and Von Siber was an ambitious man. And a man whose ambitions had been sorely disappointed. In eighteen months as a bomber pilot Von Siber had taken fierce pride in his skill, the way he identified and pinpointed military targets strictly according to the book. Then came a bitter scandal—Intelligence had charged that the baron deliberately bombed a passenger train, defying Goering's explicit order that only goods trains were eligible for strafing. For two months he stayed in close arrest, awaiting court-martial, until, by pure fluke, an agent's report from Britain had vindicated him.

Von Siber, who had always known it was a goods train— no passenger train was ever as long—accepted the loss of seniority philosophically. But the fact that they had doubted his judgment never ceased to rankle.

It was different with Leutnant Martin Reiser, who was also booked to fly this night. A veteran of 103 missions, Reiser was already, at forty-three, older than most of the crews, and lately he had felt an unbearable sense of strain. The medical officer had told him that his heart was affected and added, at the same time, that tablets must be the answer—there was only one score on which a man could be grounded now. Reiser asked what this was, and the doctor replied quietly: "Death. You know how short we are of trained crews." After this Reiser was always joking about being "the oldest man in the Luftwaffe," but he had come to accept that it was only a matter of time before he was killed.

At the Castle Roland, an old sixteenth-century château at Villacoublay, Versailles, Reiser got up late, enjoyed a leisurely bath and breakfast, then sauntered down to look at the beehives. The hives had been a fixture at the castle when the squadron took over and Reiser, a slightly-built, sleepy-eyed Bavarian who smiled a lot, had become the self-appointed squadron apiarist. Before lunch he took advantage of the sun to get a few color snaps of the cypress tree outside his bedroom window. Back in Bavaria, Maria, his wife, who was carrying on the family restaurant, would appreciate these.

The prospects of a mission that night weren't really on his mind. In the officers' mess, over a beer, a youngster did raise the topic, complaining that the summer flying kit had been issued too early; this cold ate into a man's bones. Reiser, remembering the bursting flak over London, grinned wryly: "Son, you don't need gloves over England." Everyone laughed, then they drank up and went in to the officers' mess—known as the Casino—for lunch. It was just a little after 12.15 P.M.

Above. Albert and Gladys Henley, Mayor and Mayoress of Bermondsey. *The Worthing Herald*
Right. Marguerita Stahli outside 48 Turney Road, Dulwich. The photo was taken only a fortnight before she was buried alive.

Above left. Post Warden Stanley Barlow, G.M., with Warden "Sam" Ekpenyon, the Nigerian he befriended. *Courtesy: Stanley Barlow*

Above. Mrs. Margaret Daley.

Left. Jimmie Sexton and his son photographed at the outset of the war. *Williams' Pioneer Studios, London*

CHAPTER THREE

"Sir, the Beam Is on London"

12 noon—5.20 P.M.

Just as though Field Marshal Sperrle and his plans had never existed, Mrs. Daley went on polishing her parquet, Marguerita Stahli snapped on Rex's leash for a pre-lunch stroll, Jimmie Sexton, in Fields' basement, finished crating another load of shaving sticks for the army.

At Fighter Command Sholto Douglas departed for lunch at his flat nearby. Minister of Home Security Herbert Morrison settled for a quick snack in the Members' Dining Room of the House of Commons—the Cup Final kickoff at Wembley was timed for 3.30 P.M., and Morrison planned an afternoon's relaxation.

Now that Saturday noon had come there was a true sense of holiday in the City—war or no war, the British weekend remained an institution, a cherished interlude that no Briton would relinquish easily. And from now until the end of summer the weekend would be prized more eagerly than ever; only a week back, for the first time in British history, the government had brought in the new double summertime. By moving the hands of the clock forward, the people could magically enjoy two whole extra hours of light each evening—a fact which had not gone unremarked by Field Marshal Sperrle.

If some grumbled that London was not what it had been, it was still good enough for most. In Trafalgar Square the fountains were silent, Eros was a shrouded mound of sandbags, the railings had gone from Green Park, but it was a world of enchantment to the supporters of Preston North End, after journeying 200 miles from Lancashire to cheer the home team. Blue-and-white rosettes in their buttonholes, they roamed the streets and jammed the pubs—only the rattles, now used to signify gas, were missing from an otherwise prewar scene.

Down at The Lion, Angel Lane, West Ham, Publican Bill Barker and his wife Audrey had been on the run since 11.30 that morning—several times Barker had to tell his cellarman, "One-Eyed Alf," to lay on a new barrel. Some of the demolition workers, earning £12 to £15 a week, were drinking pint after pint of sweet brown ale, although Barker knew they'd switch to double rums long before he called "Time" at 3 P.M.

Many in the pub this lunch time no longer had any house or any bed outside a shelter, but there was still a cheery fatalism. One family party was spending pound after pound of the compensation money the local council had paid out for new sheets; as if in irrefutable proof that this made sense, the husband shouted, "What use are sheets? We've no house to sleep in." Once the talk turned to Hitler, but there was little enough bitterness. As a market woman who had lost her fifteen-year-old son explained to Barker: "I couldn't hate him, guv'nor. Hate's all *he's* got to work on."

In the West End, too, people thought more in terms of pleasure. Lieutenant John Hodgkinson was arriving at the Haymarket Theatre with Diana Riviere, a dark, attractive girl who worked in advertising; like Sholto Douglas they had stalls to see the new young leading man Rex Harrison and his wife Lilli Palmer in the Broadway hit *No Time for Comedy*. Marjorie Felton, a pretty nineteen-year-old, had just entered the Queen's Hall in Langham Place, St. Marylebone, and was almost too excited to speak. This afternoon, in the famous sea-green-and-gilt concert hall, Sir Malcolm Sargent was conducting Elgar's *Dream of Gerontius*, and this was Miss Felton's first concert.

At Wembley the scene was gay enough for peacetime—new green turf to replace some scorched by an oil bomb, new gate-posts to take the place of blitzed ones, the martial music of the

Irish Guards' Band drifting nostalgically on the cold, still afternoon. At 3.30 P.M. the tightly packed crowds on the benches saw the game begin—a thrill-a-minute affair with Arsenal winning a penalty and missing it within the first three minutes. And three minutes after that, when Preston scored for the first time, a roar like a shock wave traveled far over the packed stands. For 60,000 people Goering's war had ceased to exist.

Many people found consolation in old, well-loved routines, and the war was a long way from their minds. On Sydenham Hill old Mr. Reginald Harpur, a retired electrical engineer, tut-tutted over his allotment—rain was badly needed now and sparrows and linnets had been plucking the hearts from his young cabbages. Edward Morris, who kept the dairy restaurant in Upper Thames Street, near Blackfriars Bridge, took his wife for their usual stroll along the Thames Embankment. "Look," remarked Mrs. Morris, "how low the tide is this afternoon." The tide was indeed going out; several feet of sticky black mud lay between the river and the bank-side wharves.

Some gave family affairs priority. In Hammersmith Mrs. Edna Clarke, an auxiliary fireman's wife, was packing a suitcase; her husband didn't finish duty until breakfast time on Sunday, so she was off to keep her mother company. Edward Penrose-Fitzgerald, the diplomat, and his wife Isabel, took the train to Esher in Surrey where their four-year-old daughter Sarah was evacuated. Beatrice Hynes, an Acton girl, was talking over tomorrow's wedding arrangements with her fiancé, Munitions Inspector Thomas Sinden. Miss Hynes had settled on a blue crepe-de-Chine dress trimmed with white and a pancake hat made of fresh flowers; the one thing on her mind that afternoon was marriage.

In Lisson Grove, the tenement quarter of St. Marylebone, Mrs. Rose Simons, a plump, amiable housewife, was almost wishing she had never heard of marriage. In her kitchen was a luscious fruitcake with white icing and candles that she'd bought for three-year-old John's birthday on the Sunday, but the little boy had got wind of it, as youngsters will, and was giving her no peace. Why did he have to wait until tomorrow? Why couldn't he have a slice now? In vain Mrs. Simons tried to explain that it was considered bad luck. By 4 P.M. John had got his slice of cake along with his afternoon milk.

For some it was business as usual, but it helped to take the mind off sterner things. Stoke Newington's town clerk, Ernest Bedford, was working overtime—it was the last day in the quarter for the payment of rates. At 36 Friday Street, in the shadow of St. Paul's Cathedral, Mr. Alvah Clatworthy, a sixty-year-old linen manufacturers' agent and a Baptist Sunday-school teacher, was tidying up his stock. The heavy raid of three Saturdays back had brought his business to a standstill, but on Monday, God willing, he would start again. As he got his samples together, silver-haired Mr. Clatworthy hummed a hymn tune and reflected how in these grim times fewer and fewer people wanted Duchess sets or art needlework or tapestry cushions.

Others had no chance to forget the war—for long at least. The clock in the Operations Room at Fighter Command showed exactly 4.31 when the London sector of the great control map of England glowed yellow—a "preliminary caution" warning. It was too mundane now to cause any excitement—a lone raider was nearing the coast, twenty-two minutes' flying time from London—but, as usual, the news was passed to the General Post Office. From London's 136 telephone exchanges the news was passed to more than eight hundred warden's posts.

At Post D2, St. Marylebone, Post Warden Stanley Barlow was already on the spot—inevitably, thought those on duty. Not that Barlow tried to hog the limelight—he preached responsibility and making and sticking to your own decisions until his wardens knew the refrain by heart. But somehow he had a nose for trouble, and if a big "incident" developed, Barlow was always in the thick of it. Aged thirty-five, Barlow was a slightly built man of medium height; tense, meticulous, a chain-smoking perfectionist, he had just finished his studies as an accountant when war broke out. At times his temper could flare like magnesium, but he would take chances that other post wardens ducked—some needing moral rather than physical courage. Every other post warden had ducked the rumpus that might arrive from taking on "Sam" Ekpenyon, a law student and a Nigerian chieftain's son. Barlow had taken him on, and things had gone smoothly from the start.

Despite this Barlow was respected, not liked, by most of his wardens. They nicknamed him "The Fuehrer," but he did not mind. He wanted results, not popularity. Few, in any case, were aware that Barlow was approaching a crisis in his life.

The crisis was physical fear, an enemy which was latterly giving Barlow as hard a fight as Hitler's war itself. This fear was worst when the nights were silent; even April 16, which had shaken him, had not been worse than the aftermath of one incident in New Cavendish Street—he had supervised on and off for a fortnight while the rescue men dug out bodies. And on one night patrol since a shutter banging in the May wind had sent him rushing to a basement, scoring his nails into his palms to keep himself from screaming out.

That same raid had flooded Barlow's basement flat to knee height, so that now he shaved in friends' flats and slept in corners of the post, but this worried him less. The son of a Nonconformist minister, his whole childhood had been furnished rooms and sudden moves—a rootless, insecure life. Only recently he had told one warden: "I have no friends but I've become hardened to that. Acquaintances, yes, thousands, but not one real friend. When I was a kid you swore eternal friendship to chaps, you blubbed your heart out when you left, but you never saw them again, let alone the town."

On May 10 nothing of this showed in his face as he stood in the basement of the solid concrete building on Portland Place and checked the members of the new shift on duty. At 8 P.M. there would be another shift to check and they would share his vigil until morning. Meanwhile he had to deliver a training lecture at six, check on the dozen shelters in his area at eight, and in a long evening try to filch two hours' sleep. So he waited, lighting one cigarette from another, for the "yellow" warning to change to "red"—the danger imminent, that marked the wailing of the siren. It was the same with post wardens all over London.

But nothing happened, and at 5.05 P.M. the telephonist told him "White message through." The intruder, whoever it had been, was probably just scouting for coastal shipping.

Few but the post wardens had known about it and fewer still would have cared. At Wembley a disappointed crowd was milling through the stadium gates: after forty fast-paced minutes the game had dissolved into a scrambling kickabout ending in a draw, only Fairbrother, Preston's goalie, showing much form. Things had gone better at the Queen's Hall, where Sir Malcolm Sargent, dapper and smiling, acknowledged wave after wave of applause along with singers Webster Booth and Muriel Brunskill. The London Philharmonic piled their instruments in the band room and prepared for a quick one in The George over the way.

But pretty Marjorie Felton and her friend Sheila Gardner didn't jostle to the exits with the rest—Marjorie hated crowds, so they hung back, taking their time. Suddenly the vast hall was empty and Marjorie Felton exclaimed involuntarily: "Look, we're the last people here." Miss Felton had no gift of prophecy—it was just that the sight of the historic hall standing silent somehow awed her.

But it was no time to stand and linger. In the London sky the barrage balloons still caught the gold of the sun yet the afternoon was quick; a chill breeze stirred the chestnuts in Regent's Park. Today a man would need a coat in the evening hours. The people went home to take tea. Mrs. Daley, who had spent the afternoon window shopping in Croydon High Street, had tea by the fire. Then she went to the bedroom and laid out her uniform for that night's duty. Jimmie Sexton, at a trestle table in Fields' canteen, was drinking his tea the way he liked it, sweet, strong, and orange colored, from an enamel mug, and chewing over the Cup Final result with Albert Fey, another fire watcher. In Dulwich Marguerita Stahli had a merry fire crackling in the grate of the big, old-fashioned living room— Aunt Maud still favored ferns in brass pots and velvet table-cloths. As she drank a solitary cup she told herself she had probably been foolish to expect Windsor at all.

All over the City people surrendered themselves to the age-old ritual of Saturday-afternoon tea: a quiet room, the magic of firelight, the benison of a hot drink.

And nowhere was it more of a ritual than at the Alexandra Hotel, Knightsbridge, overlooking Hyde Park Corner. In the starker world of wartime London the Alexandra was still an oasis, a reminder of more gracious days. True, the proprietor, Mark North, had spent more than fifty thousand pounds modernizing the old hotel that had been the town mansion of Princess Alexandra of Denmark before she married King Edward VII. But the atmosphere was still Edwardian, the world that John Galsworthy immortalized in *The Forsyte Saga*—a world of rigid, uncomplicated values, which held its own opinions on good furniture and silver and liked 4 per cent for its money.

The porters wore the royal crown on the lapels of their royal-blue livery and even in this time of staff shortage Mark North insisted that each employee furnish three references.

As they took tea in the Residents' Lounge on this sharp, sunny afternoon, the talk, inevitably, was of the past. Mrs. Alice Woods, a sprightly sixty-year-old, talked of the times before her widowhood, when it was good to be the wife of a wealthy Irish landowner. As Mr. and Mrs. James Murdoch of the piano family joined in the circle, Mrs. Murdoch, a former Gaiety girl, recalled their lovely house in Regent's Park and her priceless collection of porcelain, wrecked by a parachute mine.

When Mrs. Frances Morgan and her daughter Daphne got

back from Queen's Hall, the talk turned to great concerts and conductors—Chaliapin, the leonine Sir Henry Wood, all the distinguished names that the old hall had known. The easy hotel-lounge small talk of people who know one another just so well, and who don't, by tacit agreement, extend the intimacies beyond a certain point.

Not that all the residents were minded to sit back and take life easy. At seventy Mr. Andrew Verdie still put in a bustling six-day week at the family electrical engineering business near Victoria Station, relaxed by playing a whirlwind thirty-six-hole game of golf—with a handicap of nine. A six-footer, without a gray thread in his dark, wavy hair, the old Scot was a big favorite with the Alexandra staff.

Today had been just an average day for him—mostly devoted to plans for the future. Tomorrow he and his son James were making a day of it at Eastbourne by the sea; although a widower, Mr. Verdie kept the family home going for the mellow years of his retirement. And on Monday, as he had already told James, he planned to lift some policies; he didn't see why his family shouldn't enjoy them right now.

As he strode into the Alexandra at teatime that day he was thinking of the rich, full years ahead. Then, scorning the lift, he took the three flights of stairs to his room without puffing. It was good to be fit, better still to be alive.

Along the corridor, in the five-room private suites, Percy Straus, a leading chartered accountant, talked with his wife Blanche of their pleasant home at Chislehurst in Kent—the shortage of servants had brought them to the Alexandra eighteen months back. Close at hand General Josepha Hallera, minister of state in General Sikorski's Polish Government, was lost in reverie; today was the twenty-third anniversary of the Battle of the Dnieper, which he had fought and won against the Germans. The old general was one of the few who found that day's weather "warm, very close," but Dnieper had been a battle fought on horseback in snow and rain.

"Sir, the Beam Is on London"

At Castle Roland, near Versailles, the Germans prepared to fight another grimmer battle in calm white moonlight. Along with his fellow officers, Leutnant Martin Reiser was taking tea by the lounge fire when the wings commanding officer, Oberleutnant Speck, came in. "It's London again tonight."

"Are you going?" Reiser asked when the mild murmur of interest had died down.

Speck said no. He had been picked for the special low-level mission that often went hand in glove with large-scale attacks: command assigned the target, but the pilot could choose his own take-off time, bomb load, and type of plane. The one condition: not more than 60 per cent cloud.

The others were envious. Speck had drawn the Longbridge Steel Rolling Mills at Birmingham and planned to take off at 8.30 P.M. before the moon rode too high, hedge-hopping from the English coast. Such missions were riskier but they carried much kudos in the Luftwaffe of 1941.

Speck brushed this aside. He was having trouble with his observer, who operated the bomb sight clumsily—next trip he'd pick a man with a surer touch. An orderly was sent for the noncommissioned crews, billeted in another part of the castle. Then the vast chart of East London was unrolled on the big central table. "Come on—let's get the briefing over."

Unorthodox, perhaps, but by now most knew the map by heart—a quarter of Reiser's 100-odd missions had been over the capital. So this afternoon it was a mercifully swift briefing compared with that endured by some wings. For the take-off, the 25 planes that made up No. 9 Wing of 55 Group were due airborne at 11.16, a three-minute interval between planes. Crews should be alerted a good half-hour before.

Glancing around the table, Reiser checked his own crew of three present and correct—Feldwebel Adolf Schied, the pilot, a tall, dark man with a Roman nose; Uberfeldwebel Lorenz Hüber, the mechanic; last, short, sturdy Leo Schuderer, the wireless operator. Since No. 9. Wing was short on

41

personnel, tonight they would carry no gunner—one less life to risk in case of attack. Reiser knew he could rely on these men—hadn't they, without even blinking, agreed to fly three missions during the April 19 raid on London, in honor of Hitler's birthday? In the paling dawn light they had flown up to bomb Croydon, and that when they were dog tired, too.

Speck rattled off the briefing. Don't lose sight of the U-bend of the Isle of Dogs—it marked the Millwall Outer Docks to which they were assigned. Watch the heavy flak from the battery the British had sited there, and above all watch it up the Thames estuary; from Sheerness on to London the river was a series of ominous red blotches marking the main batteries. Not that the flak would trouble them too much at their allotted height, 10,000 feet; the bigger problem was night fighters. Searchlights were not much problem either—each bomber now had a thick coating of lampblack that absorbed the beams.

Pilot Adolf Schied mentioned the one drawback to this: crew members could no longer stencil a minute white fish on their planes after each mission. They called these *kleine pische* —small fry. There was a chorus of assent; it had been a cheerful way of affirming that London raids were very routine indeed.

Speck made his final point: the stack of the McDougall Flour Factory, which "Lord Haw Haw," the British traitor William Joyce, had christened "the packet of Woodbines" was a landmark to help fix the farthest point north. The allusion meant nothing to the crews, but they called it "Woodbines" just the same.

About five, when the briefing broke up, someone made the same flat forced joke that came with every such mission: "One third-class return to London, please."

Reiser took his charts to his own room, slumping by a pine-log fire to pore over finicky calculations. Wind a maximum 12 miles per hour. About eight tenths cloud earlier on but clearing fast now; the forecasters predicted "calm and fine with slight mists."

"Sir, the Beam Is on London"

If all went well, then, a take-off at 11.16 would bring them to the French coast in forty minutes. Another eighteen minutes to the English coast at Southend. Then sixteen minutes from the English coast to London. With luck they would be over the target at 12.30 A.M.—ninety minutes after the raid was under way. After that a lot would depend on his own accuracy as a navigator—and even more on the accuracy of Hauptmann Aschenbrenner's pathfinding.

The same thought was in the mind of Leutnant General Willy Haenschke, the Luftwaffe's senior signals officer, in northern France. Toward 5.00 P.M. he contacted Oberleutnant Karl Fiebach, who had command of all ground-control stations on the coast: "We should be testing the beam."

Fiebach agreed. Disconnecting, he made priority calls to the stations selected to lay tonight's guide beams—Station Anton, near Cherbourg; Station Berta, near Calais; Station Cicero, near Fecamp. Tonight these powerful radio beams were to be laid on a southwest-to-northeast axis, the two satellite beams intersecting the main "X" beam, Anton, over the industrial suburb of West Ham.

If Aschenbrenner's "Fire Raisers" rode the tone zone of beam Anton from Cherbourg, a complex receiver inside each plane would register both points of intersection. The second intersection marked zero hour without any need for tricky navigation.

The device was by no means perfect but it was accurate enough. Haenschke knew the British could pick up the beam —but not their method—and he knew they would try to jam it. But it was a cat-and-mouse game with uncertainties on both sides—the British would know a raid was planned, but what then? London was a big city. West Ham could be only the beginning.

Moreover, other stations along the coast were laying decoy beams, crisscrossing over other sectors of the capital. So no one could be certain where the bombers would strike first, or which beam to jam.

At 5.10 P.M. Fiebach rang back. The beams were laid. They were making necessary realignments for wind, but it looked as if everything would go according to plan.

The news was being shared. At Fighter Command Headquarters, London, Squadron Leader "Dickie" Richardson, the Filter Room's junior controller, got an urgent call from No. 80 Wing, the RAF's top-secret monitor unit at Harrow-on-the-Hill. Now, at 5.15 P.M., Richardson began making a series of routine calls—to Fighter Command's Sector Ops Rooms, the Gun Ops Room of Anti-aircraft Command, to Naval Ops at Rosyth, to the General Post Office, to London Fire Service Headquarters by the riverside at Lambeth.

At Lambeth the phone rang in the annex to the main control room, the office of Deputy Chief Officer Major Frank Jackson, and the major answered. Richardson, after identifying himself, said only: "Good afternoon, sir. The beam is on London."

At 5.17 P.M. Chief Superintendent Augustus May, in charge of Home Office Fire Control, Whitehall, heard Jackson's voice over the wire: "Mr. May, this is Major Jackson. I want a thousand pumps closed in on London tonight."

CHAPTER FOUR

"There's That Nasty Man"

5.20—11 P.M.

CHIEF Superintendent Augustus May was flabbergasted. In thirty-two years' service he had never before heard such a request from the chief of the former London Fire Brigade.

Minutes before Jackson rang May had had warning that the "X" Beam was laid on London; the news had come from Wing Commander Warburton, Fighter Command's Home Office liaison officer. Yet before the size of the raid could even be gauged Jackson was asking for a thousand pumps—the professional's word for fire engines.

He now told Jackson: "Sir, that's impossible. I'm down to bedrock because of Liverpool and Hull. I'll just have to do the best I can and ring you back."

As supervising officer of Home Office Fire Control, May had to see every town in Britain adequately covered in event of a fire blitz. It was a nightmare task. On the Friday night it had been Hull, all its riverside quay gutted; for seven nights on end Liverpool—the City was near to cracking. Supposing tonight's raid wasn't a fire raid? Supposing bigger raids blew up against the northern ports once May had drained them dry of engines? Yet even convoys traveling by moonlight would need to take the road now if they were to arrive in time.

A quick check on the maps showing strength returns then May rang the regional fire officer, Commander Sir Aylmer Firebrace. A handsome, aloof former naval officer, Firebrace was attached to Herbert Morrison's staff to mobilize all the fire brigades in the immediate outer London region, outside the hundred square miles of Jackson's jurisdiction.

"Sir, I've just had a call from Major Jackson. He wants a thousand pumps closed in on London tonight."

"What are you doing about it?"

"I can't let him have a thousand, sir. The most I can let him have is 750."

"What are you going to do with them?" asked Firebrace, and May already had the answer: "I propose to concentrate them on strategic points around the capital." Firebrace approved: "Let him have as many as you can." His own staff was already alerting outer London engines—with 160 closing in to the eastern sector alone.

In the underground control of the Fire Service Major Frank Jackson tried to anticipate the worst that could happen. No man was better equipped to do it. After twenty years' service with the old London Fire Brigade he was worshiped by all who knew him; even the communist-dominated Fire Brigades Union had christened him "Gentleman Jackson." They loved everything about him—his urbanity, the gentle smile even when things were worst, the same unhurried, courteous approach to all comers. "To some senior officers," one fireman recalls, "ordinary firemen were cattle. Major Jackson would walk a hundred yards out of his way to say good morning to a fireman swabbing down the floor. He would remember his name and details of his family."

Tonight Jackson foresaw many problems which it would have been hard to detail over the telephone. But most of them boiled down to a simple mathematical fact: in the hundred square miles governed by the London County Council, who also ran the Fire Service, there were 1,270 fire appliances. Another 1,242 in the outer London region—making 2,512 appliances in all.

It was an impressive total—yet on December 29 all those appliances in action, with 300 reinforcing pumps from the provinces, were not enough to check the fires that Hauptmann Aschenbrenner had lit. Even a medium fire might now warrant a ten-pump call, but on April 16 most of the 2,200 fires that raged had needed 30 apiece. Hence Jackson's heart cry, for if the beam was on London, time was of the essence.

Already Jackson could see his own mobilizing staff getting down to business at the six-bank switchboard, led by the jovial, hard-swearing Superintendent "Shiner" Wright and District Officer Ernest Thomas. First task was to alert the chiefs of the City's five fire-force districts and their divisional deputies. At Knightsbridge Station, headquarters for the southern division of Westminster, Superintendent George Bennison got the call: "Looks like a dirty one tonight, George." At Whitechapel, covering one third of the City of London and all the East End, Chief Superintendent Harold Norman heard: "Better keep your eyes skinned tonight, Harold boy."

It was enough. Within minutes the fire chiefs were changed into full working rig—blue serge uniforms with heavy leather belts, leather fire boots, steel helmets, and oilskins at the ready. Superintendent Bennison rang his watch room: "Look, no pumps on light exercise or anything—hang on to all you've got." At Whitechapel a sub officer wanting three hours off found Harold Norman unreceptive: "Nobody leaves the station until further orders." The London Fire Service were ready for action.

Almost nobody else gave action a thought. On this clear evening of double summertime the sun still lingered and the City was in carefree mood. Where a few months back people hastened to dine at six, the three-week lull had set the dinner hour back to the peacetime level of 8.30 or even nine. There was a greater willingness to risk dining out, as if, despite the portents, people were willing themselves to believe the blitz was over, turning the clock back to 1939.

There were many places where this illusion held good. Not only the Savoy, but the Dorchester, in Park Lane, whose gas-proof shelter was bolstered by twelve feet of concrete; the brochures claimed, "Experts agree that the shelter is absolutely safe against even a direct hit." And there were also Hatchett's in Piccadilly, the Ritz Bar almost opposite, the Berkeley, where the younger set went. There were still good bands to set the feet of young bloods and their girl friends tapping: the Savoy Orpheans with the American Carroll Gibbons at his white piano; Jack Jackson with his silver-toned trumpet at the May-fair.

And there were still, despite all, the staff who knew their customers. They had served them prewar and knew how they liked things done. At Lansdowne House the waiters knew the Prince von Stahremberg—whom they called the Bonnie Prince Charlie of Middle Europe—would arrive with an even lovelier girl than last night. Head Porter Chamberlain, at the Savoy, doggedly refused promotion from the Embankment entrance: it was the door that Winston Churchill always used. Mr. Bonesi, at the Berkeley, had installed pink satin curtains in his air-raid shelters. It was the same all over the West End.

Even in quiet backwaters such as the Alexandra, which was unlicensed and certainly no place for a wild party, the tradition held. Hall Porter Frederick Willis knew how General Josepha Hallera, the Polish minister of state, thought that Willis looked like Bismarck. "How is my friend Bismarck?" the old general would inquire several times a day, and Willis always played along.

At the Alexandra these little personal touches were part of a tightly knit world that still, in May 1941, tried hard to stem the tide. For instance, Night Porter Charles Mattock knew that old Lady Banner kept herself to herself and liked her chair set well apart in the lounge. In the same way, Headwaiter Joseph Larnock knew what store Percy Straus, the accountant, laid on snowy table linen, and how Paymaster Rear Admiral Martin Bennett, normally a genial man, hated breakfast-table chitchat.

As usual, no one at the Alexandra *was* dining late—7.30 was the fixed, immutable hour. Apart from the discreet clinking of cutlery there was little sound in the lofty ivory-painted dining room with its marble pillars and blue-and-gold carpet. Many were lonely people dining alone: Mr. T. Blake Butler, a descendant of the Ormondes of Kilkenny; Rear Admiral Bennett;

"There's That Nasty Man"

Andrew Verdie, who had failed to persuade his son James to spend the night—the young man pleaded a dinner date, promising to pick his father up for the Eastbourne trip early on Sunday. The men wore dark suits, a concession to formality, the women printed silk dresses and velvet bridge jackets. In the almost religious hush people gave themselves up to enjoying the food—Chef Theo Kummer had graduated under Escoffier and his sole in vermouth and veal escalop Alexandra were justly appreciated.

Upstairs something strange was afoot. Next to General Josepha Hallera's flat, on the first floor, stood a large conference room with glass-paneled doors; it didn't belong to the general's flat but was set aside for his convenience when he conferred with his adjutant. General Hallera had no need to use the room to reach the main hotel lobby, but on this night by chance he did. As he entered he was intrigued to see two officers in naval uniform bending over a large map.

To cross the room the general had to pass within feet of them—close enough to know that they were speaking voluble French and to see that the map was an air-flight atlas of London and district.

Neither man looked up, but still the general didn't like it. Nobody had warned him that the room was likely to be in use, and what would French naval officers want with air-flight charts? Going on down to the lobby, he ran into a British colonel and told him what he had seen. "Are they English or not?" the colonel asked.

The general was almost certain they weren't, so the two men went back upstairs to the first floor. Now the conference room stood empty. The officers had gone.

Back in the lobby General Hallera contacted his friend "Bismarck"—Hall Porter Frederick Willis. Willis had no knowledge of any officers other than British nationals staying in the hotel. And no one had sought the necessary sanction to use the conference room.

The three men discussed it uneasily for a little, debating

whether or not to call in the police. Somehow the thought of starting a false-spy scare and looking ridiculous made them think twice; there probably *was* a rational explanation. In the end, as usually happens, they did nothing. The general went back to his flat troubled by a premonition he couldn't define.

Few others dining early had such premonitions. The Penrose-Fitzgeralds found things almost too quiet in the dining room of their Kensington service chambers, although sometimes Mrs. Fitzgerald couldn't believe her eyes. The proprietress was serving dinner in full evening dress and long white gloves.

Lieutenant John Hodgkinson and Diana Riviere made plans for a traditional English dinner. From Diana's flat behind Westminster Abbey they rang Simpson's-in-the-Strand, famous for its trolley-borne roasts, to inquire about saddle of mutton. When a voice assured them it was on they set off by taxi only to find it was the one item missing from the night's menu. Hodgkinson registered his protest, so the headwaiter went away to return holding a very small pantry boy by the ear. "This, sir, is the culprit. He misunderstood when he answered the phone."

The lieutenant was so contrite that he told them to forget it and please to let the boy off. As they settled down to succulent chops and beer in silver tankards, Diana, woman wise, mused that the lad might hold down his job for this very purpose.

At 48 Turney Road, Dulwich, the meal was already over. An hour back Marguerita Stahli had almost given up when suddenly the doorbell pealed and Windsor was there, clad in heavy Air Force greatcoat, his forage cap bearing the white flash of an air-crew cadet. After the six-hour journey he seemed all in, and Marguerita thought with a pang of how he had wanted her to come to Blackpool instead, and have a good time. But she was due in the office first thing Monday, and you had to balance a free-leave pass against the cost of the fare. So while the youngster relaxed by the fire Marguerita fixed supper—cold ham, potato salad, stewed fruit.

Afterward they just sat on the sofa, holding hands and talking—it was six months since they had seen one another and there was a lot to be said. About their engagement—they had planned to buy the ring in Blackpool over Christmas but somehow Aunt Maud had not wanted to be left, so there had been no meeting, and still there was no ring. About old friends in the office, for Windsor had been on the administrative side of the Church Missionary Society before joining up. About how tough the wireless operators' course was proving, so that all of them at Blackpool wondered if they'd ever get through. About cycling, which was the hobby that had bound them together, and of the rides they'd had in the summer before the war—how once, in Kent, they had cycled through a village called Pratt's Bottom and Marguerita had refused to credit that such a place existed.

It was the usual half-sleepy conversation that young people in love will make before a warm fire, and it was memorable only because this was the last night on which they would ever discuss these things.

By Waterloo Station the warehouses of Fields' Soap and Candle Factory were cold, silent caverns grouped about the half-acre of stone yard. Jimmie Sexton, cooking sausages in the empty canteen, thought for a moment of going to join the other fire watchers in the basement of the north building, where Fire Guard Chief Bill Wilks had his control point. But there were more candles to be crated yet; with luck they would have a quiet night and he could work on undisturbed until midnight.

The little Cockney didn't resent the fact that life was now a seventeen-hour working day. Not once in forty years had he ever taken a holiday; times had been too tough. A week off stretched on the parched grass of Southwark Park, yes, but never a trip to Brighton or a crossing on a Boulogne steamer.

Working for his family had always been his hobby, like his dad's before him; he could remember the paydays of childhood when his mother put on a clean dress and white apron and the children lined up in the kitchen while Dad solemnly laid that one gold sovereign in her lap. His father, still living with his daughters "south the river," as he called it, had been a grand man to know—a post office engineer, fiercely proud of home and family. Once he had even chased the landlord out of the house because the man had walked in without knocking.

He wanted to bring young Jim, his five-year-old, up like that—if there was ever again a chance of getting a home together. On this Saturday night Sexton had no doubt that Britain would win the war, but how long was it going to take? His basic wage was only £2. 11. od, and only by working overtime every night of the week could he put by any savings. It did not occur to him that there were other jobs where he might earn more. Fields' was an old-fashioned firm, years behind the times in some ways, but they had given him a job in the slump of the thirties when no one else would—and it seemed only right to stay. All the five Sexton boys had worked there at one time or another. Young Jim could do worse when his time came, though he wanted something better for *him*—he could make something of himself, perhaps even get an office job.

He felt a sudden voiceless yearning for all those fathers of families in the miles of slate-roofed houses south of Waterloo who this night had their wives and children with them—Mr. Sexton's voice is still shaky as he recalls it.

At 7. P.M. by the canteen clock he washed up knife, fork, and enamel plate, tucked the stub of his unfinished Woodbine behind his ear, and trudged back to work.

Hauptmann Albert Hufenreuter felt a sense of relief. The news that No. 5 Wing was to fly did not arrive with Leutnant Reiser's wing at Villacoubly, but did arrive at 6 P.M. After a light meal he and his fellow officers piled into an open truck and jolted the fifteen-minute journey to the airfield for their briefing.

There was more ceremony here than with Reiser's outfit—more young and inexperienced pilots for one thing, and for another No. 5 Wing was booked to do more than pound the docks. Around 7 P.M. they jammed into the Briefing Room, squatting on hard benches while the Group Commander Colonel Steinweg used his pointer on the big wall map of London.

"You can branch out from the Isle of Dogs," Steinweg told them. "Use it as a landmark and work westward." He showed the center of the City, with St. Paul's as a landmark; due west was the bridge spanning Ludgate Circus, the one railway line in the whole capital connecting North and South London. It was known to carry heavy munitions traffic day and night.

This rated as priority, as did all the river bridges running south from Tower Bridge—Southwark Bridge, London Bridge, Waterloo Bridge, though not in use to traffic, Westminster Bridge. The darkened mass of the Houses of Parliament was a good landmark for this one.

The other targets Hufenreuter knew almost by heart—the Elephant and Castle road junction, because it was the main artery of South London, where all bridge roads met; Waterloo Station; almost all the warehouse property flanking the river between Tower and Westminster bridges.

For the Londoners living near these targets Hufenreuter had the same feeling as many other men in his wing. His job was to destroy industrial property but he had no hatred for the people as such, and no desire to kill them—any more, he supposed, than did the RAF pilots who came over to pound Hamburg. He never doubted that the German cause was just; eventually, he knew, London would have to crack and Germany would win. But like all the others, he felt a sneaking admiration for an enemy who could take punishment like this and keep on taking it and somehow manage to survive.

Hufenreuter's job tonight was to navigate his pilot, fair-haired, blue-eyed young Richard Furthmann, on to the Stepney—City of London boundary, but the other targets were good alternatives if cloud blew up or the fighters got too active in any particular region.

And as Steinweg talked, the room grew quieter, as if this

possibility was now sinking in. Near Hufenreuter someone muttered: "All right, then, we go—but what happens to us?"

The same thought niggled in everyone's mind. At the half-hour met session the forecaster told them, "The latitude north of London has no more astronomical darkness." Pilot Richard Furthmann didn't catch on, so Hufenreuter translated: there would be no real darkness all through this night.

Furthmann said nothing, but both men were thinking the same. Moonlight, a wonderful boon a year ago, was less welcome now. If the night fighters came up off the ground, the Heinkels would be sitting ducks.

Nobody was really scared, but somehow these last-minute preparations were always tenser than the real thing. And there were still more headaching details to come—the distribution of light signals for identification purposes, codes for the wireless operators, up-to-the minute data on changes in radio beacons. Next they drew parachutes and picked up some simple flight rations—chocolate spiked with caffeine, dried raisins, pep pills. When they got to the dispersal hut, Hufenreuter, as always, went the rounds, asking who didn't want theirs. He collected them to send home to his parents in Quedlinburg, below the Harz Mountains.

Leutnant the Baron Von Siber had more to do and was enjoying himself. His bags were packed, in the afternoon he had managed a few hours' duck shooting from a punt; the dinner had been good—the claret he had himself brought from Bordeaux. And the baron, a self-avowed efficiency expert, had organized the kitchens on a round-the-clock basis so there would be a good meal when they got back. Von Siber was one of the few fliers that night who thought so confidently in terms of getting back.

At 7 P.M., as wing leader and technical officer, he was already at Vitry-en-Artois airfield making the round of the crews. His stern edict to the 30 pilots of No. 3 Wing, 53 Group: keep rigidly to the altitude of 12,000 feet plus. To minimize the risk of collision each wing had its own allotted altitude and time span over the target, each plane a specified quarter-hour interval to find the target and deliver its bomb.

By 7.30 the crews of the 370 planes slated to make the first sortie had been briefed. There were still three hours to go, but they knew now what they had to do.

In London the predicament was different: people checking on duty, an air of quiet watchfulness, nobody really knowing what to expect.

At Warden Stanley Barlow's post the mood was typical. As he checked on the 8 P.M. shift at Post D2, St. Marylebone, Barlow was glad to find some of his best wardens on duty, but he didn't necessarily contemplate having to call on them. One by one they trudged in, slinging their tin hats on the pegs, collecting mugs for a brew-up of tea: "Sam" Ekpenyon, the Nigerian chieftain's son; dark, enthusiastic Winnie Dorow, a young Jewish tailoress just out of the training stage; pretty fair-haired Annie Hill, who by day worked in a garment wholesaler's, and Motor Mechanic Charlie Lee; full-timer Jim Grey; Joan Watson, the hairdresser; and Eileen Sloane, a handsome woman who often ran the post on her own.

Lately Barlow and Miss Sloane had been seeing a lot of one another and the ripening friendship was the subject of a lot of good-humored ribbing.

There was little of that tonight. Despite the lull, Barlow was in a prickly mood—somehow the thought of how that banging shutter had frayed his nerves was eating at his self-confidence. He rousted one warden so long over a minor breach of discipline that the post suddenly went a shade too quiet. Finally "Sam" Ekpenyon muttered: "Give the bastard a cigarette, somcone." It broke the tension; Barlow himself joined in the laugh.

It was early yet, and a few started a game of darts to kill time, others settled to poker. But there was plenty to do before the night was out. Some bunks had been broken in one of the shelters; a woman had reported for the fifth time that her Austrian maid was sending smoke signals to the Germans; Barlow himself must check with the marshals of each of the dozen shelters.

Meanwhile, he sent Wardens Patricia Arden and Elizabeth Burger on a house-to-house check. The nightly census wasn't infallible; the post area, close to Euston Station, was too colorful a checkerboard of contrasts. In these high, narrow streets, which smelled of spice and dust, fashionable clinics rubbed elbows with garment warehouses, luxury flats loomed over lace-curtained Cypriot dining rooms, red-brick tenements hung with washing backed on to gleaming office blocks. Time and again people went away for the weekend or invited friends to stay without letting the post know. The census was just the best method of trying to find who was sleeping where, a guide to rescue men and wardens if a building got hit.

Seeing Winnie Dorow check on duty, Barlow tried to think of what it was he had wanted to tell her, then gave it up—it had somehow slipped his mind. At 8.30 he set off on his rounds; even if the night stayed quiet he would be prowling on and off until dawn. He checked and rechecked each street and alley as he would have checked a ledger, unable to settle but taking comfort from swift visual impressions that all was quiet.

Most people's evenings were scarcely more spectacular. Godfrey Clarke, a North London corn chandler, was listening to the radio—the Cockney comedians Flanagan and Allen had a catchy jingle about the failure of the blitz:

> *We've won it, we've done it,*
> *We've beaten them at last*
> *Up in the air . . .*

At Clubland, Camberwell, the youth club formed to save poor children from the streets, the Reverend Jimmie Butterworth rehearsed a drama class in *Journey's End*. And there was a dance on, too; most town halls had a dance of some kind tonight, with tea and buns for the ladies, pale ale and sausage rolls for the men.

"There's That Nasty Man"

Much the same at Corbett's Lane wardens' post, Bermondsey, where Mayor Albert Henley and his wife Gladys were the guests of honor. Now the dance was in full swing, Gladys Henley couldn't really think why she hadn't wanted to come; it could only have been an odd premonition. And it was good to see Albert relax for once, after the grinding months of blitz —better than the cinema where he fidgeted all the time and picked holes in the plot. At 9 P.M., between dances, Henley mounted to the rostrum to say a few words about the War Weapons Week beginning on Monday, for which all Londoners were urged to save. Watching him, Gladys Henley was proud of the way he could make a speech without using a single note—proud that she was his wife.

They had come a long way together. Seventeen years back, when they had met as voluntary Labor party workers toiling for the General Election, Gladys Henley had not liked him at all—yet, strangely, the friendship of the broad-shouldered, fair-haired young warehouseman and dark, lively Gladys Verrell became known all over the borough. Even after marriage they had worked on every election campaign together; when Leonard, their baby came, they would put him to sleep in his pram and take him to the Saturday-night dance held to raise funds at Rotherhithe Town Hall. He was a good baby, as placid as his father; he would sleep all evening in a quiet corner.

Not that Albert Henley wasn't sometimes very angry indeed. A stubborn man at times, his lower lip could jut obstinately, the gray eyes go cold and distant. Bullying and aggressiveness made him angriest—no man hated the war more than Albert Henley, who fought it night and day. The plight of the old and friendless made him angry, too; it had taken years of campaigning before the first block of one-roomed flats for old people was built in the borough. After that Henley would walk past them every morning on his way to work. It made him angrier than anything else in the blitz when these were hit.

Somehow everything about him added up to a husband one could take pride in: a casual, friendly man, deceptively easy-going, who liked sports clothes better than dressing up, who never forgot to say how much he enjoyed his meal, especially if Gladys could produce a bloater for tea. A father who liked reading his son's comics and was still enough of a boy to hop out of bed at nights and come back crunching a lump of coconut ice. A mayor who would send the municipal car home to fetch a basket of his favorite home-grown tomatoes but who preferred to walk through the streets, chatting with the housewives on their doorsteps, seeing what he could do to help.

As her husband finished his speech, the thought came to Gladys Henley: Albert is happiest helping people, and because he is helping people he speaks from his heart.

It was an hour of dedication. In the shadowy crypt of St. Paul's Cathedral clergy and volunteer fire watchers knelt side by side as the dean, the Very Reverend William Matthews, conducted the simple service: "Lighten our darkness, we beseech thee, O Lord, and by thy great mercy defend us from all perils and dangers of this night. . . ." Then the dean, in battle dress and steel helmet, manned the control-room switchboard. Other prayers were shorter, but as much lay behind them. In Croydon Mrs. Margaret Daley donned her uniform, knelt carefully on her polished parquet, prayed as she had done through every night of the blitz: "Sacred Heart of Jesus, let me—let *us* —be safe tonight."

North of London Air Marshal Sholto Douglas had come to a decision: London's safety could best be assured by a "fighter night." At 9.35 P.M. the usual dusk patrol, a few day and night fighters, sweeping the raiders' normal routes: the Wash, between Boston and King's Lynn, the Sussex coast over Beachy Head and Selsey Bill, along the Thames estuary between Romford and Southend.

Then, if the raid built up to follow the beam warning, both day and night fighters—100-plus planes—would soar into the battle. Day fighters would patrol in layers—between 14,000 and 23,500 feet—over London and the Thames estuary. Night fighters, working under radar control, must hug the coast.

"There's That Nasty Man"

For pleasure seekers the evening had just begun. The last houses had not yet spilled out from the cinemas; the people who packed the warm, humming darkness of the West End houses had plenty of choice. Clark Gable in *Boom Town* at the Empire; Gable again in *Gone with the Wind* at the Ritz; Ginger Rogers in *Kitty Foyle* at the Gaumont. At the Carlton, which had the Jack Benny show *Love Thy Neighbor*, Linkman William Sherrington, a wiry sixteen-year-old, stifled a yawn; staff was so short he was just finishing a twelve-hour day. He looked forward to a long night's sleep in his mother's house by the Elephant and Castle.

In the twilit alleys behind the cinemas the ladies of the evening patrolled before the shopkeeper's "Business as Usual" signs in the now-almost-regulation garb—silver-fox capes, slacks, pocket torches for when it grew darker.

At the Savoy Quentin Reynolds, the celebrated American journalist, was seeing what M. Abel Alban's kitchen could do in the way of potted shrimps and grilled sole. As he dined with U.P. correspondent Ed Beattie, they discussed Beattie's quaint ambition to retire to Sarasota, Florida, because it was the winter headquarters of the circus. Next door, at Simpson's, Diana Riviere and Lieutenant Hodgkinson had reached the coffee stage. George Ronus, manager of the Dorchester, arrived at the Colony Club, Berkeley Square, to dine with Lord Donegall, the society columnist.

As the dusk deepened, the city streets came alive with a steady tramp of feet—the bustling feet of a family party; the probing of a blind man's cane; the sharp, slow step of a mother carrying a child—like an undrilled army on the march. Armed with bundles and bedrolls and flasks of tea the people thronged, laughing and chattering, toward their chosen shelters. To Mrs. Anne Russell, arranging her black-out at a Hampstead window, the scene had a holiday flavor; she thought of the villagers trooping to a flower show in the countryside of her childhood.

For John D. Allen, an alert twelve-year-old, tramping to

Elephant and Castle Underground with his parents, it held less charm. Once below, the warm, swirling wind died to a stifling animal heat. The twisting, tossing sleepers, packed head to foot, the platforms, gritty and buff-colored with trodden sand, the reek of the latrines—they all added up to a new and unwelcome world.

Many hundreds were bedding down with friends or in buildings where they knew the watchman; Commissionaire Bill Laycock had a dozen regulars and a black retriever using his rest room at the Elephant and Castle Cinema. At least thirty jammed in the basement of Fields' Soap and Candle Factory, where Jimmie Sexton had his bed.

As they trooped through the shadowy streets they were a polyglot company—in Warden Stanley Barlow's area by Euston Station the shelter rules were in eight languages. It all showed an informality revolutionary for Britain, although many shelters had by tonight become as exclusive as clubs. Wealthy West Enders had wardrobes and even pianos in the shelter near the Dorchester in Park Lane; the taxi drivers were a clique sticking to Leicester Square; Jews to Mrs. Bertha Roston's wine parlor in Stepney; down-and-outs to the Hungerford Arches beneath Charing Cross Station, where Superintendent Bernard Nicholls's Anglican Pacifist unit collected the resultant vermin for typhus research.

Jews and Gentiles, rich and poor, the brave and the fearful, they added up to only 70,000 Londoners using the public shelters this Saturday night.

To the men who knew this was a bad sign. In Poplar, Chief Warden Ted Smith realized people had got more confident—the rescue services would have their work cut out in a raid. Camberwell's ambulance superintendent, William Harrison, put it down to local prejudice; a street shelter had been hit and many had died several weeks back. Now the locals distrusted shelters. They were taking a chance at home.

Three miles up in the sky Hauptmann Friedrich Karol Aschenbrenner was also taking a chance, and holding his breath. At 10.45 P.M. the 20-strong spearhead of K.G.100 was just crossing the English coast line east of Lulworth, Dorset. Aschenbrenner and his pilots were riding the tone zone of beam Anton, the frequency a steady, regular pulsing in each wireless operator's ears, and for nothing on earth could they now alter height or course or take evasive action. For fifteen full minutes they must fly unwaveringly in Indian file—each pilot walking a kind of aerial tightrope.

From Lille and Laon the first detachments of K.G.26 and K.G.77 were winging to the rendezvous, and on twenty airfields from Holland to Cherbourg bomber engines were blazing into life. As British radar stations showed the first blips dancing forty miles into France, Squadron Leader Cyril Leman, in Fighter Command's operations room, rang Air Marshal Sholto Douglas: "There's something big on tonight, sir."

In the underground filter room, next door, Squadron Leader "Dickie" Richardson struggled to sort order from chaos. Below Richardson, perched in the controller's gallery, a tense team of plotters, tight-packed around a giant map of the coast line from Penzance to Aberdeen, kept nightly touch by head-and-breast sets with the radar stations girdling the coast.

But tonight the reports were mounting so fast it was hard to tell what was going on. First the Highstreet, Norfolk, station; then West Bromley, Suffolk; Canewdon, on the Thames Estuary; Poling, Sussex; Canewdon again, the controller there reading quick sense into the white scallops of light dancing on the opaque glass radar screen: "M for Mother 2301, 20-plus at 12,000."

To Section Officer Sadie Younger, the filter officer covering the estuary corner, the rigmarole made disquieting sense. The grid reference marked Canvey Island on the Thames Estuary —20 or more unidentified aircraft had roared over the point, flying at 12,000 feet above the river. Five minutes later, more detail: still hugging the river, the planes were moving west.

From the gallery Richardson called the snap decision he

would make more than threescore times that night: "Slap a hostile on that one."

It was suddenly a frantic race against time. WAAFs were shifting the small magnetic iron plaques marked "Hostile" on the track; a WAAF beside Richardson with a fourteen-circuit head-and-breast set was intoning plot after plot: "Hostile 20-plus at 12,000"; the news passing to the ops room next door, to Fighter Command's Sector ops rooms all over the south. All the time the filter officers kept up a barrage of instructions: "Get another plot on that one." "Tell them to check that height."

As K.G.100 droned steadily over Woolwich, height was important to Aschenbrenner, too; at 15,000 feet the guns could reach them so very easily—and spoil everything. Time was running out; to the radio operators the beam tone had changed to a long-drawn-out throbbing—the first intersection past. As the planes came onward, London by moonlight seemed strangely lifeless: the Thames coiling like a ribbon of quicksilver, the pale miles of massed roofs, the river bridges like a child's matchwood models. To Aschenbrenner and all his pilots the silence was uncanny. It was as if the city were dead. Soon the guns *must* open up.

Below all was calm, like any serene moonlight night before the war. Only a few felt a gnawing presentiment. As Sheila Russell, a pretty secretary, modeled some tennis shorts in the hall of her mother's Hampstead flat, a neighbor urged through the half-open door: "Sheila, put on your siren suit, this is no night for tennis. The moon's like day!" Miss Russell had a surer yardstick: her sister Pat was about to take a bath so the sirens were bound to blow.

At Corbett's Lane Wardens' Post, Bermondsey, Gladys and Albert Henley had answered the final volley of good nights. As they strolled peacefully back to the mayor's parlor, Albert decided: "We must go to the shelters and tell people about War Weapons Week."

Nearing the town hall, Gladys Henley remarked: "I wonder if they'll come tonight."

"Of course they will," Henley replied. "There's a full moon."

Some seized on smaller clues. At Westminster Control Center, "Blitz," the black tomcat mascot suddenly took a flying leap, landed smack in Special Officer Angela Elliston's in basket. There were knowing glances—Blitz used his own and normally infallible radar.

At five minutes before 11 P.M. London was a strange city— the few knowing or guessing what lay in store, the many utterly oblivious.

At 11 P.M. no one could be in doubt. In Fighter Command's ops room, as hushed and subdued as a city counting-house, Sholto Douglas and Squadron Leader Leman watched from the circular gallery: across the map of England the WAAF plotters with their long-handled paddles eased an urgent thicket of red metal arrows toward the capital. On the gallery's wall map the suffused lighting round the London region changed from yellow to red—danger imminent. Nearby, along the gallery, Air Raid Liaison Officer Ronald Squire pressed one of a battery of buttons connecting with the War Duty Officer at Scotland Yard. The news passed to 500 police stations.

For one long minute the cold, high voice of the siren wavered and cried over the gray miles of rooftops.

As it reached its peak over North London, Mrs. Emmy Shaw, an Islington housewife, racing panic-stricken for the shelter, hit the brick wall of a factory head on. She could have known nothing as the world fell in on her little life. No bombs had fallen as the blitz of May 10 claimed its first victim.

Most people took it more stoically—after the first primitive coiling in the pit of the stomach came philosophy. So often the raiders never came at all—it might be localized—or the guns could turn them back. At the Savoy, Claire Luce, the American actress, settled to a quiet game of chess in the Press Bar with the Chicago *Tribune's* Larry Rue. Signor Giacomo Prada, owner of the Soho gourmets' paradise Casa Prada, descended on foot, as gravely as always, to his wine cellars, to the choice Burgundies the staff called "Signor Prada's babies." He knew no fear; merely if they died, he went with them.

In the Savoy's restaurant Quentin Reynolds and Ed Beattie exchanged glances, and Beattie sighed: "There's that nasty man." Across the crowded dining room Band Leader Carroll Gibbons took thought of Hitler; his fingers rippled over the keyboard as he swung the band into "When That Man Is Dead and Gone."

At 11.02 Squadron Leader Cyril Leman, in the ops room gallery at Fighter Command, saw that the dark sprawl of the metropolis had vanished from the gridded map—swamped by red arrows. Aschenbrenner was over London.

Field Marshal Hugo Sperrle who planned London's greatest fire-raid. His motto was: "Is there a foe that bombing cannot break?" *Luftwaffenakademie, Hamburg*

Lieutenant Martin Reiser, Luftwaffe, Villacoublay Airfield, France

Above. Only a windbreak of hawthorne prevented Hauptmann Albert Hufenreuter's Heinkel 3 from exploding against a line of oak trees near Ashford, Kent. *The Kent Messenger. Below.* Men of the R.A.F. Squadron walking to their planes on the night of May 10, 1941. *Courtesy: Air Chief Marshal Sir Thomas Pike, K.C.B., C.B.E., D.F.C.*

CHAPTER FIVE

"*Why, It Must Be One of Ours*"

11—11.30 P.M.

Down at The Lion, Angel Lane, West Ham, Publican Bill Barker was a busy man at 11 P.M. on Saturday, May 10. Normally the big Victorian pub with its engraved glass and mahogany furniture should have closed half an hour ago, but these were not normal times; the police and ambulance corps often used the pub as an emergency center, and the padded leather benches had seen service as a mortuary. Now Barker was washing and polishing glasses as fast as he could, the four bars were jammed out, and Audrey, his wife, was at the piano leading an ear-splitting singsong. Already the company had rollicked through "Bless 'Em All" and "The Quartermaster's Stores." Now, as the clock struck eleven, Audrey swung into a tune with a note of optimism—"There'll Always Be an England."

Although the siren had sounded, Barker was not worrying that Temple Mills Sidings, then Britain's largest marshaling yard, lay only 400 yards from his front door. The East Enders' belief in Kismet was contagious, and the noise of the piano was drowning out any planes that might be overhead.

At 11.02 P.M., seconds after Aschenbrenner's observers were signaling "Bombs gone" over their intercoms, the first incendiaries came whistling from the sky. Barker and everyone heard that high-pitched whine; within a second someone shouted "Drop!" Glasses went flying and everyone spreadeagled on the floor, burying their faces. Suddenly they were scrambling to their knees, laughing shakily, because Audrey Barker, slightly deaf in one ear and with her back to the room, had heard and seen nothing. The defiant notes of "There'll Always Be an England" were still thumping out above the din.

At once the pub woke to action, but caught off guard it was easier to act than to think. Across the way some incendiaries had taken hold, and a butcher's shop was blazing—too small a job for the Fire Brigade, so Barker's customers waded in: laborers, railwaymen, stall holders. A couple grabbed a stirrup pump and bucket and had been pumping for a full minute before one rounded furiously on the other. "You bloody fool, there's no water in the bucket!"

Other bombers were moving in and more incendiaries were falling—not over West Ham alone. All along the eight and a half miles of riverside between Barking and Tower Bridge they came showering—seconds of thin, high, whistling, then the sharp clattering as they struck home. To those who watched, the scene was indescribable. They fell in tenement gutters and on warehouse roofs; among 250 acres of resinous timber stacked 20 feet high at Surrey Docks; on pavements and in roadways; lodging in drainpipes, on window ledges. They burned with a sizzling blue-white glare; above them the chandelier flares came dripping beautifully down like Chinese lanterns, bathing the river, the dockside, the miles of slate roofs, in a purer, whiter glare than moonlight.

Near the City of London—East End boundary Police Sergeant Fred Scaife was transfixed by the unearthly beauty: he thought of diamonds glittering on dark velvet. To Station Officer Albert Garrod, in Clerkenwell, the incendiaries seemed like a swarm of vicious gnats.

Even trained observers were aghast. In the East End Stepney Warden John Connolly stood paralyzed. Never in all the blitz had he seen incendiaries fall on this scale. Young William Sherrington, the sixteen-year-old linkman from the Carlton cinema, had just seen his mother to the shelter when the flares came billowing over the Elephant and Castle. The lad felt his heart in his mouth. "Now we're in for it."

Elsewhere all was still quiet. In the old walled City of London, the rich, square mile of office blocks, the Police Commissioner Sir Hugh Turnbull was on the roof of Police Headquarters, scanning a peaceful night sky. For ten minutes after the siren had gone there was no sound—so quiet that the commissioner's batman, P. C. Thomas Farquharson, could hear, from miles away south of the river, a dog bark. Nearby, on the top of Martin's Bank, Lombard Street, Fire Watcher Len Hill was also on the lookout. At 11:10 P.M. Hill phoned Control: a plane had droned overhead from the east heading for St. Paul's. No sound of gunfire followed.

To Sir Hugh Turnbull the fact seemed reassuring. "Why, it must be one of ours—no one's firing at it." Nobody answered; at Police Headquarters and all over the City of London it was a time for listening. Presently another plane passed overhead, moving in the same direction as the first. Ten . . . fifteen . . . twenty . . . the minutes ticked by; still no sound but the planes' droning—farther and farther away by now. Then one of the planes did a left-hand turn and came back again. Still no gunfire. P. C. Farquharson thought of the times he had read how suspense could make the sweat slide down a man's back. He had never believed a word of it until tonight.

As much as anything it was the long silence after the sirens had gone that men remembered that night—the sick minutes of silence that frayed the nerves.

Since tonight was a "fighter night," Air Marshal Sholto Douglas had decreed that the guns could engage targets only at 12,000 feet and below—2,000 feet below the bottom layer of fighters. If the bombers stayed above that level they might enjoy comparative immunity, unless the fighters were lucky.

A few had premonitions. Engine Driver Leslie Stainer, bringing his engine out of Bricklayer's Arms Goods Depot in readiness for the Cannon Street–Dartford run, had "a sense that something awful was going to happen." At Borough Market, near London Bridge, incendiaries rained across the track, and Fireman Harry Osborne leaped from the footplate to douse them with water from the engine. Soon Stainer had had enough.

"For the Lord's sake, let's get on into Cannon Street."

Private Arthur Simons, home on short pass, had the same idea: "Come on, gel, it's one of them moonlight blitzes." Brushing off Rose Simons' protests, he strapped three-year-old John into his push chair and hustled his family off to the street shelter, leaving the birthday cake behind.

Yard Inspector Robert Bromley, of Bishopsgate Goods Depot, East London, found the same fact reassuring. As he drank his beer in The Unicorn, Shoreditch High Street, a second before the siren, he told himself the Germans would never dare come by moonlight.

In the mayor's parlor at Bermondsey Town Hall Albert Henley was changing into uniform. Turning over his small coin, he found he had only 2s. 8d. but thought he might as well take it along. As he set off for Control to find what incidents were brewing up, Gladys Henley chaffed him: "Fancy a mayor walking about with only 2s. 8d. in his pockets."

Mrs. Henley did not realize that her husband had gone on duty without what he called his "lucky sweater"—a handsome Fair Isle slipover whose glowing colors had even drawn a comment from the Duke of Kent when he visited the borough. She had no premonition.

Stanley Barlow, hastening to Post D2, St. Marylebone, felt a shade uneasy but couldn't tell why. As he passed the Bay Moulton pub in Great Portland Street, two of his wardens were just leaving—Motor Mechanic Charlie Lee and Winnie Dorow, the young trainee. The girl hailed him: "We left a drink for you on the counter." Too late Barlow remembered that he had promised to meet them for a quick one. Hastening on, he called over his shoulder, "I'll pick it up tomorrow."

Over King's Cross Station the searchlights switched on, wheeling and coning in the pale sky. Assistant Yard Inspector Frank Marshall could guess what was coming. He told his chief, Jabez Stevens: "I think they're going to make a main-line hit for us tonight." At Waterloo Stationmaster Harry Greenfield took one look east, then scribbled a note in the official diary:

"Why, It Must Be One of Ours"

"Guns and planes—hundreds of them."

Three miles away, in the West End, the reaction was slower. If the sirens had sounded, the night was young—and it could so easily be a docks raid again. At the Ritz Bartender Michael Gonley was laying out fresh saucers of olives and potato chips and reflecting how these days you always knew a first-timer—the swift glance at the ceiling on entry to gauge how solid was the roof. Bartender Charlie Pearce, at the Queen's Brasserie, bagged the autograph of Wing Commander Stanford-Tuck, the fighter ace.

In the night spots the mood was one of sophisticated melancholy—and the setting was perfect. At the Cocoanut Grove a pink spotlight picked out the seductive Hungarian Magda Kun as she lilted into a favorite number:

> *"I've got a cozy flat*
> *There's a place for your hat*
>
> *I'll wear a pink chiffon negligee gown;*
> *And do I know my stuff,*
> *But if that's not enough*
> *I've got the deepest shelter in town . . ."*

In the Garden Room at the Mayfair cigar smoke lay in blue rope-like coils in the warm air; the chandeliers shone as discreetly as altar lights; the champagne in the ice buckets was deliciously cool and at 25s. a bottle cheap. When a pretty girl asked for "A Nightingale Sang in Berkeley Square" Bandleader Jack Jackson grimaced at Pianist Freddie Aspinall. It wouldn't be the last time that evening and just as surely they would want "Room 504" and "The Last Time I Saw Paris."

On this Saturday night nostalgia was still the surest substitute for peace. On the BBC's Forces' Program the Rendezvous Players were signing off with a memory of 1917, "Let the Great Big World Keep Turning."

A few took precautions—more to be on the safe side than because danger seemed imminent. At St. Luke's Hospital,

Chelsea, Clerical Officer Edward Glading kept rootling for his identity card—if anything happened he wanted to be sure they'd identify his body. Harry Weinstock, a City of London auxiliary fireman, carefully emptied his pockets into the dormitory locker: a bunch of keys and thirty shillings. They were all his worldly goods, but he didn't want them going to waste. The chief warden of Stoke Newington, Major Charlie Creswick-Atkinson, left his false teeth in the Control Room—you never knew what blast might do. Then he set off on patrol like a country squire inspecting his coverts—tweeds, walking stick, golden retriever Punch trotting at his side.

On Fields' factory roof by Waterloo Fire Watchers Jimmie Sexton and Albert Fey were garbed more prosaically—overalls, steel helmets, gum boots. In the light of the full moon everything was as sharp as an autumn morning, the tall brick smokestack of the factory with its warehouse buildings looming above the main lines at Waterloo. The factory really consisted of two main buildings three stories high set 30 yards apart across a stone courtyard. When the siren went Sexton and Fey had already been standing guard for an hour on the south building nearest the railway lines.

Now Jimmie Sexton glanced nervously at the big twenty-ton vats of candle wax and palm oil stacked across the roof. If these caught hold, he thought, the factory itself would burn like one vast candle. To date no incendiary raid had ever come close enough for that.

At first it was like any other night—the slow, wordless patrol on the flat roof, stamping your feet and windmilling your arms to keep the blood coursing; the prickling moment when the siren went and a deeper chill seemed to invade the body; that same too-long silence. Then Fey rang his first routine report to Fire Chief Bill Wilks in the basement of the north building that served as Fire Guard Control: "They're dropping 'em up east somewhere—flares and incendiaries—and there's a few gone down over the Elephant."

There was more to come; Hauptmann Aschenbrenner was

taking good heed of the instructions of his commanding general, General Pflugbeil: "Get the City well alight for the first wave." Now the "Fire Raisers" wheeled south of Tower Bridge, striking down the river for Waterloo and Westminster. They came in low, cruising at 10,000 feet, and for the first time the guns south of the river opened up and the searchlights came on.

At the Savoy the band was still lively but the mood had gone flat—one by one the diners were drifting out in search of taxis. Journalists Quentin Reynolds and Ed Beattie, in quest of news, made for the back of the hotel, out by the sandbagged rear entrance to the street. To the east, in the warehouses on the southern shore, angry fires were licking to the sky. They saw the red splinters of shells, the darting searchlights, and heard the roar of many planes.

The same thought hit them as had hit Stationmaster Greenfield. "Christ," Reynolds said, "it sounds like there are hundreds of them."

As yet there weren't, but they were coming: already Canewdon and other radar stations en route could report only "mass plots" to Fighter Command's Filter Room—so many aircraft winging west that the dancing white scallops on the radar screens fused into one colossal "blip." Section Officer Sadie Younger recalls with feeling: "We worked only four-hour shifts but that was enough—a night like that sent you crosseyed."

And still the bombers came. At 11.10 Sadie Younger called to Squadron Leader Richardson: "There are more here than we know—they *all* say they're saturated." Now Richardson told the Sector Ops rooms, who controlled the battle for the sky, "You'd better put on everything you've got."

They were doing their best. At Martlesham airfield on the Suffolk coast the first Hurricane of 242 Squadron had already skimmed along the runway, vanishing westward into the empty sky. First away was Squadron Leader Whitney Straight, prewar racing motorist, who had taken over the squadron from Air Ace Douglas Bader. With a shining Battle-of-Britain tradition, the squadron rated as one of the most lethal in the RAF. French, Poles, Norwegians, Canadians, Czechs—every pilot an officer and a dangerous adversary to meet in the London sky.

Nonetheless, Straight thought they would need more than skill tonight—they'd need luck. At just after eleven he had swung southwest toward the Thames, climbing steeply; at 14,000 feet he passed through cloud. Once above it, flying at 16,000 feet, the scene was unforgettable: the miles of pale sky; the silver orb of the moon; the clouds reflecting the moonlight like snow-capped mountains. At 11.15 P.M. he saw the dark outlines of the Ford factory at Dagenham, then swung west toward Tower Bridge.

Two miles away in West Ham the first bombers were pounding London; the clouds gave back the coppery glare of rising fires, and somewhere in the miles of night sky around more bombers were moving in. Straight's problem was how to see them; the spurting exhaust of the Hurricane dazzled his night vision, to say nothing of the flak. The glowing orange balls came whirling up from the ground, slowly at first, then faster like bubbles rising to the surface of a glass—4,000 feet below but near enough to be distracting.

Incredibly, Straight's first awareness of the enemy was bombs: through a rent in the cloud a stick of three was suddenly hurtling away beneath him. Now his eyes probed the false daylight but he could see nothing—no sign of an aircraft. The bomber could be anywhere—at 25,000 feet or even at his own altitude. He flew on, one of a dozen day fighters already stalking the night sky in search of prey—and luck.

In the East End they needed more than luck. By 11.25— twenty minutes after Aschenbrenner arrived over the target— what looked at first like a dangerous fire situation was building up in the drab gray streets of West Ham.

First the Royal Albert Docks; next the railway sheds and sidings at the King George V Dock; then a major fire at Mitchell and Snow's, the cork merchants. At West Ham Mobilizing Control it didn't seem to Fire Chief Herbert Johnson that he had enough fire engines to cope with the gouts of fire springing up everywhere. Of the 80 engines on the spot, most were already busy with fires that had started, and he had to think of his own area first. It was in any case accepted practice to order more engines than you needed, as something unexpected might blow up. At 11.44 Johnson called Sir Aylmer Firebrace's mobilizing staff, who were also housed at Lambeth, and asked them to have an extra 20 engines standing by. Seven minutes later Johnson signaled "Third Stage Help"—he wanted those engines drafted in.

At Fighter Command the Filter Room had struck the night's knottiest problem. As early as 10.23 the WAAF plotting the northern sector of coast line had a sudden call—one of the radar stations showed a single plane crossing the coast line northeast of Alnwick, Northumberland. "Hey," Sadie Younger heard an irate plotter call, "what's that type doing up there? They should have told us there were some more coming in."

But as the minutes ticked by it seemed that there weren't— just one aircraft, hugging the North Sea coast line at 300 m.p.h. Two fighters, trying to intercept it, had as promptly lost it.

Squadron Leader Richardson rubbed his eyes. It made no sense. A quick glance at the Movement Control Sheet confirmed what he really knew—no friendly aircraft was scheduled within miles of the spot. Yet it couldn't be a German bomber; no bomber in the Luftwaffe could touch above 180 m.p.h. His chief, Air Commodore Tom Webb-Bowen, came to the only decision he could: "Stick an 'X' on it."

This stamped it doubtful, to be watched but left alone; there was little else to do. To mark it hostile automatically called the local guns and fighters into action—and it just conceivably could be a friendly fighter in trouble.

Next door in the ops room Air Marshal Sholto Douglas got curious. He told Operations Officer Cyril Leman: "Find out what it is—what it's doing." On the Ops Room Control table the plane was marked by a red metal arrow; as the men in the gallery watched the WAAF plotters, earphones primed for each fresh course the Filter Room gave, were getting busy. Slowly the long-handled paddle was easing the plane north toward Edinburgh.

But Leman had one ace up his sleeve that the Filter Room couldn't play—the dozen-odd Observer Corps posts scattered across the moorland between the Northumbrian coast line and Edinburgh. If someone could just glimpse the plane it might solve the whole problem. At 10.30 came bewildering news from Post A3 at Chatton: "We've got a visual at 100 feet—it came from behind cloud. It's a Messerschmitt 110."

Sholto Douglas heard the news and shook his head. "Impossible. No Messerschmitt would have the fuel to get to Edinburgh and back. Get another fix on it." Again Leman uncradled the phone, convinced in his own mind that Hitler had developed a new bomber. Within minutes came confirmation from Jedburgh. It was a Messerschmitt right enough, at times flying as low as 50 feet.

Douglas, a fast enough thinker, made up his mind: "Get the fighters up after it." Then a strange thing happened. For a while the plane became confused with the track of an RAF Defiant flying in the same area. At 11.09, before the fighters had had time to make any contact, the observer post from Eaglesham came on the line. The plane had been shot down at Bonnyton Moor, a few miles southwest of Glasgow. More phone calls—and the mystery deepened. No. 14 Group, RAF, controlling all fighters in Scotland, knew nothing about it.

The minutes passed but no more news came of the Messerschmitt. Douglas felt a strange sense of disquiet. Why had it made that lonely northern run—and who had shot it down? At 11.20 a WAAF removed the red metal arrow from the board—the pawn was out of play. But at 11.30 everyone was more preoccupied by that one mystery plane than by the hundreds now milling over the target.

Whoever it had been, it wasn't Leutnant the Baron Von Siber. At 11.28 his Heinkel III, "L for Lucy," was just crossing the English coast line north of Southend, dead above Foulness Point. The stocky fair-haired baron was feeling good; he was anything but a superstitious man, but all the omens were right. The Heinkel, with its load of eight incendiary canisters and two 250-kilo high explosives, was behaving well. He had driven to the airfield in a British Ford left behind at Dunkirk—in the Luftwaffe it held much cachet to own a British vehicle. And at 12,000 feet, flying at a steady 180 m.p.h., they would reach London almost dead on time, just before midnight.

The baron's plan was clear cut: approach from the north, then swing sharply southwest across London in the general direction of Buckingham Palace. Deliver the first load, get back to base fast, bomb up, refuel. Then try for the palace again.

If he felt the slightest tension, the baron wasn't admitting it, even to himself. He knew his duty better. At twenty-five he was still the senior man and the officer—it was his duty to remain calm. A few of his crew, like Unteroffizier Wylezoll, the seventeen-year-old gunner, had wheedled some winter flying kit; it was cold, and if they were shot down over the sea they would stand more chance in fleecy winter jackets. The baron, though, wore his summer flying kit. He did not feel the cold; he did not allow for the risk of being shot down.

Nor for the night fighter on his tail—presumably nobody did, for both Gunner Wylezoll and Oberfeldwebel Schneider, the mechanic, had been briefed to keep a sharp lookout in the rear turret. Without warning there was a rending clatter followed a second later by a soft yellow whoosh of flame from the port engine. In the second of turning the baron saw dimly the second burst, coming from less than 50 yards away, and thought he recognized the long mullet-head cowling that housed the Spitfire's engine.

There was no time to see more. The Heinkel shuddered and yawed violently with a third and final burst of tracer. Glass sprayed everywhere, and a great rush of cold air came swooping into the cockpit. Most of the instrument panel had gone, blown to smithereens. Probably the Spitfire was trying for the starboard engine—instead, it had blown away most of the cockpit and half the nose. In the rear turret somebody cried out, and there was a strange moaning. Then silence.

Hastily the baron cut out the port engine, then called over the intercom. No answer. He called again. Still no answer. In fifteen seconds flat three of his crew had died. Only Feldwebel Josef Fischer, the compact, swarthy little navigator who sat just astern, was still alive. For the first time Von Siber felt a sudden chill.

But only for a minute. It was by guess and by God now—no more instrument flying with the panel shattered, just the hope of keeping "L for Lucy" airborne long enough to reach the Channel and ditch her in the sea, near enough the coast to be picked up by German air-sea rescue. With the Heinkel dipping heavily to port, the baron told Fischer to fuse and release the bombs. They would not harm Buckingham Palace now, but the aircraft was lighter as they went. They had gained height.

With the increased wind resistance to the burning port engine, the Heinkel was still yawing to the left. Suddenly the oil temperature soared frighteningly. Luckily that gauge was still working, but it meant a hit scored that the baron hadn't recognized: the oil radiator of the starboard engine. There were violent bumps and shudders. Waves of flames washed back at Von Siber, and the sickly-sweet smell of burning alloy.

He tugged with all his might on the stick, trying to keep "L for Lucy" up, then saw, from the corner of his eye, a stab of flame somewhere in the fuselage astern. Somehow some petrol must have got fired in the rear turret, and from the way the Heinkel was jerking he gauged they were losing height rapidly —perhaps 12 feet a second.

The baron was not rated a good pilot for nothing; in a case like this he knew where duty lay. Fischer was a good observer, one of the best he had known, but he could not help now, and no pilot who abided by the Luftwaffe's rigid code of honor could needlessly risk the life of his crew. At midnight the baron ordered Fischer: "Bale out." He and his crew of three dead men would go it on their own.

At Fields' factory, by Waterloo, Jimmie Sexton felt almost as lonely. True there was Albert Fey to help him but suddenly, at 11.40, they could have used half-a-dozen men on the roof of the south building. As the incendiaries came raining down the little handyman was ducking and darting in all directions, dousing them with sand. In his mind Sexton kept up a kind of chant: "We've got to hold on. Soon they'll switch to another area. We can save the factory if we only hold on." As a heavier bomb dropped near at hand they ducked between the iron vats, holding their breath.

As if to refute Sexton, the roof telephone buzzed, and Fey answered. It was Fire Chief Bill Wilks, asking if they possibly could hold on. Fey said he thought yes, then asked why. Quietly Wilks explained that the bombs that had fallen had wrecked the twelve-inch water main in York Road and the twenty-four-inch in Waterloo Road. The whole area was virtually without water to fight the fires.

Sexton looked east along the river, and his heart sank. He could imagine nothing worse than what was now happening to West Ham, but was their turn still to come?

Closer to, it looked more eerie still. To Thomas Sinden, the bridegroom-to-be, the only passenger on a bus traveling east, the whole scene was like fairyland: the white dripping flares, the dim blue lighting of the bus, the buildings silhouetted as if against a sunset. Farther, toward the docks, he counted the fires in hundreds. His first thought—it was the end of London. The second and worst—he would never marry Beatrice in the morning.

On the face of it the firemen had a tough time ahead. On the roof of The Lion, West Ham, Publican Bill Barker saw the great orange wall of flame as a timber dump took fire across the Temple Mills Sidings. As he watched, a watertower poked up against the blaze like a steel finger, the firemen at the top clinging grimly to the jet. Suddenly a German plane zoomed low from the clouds; machine-gun fire cracked sharply. The firemen didn't even deign to look around, and presently, as if abashed, the plane went away.

Some professionals took a cheerier view. To Sub Officer Charles Tharby, dashing from dock fire to dock fire, it seemed a light night for West Ham—on one occasion they'd had 38 land mines. But the mains were standing up, the borough was networked by natural rivers, there were many small fires, but most of them well in hand.

Away from Control, Tharby didn't know that his Fire Chief Herbert Johnson had called in 20 extra engines—and was on the point of calling for 20 more.

Back in Paris, at the Luxembourg Hotel, Field Marshal Sperrle and General Koller heard the news which Aschenbrenner had radioed back: 100 bombers were over the target, more were on the way, big fires were piling up. The field marshal decided that supper and a cabaret would not come amiss. General Koller, more studiously inclined, went home to read the German poet Heine. There was, in any case, nothing more that either man could do.

CHAPTER SIX

"Somebody Will Be Late for Their Breakfast"

11.30—12.25 P.M.

THE message from West Ham meant one thing to Major Frank Jackson at Fire Service Headquarters—he must go there and see for himself. If the blitz moved westward, London would need all the fire engines there were. There could be no question of them lying idle tonight.

Before leaving Lambeth he rang Chief Superintendent May at Home Office Control, and May repeated his earlier assurance; at a pinch he thought he could manage 750 reinforcing engines.

May sounded more cheerful than he felt. Since Jackson's first call—six hours back now—he had been mobilizing every engine he could, but it was slow, backbreaking work. As on every other night it was the same story: men were on leave; the engines weren't all serviceable; the local fire chief would have to ask the mayor's authority first; a succession of men standing on petty dignities as the minutes raced by.

The trouble was that Britain's 1,600 local fire brigades were a law unto themselves—different uniforms, different standards of training and equipment, different pay. The system was being scrapped in favor of a National Fire Service, one unified fighting force, as Minister of Home Security Herbert Morrison had announced that very morning.

In fairness to Sir Arthur Dixon, chief of the Home Office Fire Department, no authority had been obliged to maintain a fire brigade until he changed the legislation in 1938. But although the idea of nationalization was scarcely new—the technical journal *Fire* had been urging it for sixteen years—Sir Arthur had had his own ideas. As late as March 1941 he had declared: "Nationalization is impossible. The whole of history is against it."

Morrison, too, had been wary of the project, foreseeing bitter opposition from local councils. It had taken a powerful caucus led by Lieutenant Commander John Fordham, one of Jackson's deputies, two months to persuade Morrison that Sir Arthur was wrong. And the struggle had involved such powerful allies as *The Times, The Daily Telegraph*, Norman (now Sir Norman) Brook, secretary to the Cabinet, Lord Beaverbrook, Minister of Information Brendan Bracken, and William (now Lord) Rootes, the car magnate.

None of this was much help to Chief Superintendent Augustus May—or London—now. Until the National Fire Service was a fact in law, local authorities could be as awkward as they pleased, and never had they seemed so pigheaded as tonight. One local fire chief said flatly that he had no engines, until May countered by quoting from his all-England strength returns: the chief had ten to spare and London needed them.

Now the argument changed: "I want them myself." No wonder May shouted back: "Never mind what *you* want, someone else is in worse trouble than you. I'll look after *you* when you're in trouble."

Worse, it was still too early for May to decide what to do for the best. A week of attacks on the northern ports meant that he dare not call in engines from farther north than Birmingham. Luckily Birmingham had been retaining some London engines for emergency use. These could be brought back to base right away.

Already word had gone out. A hundred miles away, in Birmingham Fire Station, Sub Officer Charles H. Gibbs was wolfing canteen sandwiches and coffee after a dance when an excited fireman burst in: "Hey, Sub, come on, form convoy." Twenty minutes later Gibbs had clambered aboard one of fifty gray-painted engines lined up on the Coventry Road. At midnight, chugging at 25 m.p.h. along blacked-out roads, they were heading for London—the first relief convoy to set out for the capital that night.

It was none too soon. There had been that deceptively slow, almost insidious start; now, ten minutes before midnight, the raid came ferociously to life. The bombers were moving westward; over the City of London; over the warehouses of Clerkenwell and Saffron Hill, the Italian quarter; over the quiet Bloomsbury squares. But pinpointing wasn't easy. Although Euston Station was priority, the incendiaries, instead, caught the British Museum a mile south, plowing through the old copper roofing, burning fiercely in the high, timbered rafters between roof and plaster ceiling.

As the first fire engines came racing across the courtyard the Museum's director, Sir John Forsdyke, went pelting to meet them, the doughty little Greek scholar taking a header on to the running board.

It took only twenty minutes to realize that the position was hopeless. Not only the rafters were burning but the Roman Britain Room; the Prehistoric Room; the Greek Bronze Room, empty now of art treasures but an integral part of the threatened building. On the roof choking black smoke drove Sir John and the firemen back.

Suddenly, with a roar, the flames wrapped around the southwest quadrant bookstack, climbing like a beacon to the sky. Sir John and a fireman struggled across with a jet but after a minute they gave up. "We might as well be spitting on it."

At least no lives were lost. Less than a mile away the first bombers of Colonel Rath's K.G.4 orbited between King's Cross Station and the New River Head reservoir of the Metropolitan Water Board, and the first two of that night's parachute mines drifted slowly as thistledown across the pale sky—nine-foot cylinders packed with 1,500 pounds of high explosive. By chance they struck neither target but landed in quiet Holford Square, Finsbury, where Lenin had lodged thirty years before. Three miles away, in Hackney, Reginald Bell, coordinating officer of No. 3 Group, London Civil Defense Region, saw the two immense magenta flashes hang glowing and throbbing in the sky—instinctively Bell, a gardener, thought of sweet sultan blossoms.

Near at hand street Fire Guard Harry Wright, who had thrown himself forward, felt the pavement recoil three times, punch at his stomach. Stretcher-bearer George Eiffel, one of the first there, found an unimaginable scene: 60 dead and 116 badly wounded; a crowd of 300 strong milling and screaming; human hair matted gray with rubble; faces a mask of blood; yellow dust hanging as thick as smoke over acres of shattered buildings.

A barrage balloon site, a brewery, a convent, two pubs, and sixty houses had been atomized within seconds—and the night was only beginning.

The full fury of it was starting to register now. At Martin's Bank, Lombard Street, Fire Watcher Sidney Smith was one of the first to detect the pattern of Sperrle's new technique—the high explosives and incendiaries raining together without a pause; wave following wave in tight-knit formation; the planes seeming to scream in at housetop level, lower than they had ever done before.

On the roof of the Savoy Quentin Reynolds was convinced that the whole city must burn, but on such a scale that he was awed, not scared—it was all like some gigantic Hollywood spectacle. From the terrace of a Hertfordshire country club Captain Clifford Mollison, Fighter Command's Home Forces liaison officer, watched vortices of blast eddying above the City like ripples thrown upward from a pond. The savagery of it appalled him. "It's that bastard Goering. He's really lost his temper."

Some felt more detachment. Sixty miles away cars had parked on Cuddesden Hill, Oxford, and a group of sixty-odd people had settled down to watch the show. Theological Student Bill Baddeley, who'd been roped in by friends, felt somehow conscience-stricken. Many had even brought hot coffee and sandwiches to complete their Roman holiday.

"Somebody Will Be Late for Their Breakfast"

The livid flames could be seen farther than Oxford. Leutnant Martin Reiser and the crew of his Heinkel III, "B for Berta," were 160 miles away over Rouen when they first sighted that red shifting skyline. Over the intercom Reiser told Pilot Adolf Schied, "Fires like that and moonlight, too—they must have been crazy to send us." And at 12.22, well north of Brighton, it seemed as if Fate agreed—a violent explosion in the sky far to the east, then a plane plummeting into space, trailing fire as it went.

Reiser, of course, couldn't know it, but the Baron Von Siber was in trouble.

For minutes after ordering Observer Josef Fischer to bale out, the baron had fought to keep "L for Lucy" airborne. Now he knew it was hopeless; the Heinkel was starting to spin dizzily; he, too, must bale out. It was easier said than done. Although he had made sure Fischer opened the pilot's escape hatch, he had forgotten to ask help with his seat belt. To loosen it he had to detach one hand from the stick, which was nearly fatal. Flames, the moon, the shattered cockpit swam before his eyes as he tugged.

Somehow he managed to crack his head badly; as he wrestled through the escape hatch, pain was fast drowning consciousness. He dropped like a stone, tugging the ripcord with one last effort; only the jerk of the flowering parachute snapped him back to sanity. As he fell, he saw clearly below a steely gleam in the moonlight, and his body braced for the shock. He was going to land in a river.

Actually it was the Medway at Upchurch in Kent, but either way it spelled trouble to the baron. First the icy water knifed the breath from his body—at midnight the air temperature was one degree below freezing. Then somehow a trailing lead from the Heinkel's intercom had got snagged in his parachute's release mechanism; several times the wind, ripping across the river, pulled him choking beneath the muddy black water. By the time he had yanked out his knife and cut it free he was well

83

out in midstream and it was a numbing 500-yard swim to the shore.

As he scrambled through the mud a Home Guard detachment loomed up; the baron was about to announce he was a German officer, but apparently they knew. They seized him, pounding him almost insensible with fists and rifle butts. The blitz that was just starting for so many millions was over for the Baron Von Siber.

For Hauptmann Albert Hufenreuter the trip was presenting complications, not the least of them being his pilot, Richard Furthmann.

The first trouble had come at 10.30 P.M. on Lille North airfield when the crew settled at take-off stations for cockpit drill: Furthmann revving the engines up to zero boost, testing the magnetos, bomb doors, flaps. First the port engines whined and snarled, blue smoke curling, then, after a few turns, the starboard, too. Somehow Furthmann didn't seem satisfied; again he punched the buttons of the booster coils. First the port inner, then the starboard inner, port outer, then starboard outer.

Hufenreuter, seeing him grow pink and start to sweat, called, "Is it all right?" The young pilot didn't answer, just kept testing, until finally Hufenreuter yelled, "Well, is it all right, or isn't it?"

At last Furthmann said reluctantly, "Well, yes," and then a moment later, "Stand by for take-off." He checked through to all the crew on the intercom—Karol Gerhardt, the wireless operator, even younger than Furthmann himself; Mechanic Josef Berzbach, dead keen and reliable; Eggert Webber, the gunner. Then the chocks were waved away and they taxied out to the down-wind side of the airfield. Hufenreuter looked at his watch—10.28. Two minutes to go.

Then the Heinkels scheduled before them had gone. Furthmann flicked off the brakes and they were rolling, picking up speed, and the airspeed indicator was quivering at 125 m.p.h. as the long, concrete runway raced away beneath. Then they were climbing, four incendiary canisters and one 1,000-kilo bomb destined for Stepney secure in the bomb bays. At 300 feet they turned on course.

Now more trouble arose. Tonight, Hufenreuter, ignoring the briefing, was making his own course and the pilot didn't like it. Once Furthmann, a good, cautious pilot who went by the book, voiced a protest—the briefing was due north, over the Dutch island of Tschelling, then a course of 203 North magnetic. Hufenreuter snorted: "The same way as all the others are going? You want to make it easy for the British?"

It almost seemed to Hufenreuter that the others did. Without observing them, he could feel their tension growing as the Heinkel neared the French coast, could feel them waiting for him to flash the signal pattern that established their bona fide with the German anti-aircraft batteries.

Soon Furthmann asked what the matter was. Wasn't he going to give the signal? Hufenreuter admitted not if he could help it. If the batteries let the formality slide, it would suit him better. He argued, "If they can see it, the batteries over at Dover can see it, too, can't they?"

A moment then Furthmann became agitated. "Give it, please give it. Look, they're signaling to us, can't you see?" Reluctantly Hufenreuter gave the signal. Mingled sighs of relief came over the intercom and Gunner Weber urged: "For heaven's sake, don't play monkey tricks like that. You'll have us all shot down."

At 11.15 P.M., as Cape Gris-Nez came in sight, Hufenreuter had privately confirmed what he had half-suspected all along: he would have to see this flight through himself, to inspire this keen but untried crew with the strength of a prewar Luftwaffe pilot.

He settled down to map reading, charting pinpoints, working out a new wind. The moon swam up over the North Foreland, so bright tonight that he didn't even need a flashlight to map read. Twelve thousand feet below the Channel was a shelf of green luminous glass and there were small white waves creaming against a foreign shore—England. . . .

Hufenreuter spoke. "Your ground speed is exactly 164 miles per hour. We shall be over London in exactly thirty-five minutes and ten seconds. ETA Hastings up in ten minutes. We ought to cross the coast dead on track."

No one answered. Each man sat quiet, waiting, alert for whatever was coming, his ears filled with the alternating irritating drone of the desynchronized engines. The uneven note was supposed to make it harder for the sound locators but they knew they would be registering some kind of blip on a radar screen by now. And the orders would be going out to the flak and the fighter fields.

Then they had crossed the coast; blacked-out Hastings lay to starboard; beyond trees were thin striped shadows on the moonlit downs. Furthmann asked: "What now? Lay track to Maidstone and then straight to target?" But Hufenreuter grunted a negative; on a night like this only a zigzag course would help. He had worked it all out as he always worked out his courses, in solitude that afternoon, telling no one until the time was ripe. Northeast now to Canterbury, as if they were heading out over the North Sea. Then lay track for Croydon on the west. Then due north to pick up the Thames at West Ham.

He told Furthmann: "But I don't like this moonlight. Better climb—take her up to 16,500. I'll tell you when to start losing height."

The Heinkel flew on. Lying on his stomach in the nose, Hufenreuter methodically tested switches, lights, bomb-sight settings. From time to time he intoned: ETAs . . . Canterbury . . . Croydon . . . West Ham. And they caught their breath with awe. Along the Thames the red smoky fires had merged into one—the riverside seemed alight for miles. Never had they imagined a city could burn like this. The Thames glowing like blood with the reflection of the fires, buildings outlined like mountains of red-hot cinders; the white probing fingers of the searchlights; the droning of hundreds of engines, spaced neatly 150 feet below and above them, that seemed to shudder and vibrate in their own fuselage. For a moment Hufenreuter thought: This is it. We're seeing the end of a city, then turned his mind to other things.

He told Furthmann: "Bring her down more—a bit more. Height 9,500—turn east. We're right dead on track and the target should be coming up any minute."

Furthmann seemed anxious to be gone. "Are you going to bomb?"

"No, I'm not." Hufenreuter was adamant. "We're going to identify the target area first and make damn sure we get something worth-while. We won't need a flare—there are too many of them as it is."

To Hufenreuter it seemed that K.G.100 was gilding the lily. All along the Thames for miles the flares were dazzling and blinding, thousands of small magnesium expansions—so many that it was hard to see the target at all.

Prone on his stomach, Hufenreuter wrestled with the last-minute niceties. From 10,000 feet the bomb would take about twenty-five seconds to fall. Now they had dropped to 9,000 feet, sacrificing height for speed—120 m.p.h. now against 100. By the time the bomb had fallen they would have moved perhaps a mile. He set the five complex readings of the bomb sight —they must be three miles from the aiming point now, which was just right—they needed all that for the run-up. The searchlights weren't catching them, the lampblack eating up the beams like velvet. Only a few flashes of ack-ack farther east. So far so good.

A thousand feet below a parachute flare splashed into life; at once Furthmann made a steep bend to port.

"Why that?" Hufenreuter grunted. The boy seemed nervous. "There were flashlights." Hufenreuter assured him: "It's all right. They're lower than us." Over the intercom he called back to Berzbach and Weber: "Still awake, you two?" He thought they sounded very wide-awake.

Now Hufenreuter was almost ready. "Left, hard left," he told Furthmann. Slowly the Heinkel eased round, Hufenreuter craning for a visual; the red river curving; white, blinding flares; the soft, steady drumming of the engine. It must be Stepney all right, miles of huddled buildings, but it was hard to find a good target in this dazzle. "Left farther still," he told Furthmann, "about twenty degrees."

The pilot countered, "What's the time?"

"Twelve-five. Why?"

Furthmann seemed agitated. "Please hurry—our time was up minutes ago."

"If we stay here another ten minutes," Hufenreuter replied, "we're going to find a target. That looks promising—a warehouse or something. Right a little now. Steady."

Bombs fused, bomb doors open. Now Hufenreuter jabbed the push button on the end of the trailing wire not unlike the button suspended at a hotel bedside. Then "Bomb's gone," Hufenreuter yelled over the intercom, but there was no need. The bomb went hurtling toward Stepney. The aircraft soared like a balloon in a squall, 1,000 pounds lighter.

Yet Hufenreuter felt the old frustration. He had dropped eighteen 1,000-pounders in his time and it was always the same: relentlessly honest, Hufenreuter was never satisfied unless he could assure himself he had chosen and hit an orthodox target. To the observer it seemed that wartime crews were the same, too: ditch the bomb and get out of it, never mind whether it was a military target or just a street of houses.

At 12.07 he told Furthmann: "Keep her on the river. We'll see what the incendiaries will do."

They cruised gently, following the shimmer of the Thames toward the City of London. The fires were getting away now, red licking tongues along the northern shore above Southwark Bridge—Upper Thames Street, the wharves by Cannon Street Station. Back at the bomb sight Hufenreuter felt better; with incendiaries you knew where you were. It was a certainty that they'd start up something worth-while and if the pilots following up knew their job, they would land something heavy near it—to spread the fire or hinder the fire brigade, who cared?

And over the City you couldn't miss—there wasn't that inner niggle of dissatisfaction which you got with more isolated targets that you might be wasting incendiaries on a plowed field.

The Heinkel droned on, Hufenreuter intoning at intervals, "Left, a bit . . . steady . . ." Four times he pressed the button; four times he signaled "Bombs gone." The incendiary canisters went spiraling down over Roman London. Then they were curving with the Thames, the great fires mirrored in the shining water.

After a bit Furthmann asked, "Where are we?"

Hufenreuter grunted and consulted the map. "Over Wandsworth. Why?"

For the first time that night Furthmann chuckled. "Funny—I was born there. My father was a bank clerk."

They joked for a bit as to whether that made Furthmann British, owing allegiance to King George and Winston Churchill, although he spoke no word of English. Then Hufenreuter said: "All right, we've had our fun. Course 189. Let's go home."

On the ground it was hard to tell what was going on. In Turney Road, West Dulwich, Marguerita Stahli had damped down the coal fire, donned an old weatherproof, snapped on Rex's leash.

Now, with Windsor by her side, she was patrolling, steel helmeted, up and down the street in case of trouble—a voluntary roster the residents themselves had arranged. They could see the fires to the east and north, but at 12:30 there seemed little chance of the raid spreading this far south of the Thames. They arranged that presently Windsor would borrow Marguerita's bike and cycle home to spend what remained of the night with his parents at Croydon, seven miles south.

Whatever the vantage point, the feeling outside the East End was much the same. Warden Jack Smith was just setting off on his beat near the Alexandra Hotel, Knightsbridge, when he ran into fellow Warden Major Kennie. "Ah, well," the major said, "another quiet night, I s'pose."

On Sydenham Hill old Mr. Reginald Harpur, snug in his shelter, was making up his diary; the man next door was pushing a wheelbarrow, gardening by moonlight, "as though the days are not long enough, even now."

At St. Luke's Hospital, Chelsea, the medical superintendent, Dr. R. Thane Taylor, debated whether to move all the patients from the upper wards to the basement, then decided against it. This wasn't really Chelsea's raid.

Mrs. Margaret Daley and the twenty-five workers at St. Augustine's Depot, South Croydon, shared that viewpoint. As she checked on that evening, in blue serge tunic and slacks, blue peaked cap set on neat brown hair, the old query rose again to Mrs. Daley's mind: Would this be *the* night? Then she saw dark nineteen-year-old Olive Ward, her attendant, detach herself from the throng in the gloomy raftered hall. Temporarily she forgot it as they exchanged greetings.

Around the hall the others wondered about Mrs. Daley. Although they liked her well enough she was always something of an enigma—a few were certain she had been "a lady's maid in a big house." She would pitch in and help anybody, she liked a joke, but she wasn't a woman with whom you would take liberties. At the end of a long, grimy shift she was as neat, as unruffled, as reserved as when she started.

Meantime Mrs. Daley had plenty to do. First the big converted Chrysler had to be cleaned—one of a dozen ambulances and sitting-case cars parked in the moonlit yard behind the hall. Then a careful check on the petrol, water, batteries, while Olive Ward worked over the equipment—four pillows, blankets, splints, hot-water bottles which needed refilling every hour of the night.

Again she wondered about tonight. Was it going to be Croydon's raid? Somehow it didn't seem likely; the planes muttered overhead, and to the north the sky was trembling, but it was twelve miles away at least. Later would come duties they all shared, the hall and toilets to be swept out, stoves to be lit, taking turns in the canteen, but maybe by 2 A.M. the all-clear would go. If it didn't, it meant a long night up playing darts or table tennis. Even curling up in blankets on the bare boards of the hall, the only sleep possible, was forbidden if a "red" warning was up. And if trouble did come, she must just have faith in God.

After all, God had protected her the day Bernard's motor-cycle had gone out of control, crushing her against the iron gates of her home. She had been pregnant at the time, but God had not let her die, even though the result had been a miscarriage which had begun the slow breakup of her married life. And God had protected Bernardine, her daughter, even when she was too ill with rheumatic fever to be moved to hospital and the blitz had shaken the house all night. Sitting by the bedside, holding Bernardine's hand, Mrs. Daley had talked to God. "Please, God," she kept saying, "don't let my Bernardine die." She knew her prayers had been heard, because Bernardine lived.

By midnight she had decided, as she always did, that there was no use worrying. The raid probably wouldn't come their way at all.

Closer to the target area there was still the same illogical feeling—danger was what happened to other people. In Bermondsey Auxiliary Fireman Percy Madden heard the first bomb drop, sang out idly, "Oh, pack it up, old boy, we're just going to bed." At St. Pancras Station Porter Walter Rainberg was quite enjoying the spectacle with Porters "Yorkie" Merriman and Andrew Fuller; the raised terrace outside the great Victorian-Gothic station offered a grandstand view. As a chandelier flare came floating down, Rainberg called, "Not half a treat—like something in a pantomime." When the funereal whistle of the bombs followed, the others heard the disbelief in his voice: "Hold on—they're coming in the station."

They were indeed, and 15,000 panes of glass were coming with them. When Rainberg and the others picked themselves up from the archway they'd dived into, there was a ringing in their ears that lasted for weeks; the soot from the shattered Victorian roof inside the main station was like black whirling snow; a crater with the lights of the Metropolitan Railway winking 100 feet below; ten-ton concrete slabs piled 300 yards away.

As this debris spattered on the roof of Euston Station half a mile away, Arrivals Foreman Ted Streeter couldn't believe his ears either. He told his mates, "I think it's raining."

Shortly Assistant District Controller William Walton at Kentish Town Control up the line signaled to every station on the northern run: "All platforms St. Pancras to be considered out of commission."

More and more people were finding that danger was their heritage. All through the blitz Driver Leslie Stainer had breathed a pet invocation, "You can have it, we don't want it," when he heard a distant bomb. Now, at midnight on May 10, it was Stainer's turn—bombs raining on Cannon Street Station where he stood frozen on the footplate of Engine 1541 ready for the Dartford run. The aspect signal lights blasted out; bomb after bomb falling; the station roof alight. When Stainer next looked skyward the moon had gone—blotted out by the smoke from the fires. Soon Foreman Foote came running with fresh orders. Vast brands from the blazing station roof were falling everywhere; the safest place for the trains was out on the railway bridge.

Tonight all safety was comparative. With Driver Percy Collins, Stainer and Fireman Osborne coupled up another engine, pulling out of the platform on to the bridge above the river—in time for a stick of three to come screaming almost on top of them. One landed in the river, so hard that a column of water geysered 80 feet high, clean over the top of the signal box. The third was closer; for one moment Stainer and his fireman, bunched on the footplate, felt the 54-ton engine lurch clean from the rails.

"Look out," Osborne shouted, "we're going in the drink." As the engine righted itself, Stainer was still dizzy with the explosion. "Old mate, I thought my back week had come."

Next they realized they were trapped—the other engine be-hind them had caught a direct hit, "opened up like a sardine tin," cordite and scalding steam boiling everywhere. As they ran back to check that Driver Perce Collins and his fireman were safe, they saw their own train burning too fiercely for buckets of water to help. There was only one thing to do: uncouple the engine from the train, scour the engine, and leave the train to burn out. Now Stainer told Osborne: "If we stop together, a bomb'll come down and wipe us both out. If we separate, we've got a chance."

By 12.20 Stainer had doubled to the far side of the bridge. Huddled in its lee, lonely and cold, he waited for the dawn, and watched Cannon Street burn.

Two railway termini out of commission—and Sperrle's bombers had been west of Aldgate Pump, the East End–City of London boundary, just twenty minutes.

Both stations, of course, were priority targets, easily spotted from the air. Other hits were more fortuitous, but they registered just the same. It was as if on this night, as never before, the Luftwaffe had everything its own way.

At Group 3 Headquarters, Hackney, on the farthest fringe of the East End, Reginald Bell tried to sort out the tangle. The coordinating officer for Group 3, Bell was a government official responsible for the City of London, Holborn, and the six high-risk East End boroughs—Stepney, Poplar, Hackney, Bethnal Green, Finsbury, Shoreditch. From his own basement Control Bell kept in minute-by-minute touch with the controls of each borough—just how badly each was faring. With a tally of available forces Bell could switch rescue workers, ambulances, even relief wardens, from one district to another as needed.

At 12:20 Bell heard the voice of Stepney Controller Roger Corderoy over the wire: "The buildings above our main access are well alight and you've got to run the gantlet to get in. They've got some water on to the fires somehow but there is only one pump."

Bell listened gravely. Stepney Control Center lay underground between an electricity generating station and a sandbag store. Now both were in flames. Without lights or ventilation Corderoy's staff was working in suffocating darkness, unable even to see one another for the smoke pumping into the basement.

Bell tried Fire Brigade District Headquarters at Whitechapel. Only ten minutes back on his way east Major Frank Jackson had told Whitechapel's Chief Superintendent Harold Norman, and his Station Officer Cyril Tobias: "I'm very worried about the West Ham situation. I think they asked for help earlier than they need have done."

Now, although Jackson was on his way to sort things out, Whitechapel still had no engines available. Bell rang back to Stepney: "What about evacuating to your reserve control?"

Corderoy seemed almost resigned. "No good. It's damaged by blast and out of action. We'll just have to carry on."

Bell worried about it, hardly knowing what to do for the best. How much was Stepney going to need in the night ahead? With their Control fighting to keep going, it was hard for them to reckon up what was happening in their own area. Should he divert services from Poplar to help them out—or was Poplar due for a heavy night? Finsbury was out of it—just to cope with those two land mines in Holford Square they'd had to call in troops.

The City? Holborn? Shoreditch? Bethnal Green? At 12.25 Bell didn't know. His telephone links with all of them were severed.

It was the same south of the river. At midnight Southwark's Deputy Controller Cyril Platten, a tall, handsome solicitor, was calling Control from his Edgware home, ten miles away. But now every line seemed dead, and there were twenty lines serving Control through four exchanges. Platten jumped in his Rover and set off for Southwark; this raid might prove too much for them. The road was black but clear of traffic as far as St. John's Wood, then the full hysteria of the raid struck home.

"Somebody Will Be Late for Their Breakfast"

Now the glow of the sky lit up the road for him; he knew that the bombs were falling but couldn't hear them inside the car; frightened to death, he began to drive faster and faster. By Waterloo Station a flaming gas main barred the way, pulling him up with a scream of tires. Mr. Platten had a weird fancy: "It was as if the Angel Gabriel stood there with a drawn sword."

After a nerve-racking ninety-minute drive Platten reached Southwark, to find the lines weren't dead, just choked out with calls for help. For the first time in the blitz Control Room Officer Richard Edwards had persuaded Group 5 Headquarters at Brixton to slash red tape—with every rescue man and ambulance worker the borough possessed already in the field, Group were laying on mobile reserves for Edwards himself to direct as the need arose.

For the first time in centuries the façade was stripped aside to show London for what it was—a series of small stone villages which chance had gummed together. Now, like villages in a blizzard, they were cut off from one another—by severed telephone wires, by roads blocked head high with rubble, by the sheer risk of running the gantlet of bombs.

Shut off in their private worlds, men did the best they could. Down at the Elephant and Castle incendiaries fell so fast that sixteen-year-old Bill Sherrington dashed to the nearest shelter for help, but found only sour looks—he must be mad to venture abroad on a night like this. So Sherrington battled heroically on his own, darting into houses the owners had left; stamping out some bombs, using a stirrup pump on others; tipping a flaming flower box into the street seconds before the windowframe caught. At Lambeth Hospital, where the top floor had caught, Assistant Matron Margaret Pirie saw a furious eighty-year-old leap from bed in a nightshirt, and quench the blazing black-out curtains with a deftly aimed urinal.

In Westminster there was more punctilio. John Hodgkinson was wooing sleep in the air-raid shelter beneath Diana Riviere's apartment block when a lady appeared. "Would you be so good as to look at something in my garden?" Shaken by the sight of his first incendiaries licking at some trelliswork, Hodgkinson couldn't locate sand or stirrup pumps; he had to snuff them out with his steel helmet. Next the porter for the block appeared; some incendiaries had fallen on the roof and he wanted help. As he guided Hodgkinson through a mass of stairways and attics the man, a servant of the old school, kept up a running commentary: "Up this way, sir . . . mind your head . . ." Finally they swamped the incendiaries with some boxes of mold standing handy. "Such a pity, sir, someone had planned to raise tomatoes in these."

Even Field Marshal Sperrle and his group commanders could hardly know how bad things were for London. At 12.30, when some of the first planes were arriving back, the crews *did* report that they had bombed visually with good results, but many commanders didn't know this. At Dinard, Brittany, Colonel Herhudt von Rhoden, chief of staff of No. 4 Flying Corps, had gone to bed, ordering: "Don't wake me unless the weather changes—we might have to divert some planes to other airfields." At Castle Maria Kerke, Ghent, General Paul Deichmann, No. 2 Flying Corps' chief of staff, at least waited up for the first report, then turned in.

It all sounded good—four large fires at the western end of Victoria Docks, others in Millwall Outer Docks—but fairly routine. The general didn't even call his chief, General Loerzer, to pass on details.

Not that it would have conveyed much if he had. General Loerzer's knowledge of the situation in London was typical of every Luftwaffe officer—superficially good but sketchy. Details of damage to communications, electricity cables, gas mains, almost never filtered through to those who would have liked to know. The only clue as to potential difficulties had come some months back in a dispatch routed through Portugal from the Germans' most reliable agent in Britain, a Danish-born mechanic named Hans Schmidt. Then Schmidt had reported London's water supply "not very adequate for fire fighting."

Goodge Street, near St. Pancras Station, was one of the 2,200 fires out of control before midnight. *Mirrorpic*

Heart of a conflagration. This was Fetter Lane, off Fleet Street, one of nine conflagrations started by Nazi incendiaries. *Mirrorpic*

Left. Fire streams from the spire of St. Clement Dane's, Wren's "Oranges and Lemons" church, one of the last targets to catch fire. *Mirrorpic. Below.* Firemen playing their hoses on the ruins of the Salvation Army headquarters in Victoria Street. *Radio Times Hulton Picture Library*

"Somebody Will Be Late for Their Breakfast"

The Luftwaffe High Command had brushed this aside; too vague to be of much use.

It was a masterly understatement. In a large-scale raid, if the fires got away, even the square mile of the City of London needed 600,000 gallons of water a minute to keep things in check. The chances of tapping this quantity from the public mains were slender—and not merely for reasons of pressure. The mains lay rigid in the ground, barely three feet from road level. Even a 50-kilo bomb landing close could snap them like a carrot.

Two years' prewar haggling between the Home Office and the London County Council as to who should foot the bill had resulted in two twenty-four-inch emergency mains, with a third under way, being piped through high-risk areas— £500,000 worth of engineering. These, too, were cast-iron mains three feet below road level.

Back at Fire Brigade Headquarters Major Jackson was sorting out the picture. At West Ham Jackson had found all his fears justified: in his anxiety to keep his area covered, Fire Chief Herbert Johnson had overordered. At West Ham's three principal stations, Stratford, Prince Regent's Road, and Silvertown, fire engines had been lying idle. Now West Ham had been ordered to dispatch surplus engines without delay to the sorely pressed Whitechapel area.

But Jackson saw that it would need more than West Ham's fire engines to put things right. The news was as grave as it could be. At midnight a bomb had fractured the City Main, connecting the Thames near Cannon Street Station with the Grand Junction Canal, northward, by City Road—just as it had done on December 29. And the West End main, from the Grand Union Canal in Regent's Park to Shaftesbury Avenue, was out, too.

Between them these mains had reinforced the public mains at a rate of 30,000 gallons a minute.

But the emergency mains had been constructed like any

other water main; like any other water main they had suffered the same fate.

What did this mean? Rocking backward and forward on a chair, feet, as usual, jammed into a wastebasket, Jackson talked it over with his water officer, District Officer S. J. Hender. It amounted to this. Jackson could keep the fires in check if the emergency mains stood up. He could check them with the public mains in commission. He could even check them with the Thames at normal level.

But look at it which way you would he could not hope to keep the fires in check with the emergency mains gone, the public mains fast going, and the Thames at its present level.

Actually the river was not at lowest ebb tonight—18 feet six inches as against the "mean" spring minimum of 16 feet—but it was still out of reach to most fire engines installed on the high embankments and bridges. And at low tide the river would be separated from its bank-side wharves by 50 feet of treacly black mud. Even trailer pumps lowered by ropes or man power to set their suctions into the ebbing tide would be inextricably bogged down.

Despite all the blitz the capital had been in most ways superbly lucky. Most attacks had been localized. The fire raid of December 29 had seen 1,400 fires but mostly within the City's square mile. And March 19 had been like September 7—the docks had suffered most. Now Superintendent "Shiner" Wright's mobilizing board with its rows of colored tallies showed the situation plainly.

There were fires beyond West Ham, stretching almost to Romford; fires six miles to the west in Hammersmith; fires eight miles south at Norwood; fires far to the north beyond Hampstead. And in the miles between these lateral points tongue after tongue of orange fire was licking to the sky.

At Roseberry Avenue, Clerkenwell, the Italian quarter, the building next to the Fire Service's "B" District Headquarters covering the bulk of the City of London had taken a direct hit, putting out the switchboard. For the moment seventy-five sub-stations in one of London's highest-risk fire areas were cut off from their mobilizing headquarters—with no knowledge of the worst fires, with no instructions on how to deploy their machines.

Even these were routine jobs compared with what was to come. While Jackson was still chewing over the problem with District Officer Hender, Superintendent George Adams, a seasoned patriarch of the Fire Service, was checking in to the District Headquarters he commanded at Southwark Bridge Road. A glance at his Control Room tallies told Adams that the biggest fire yet developed in "F" District—which covered the Thames and its immediate area from Teddington to the Nore—was a ten-pump affair beyond the Elephant and Castle. Adams told his driver, S. S. Chapman, "We'll have a look-see."

It was only a five-minute run in the staff car, and Chapman took the direct route—south down Southwark Bridge Road, away from the river, to make the oblique right-hand turn on the far side of the Elephant and Castle traffic junction. Suddenly, as the car jolted through the deserted crossroads, Chapman jammed on the brake. To Adams it seemed the skies had opened to rain white fire: scores of bursting incendiary canisters, dazzling white parachute flares, flares that splashed into blue and gold, red and green marker flares. Next instant the six roads stemming like spokes from the central wheel of the Elephant exploded into flame at the same moment.

"For the love of Pete," growled Superintendent Adams, "what the hell can I do with this lot?" Driver Chapman, imperturbable, called on some useful philosophy: "One thing, guv'nor, somebody'll be late for their breakfast in the morning, and that includes us."

Adams stood thunderstruck. He was appalled by the near-celestial grandeur of the scene. And still the incendiaries were raining on the well-loved territory—on the roof of the Elephant and Castle pub with its elephant-and-castle trade sign molded in red clay; on the roof of Spurgeon's Tabernacle, where Charles Haddon Spurgeon, the American Baptist, had preached;

on the railway arch, on Freeman, Hardy and Willis's boot shop, on acres of soot-stained houses; on back-street grocery stores and poky cobblers' shops, on gin palaces, and factories and eel-pie shops. More than just the main artery, where all southern roads to the Thames bridges intersected, the Elephant and Castle was the symbol of warm, rumbustious South London Cockney life.

It was now 12.19. Adams knew that he had to get a message back, and fast. Like every senior officer, he had a despatch rider following his car on a motor bike; now he grabbed his man. "Get back to Control and tell them: Make pumps ten. Say if I'm not careful I'll have a conflagration on my hands down at the Elephant." Adams knew that he would need many more than ten pumps to hold these fires in check—but they would do for a start. And the night's first potential conflagration, he thought, should rate top priority.

Superintendent Adams was wrong on one detail. Back at Lambeth Control, as his report was logged, neither Superintendent "Shiner" Wright nor District Officer Ernest Thomas even raised an eyebrow. It was the sixth embryo conflagration they had logged in eighteen minutes flat.

CHAPTER   SEVEN

"*Another One In, Another One Out . . .*"

12.25—12.45 A.M.

HIGH above the East End of London another wave of bombers orbited, and a trail of incendiaries fired the Anglican Church of St. Mary of Eton by Wick Road, Hackney. Impotent with rage, a street fire guard shook his fist at the sky, loosed off a torrent of oaths, then realized one of the curates was right beside him.

Shamefaced, the man mumbled: "I'm sorry, Father, I didn't realize . . ."

The priest's eyes twinkled. "That's all right, son, you can say it. I just have to think it."

As yet not many Londoners felt so involved emotionally. At 12.25 it was still, for more than a dozen boroughs, the other man's raid—a source of pity, not fear—and even the areas hardest hit told themselves things might soon slacken off. In East Ham Truck Driver Edwin Wheeler saw a German bomber bobbing in the hard white fountain of a searchlight and felt a twinge of pity: whatever the pilot had done, he didn't deserve to die. As the batteries hammered from Regent's Park, shelterers by King's Cross Station chorused, "Good, we're giving it to 'em." District Warden Rob Connell asked, "But s'pose a Jerry baled out in your back garden, what then?" Again reaction was unanimous: "Oh, that's different—offer the poor lad a cuppa char."

Four hundred miles away, on Bonnyton Moor, near Glasgow, Mrs. McLean, a sixty-four-year-old crofter's widow, was doing just that. It had been a long, hard day on the little farm, and by eleven Mrs. McLean and her daughter Sophia were in bed; only David, her plowman son, lingered by the dying fire. Suddenly from the depths of sleep Mrs. McLean heard a strange droning; it went on and on as if half-a-dozen planes were circling the house. By this time David McLean had snuffed out the oil lamp and dashed to the window in time to see a plane rip violently into the ground 500 yards away. The shaking yellow flames lit up the silhouette of a parachutist floating gently down over the McLeans' cottage.

So McLean grabbed a hayfork, dashed to the scene in time to find an aviator in full flying kit alternately nursing a hurt ankle and fumbling with his parachute harness. When old Mrs. McLean saw David struggling back to the cottage, supporting a handsome black-browed stranger who admitted he was a German, she felt "none too friendly," but somehow Scottish hospitality won the day. The poor man looked pale and tired and his ankle was so swollen that she just had to get the kettle boiling and offer him a cup.

"Thank you, I never drink tea as late as this. I'll only have a glass of water," was the courteous reply.

So they settled down to chat—as strange a tea party as existed anywhere in Britain that night. The stranger gave his name with disarming frankness—Horn, Hauptmann Albert Horn of Munich. How long had he been in the air? He thought more than four hours. Almost diffidently David McLean explained that he'd have to get in touch with the police.

"Please," said the visitor, "I think that would be best." Later he pulled out a pocketbook to produce a snapshot of a four-year-old boy. "That's my son. I saw him this morning. God knows when I shall see him again."

Now David slipped off to phone the police, but still the visitor sat chatting, seeming grateful for the comfort of a peat fire. He was so obviously a gentleman that old Mrs. McLean was fascinated—by his perfect English, his gold watch and bracelet, his easy manners. His one apparent concern was his parachute. "I should like to keep a piece as a souvenir. I am very lucky to be alive."

Presently, in answer to David's summons, two armed privates arrived. Watching him, David McLean thought the visitor seemed relieved to find them British. Asked if he was armed, he spread his hands in a gesture. "You see all I have. My plane was unarmed also."

As the soldiers searched him the McLeans stood silent, almost embarrassed. It was as if, through no fault of their own, the hospitality had gone sour. But there wasn't a lot to find—a box of German matches, personal papers, various capsules of medicine. The one thing that struck them was the number of photographs of himself and his family that the visitor seemed to carry. To the end he remained calm and smiling; when the time came to go he again bowed stiffly to old Mrs. McLean and Sophia and thanked them profusely for all they had done. As if to atone for the formalities of the search, one of the young Tommies presented him with a bottle of milk which he had brought for his guard duty.

By 12.30 the McLeans had washed up the tea mugs and retired to bed, a little dazed by the night's drama, unaware that they had done anything more unusual than entertain one unlucky German airman.

About the same time, in Fighter Command Ops room, Air Marshal Sholto Douglas was starting to get a different picture. Not that he fully accepted it, for it was so incredible that it didn't make sense. An hour and a quarter had passed and he had almost forgotten the mysterious Messerschmitt when the phone jangled. The commander of No. 34 Group, Royal Observer Corps, calling from Glasgow: "We've got the pilot of the M 110, sir. He admits he's Rudolf Hess and he wants to see the Duke of Hamilton."

Events might not have moved so fast if it hadn't been for the speedy sleuthing of Graham Donald, Glasgow's assistant group officer. Eager to vindicate his observer posts' identifications, he had driven to the scene, to find the wreckage of a Messerschmitt strewn over an acre and a half. Curiosity took him to meet the pilot at the local Home Guard Headquarters—even with extra petrol tanks the man could never have made the return trip. And as they chatted, something about the pilot's face struck him as familiar.

Still, Douglas couldn't believe his ears. Walter Richard Rudolf Hess was deputy fuehrer of the Third Reich—ranking as Nazi No. 3 after Hitler and Goering. He had fought with Hitler in the Beer Cellar Putsch of 1923 and since then the two men had been inseparable. Why, Hess was reckoned responsible to Hitler alone, the man who truly wielded the power in the Nazi party. Now he had come to Britain to see, of all people, the Duke of Hamilton whose Scottish estates bordered the scene of the crash.

One factor was easily settled: the Duke of Hamilton, the first man to fly over Everest, was now a wing commander in the Royal Air Force, in charge of Douglas's fighter sector at Turnhouse, East Scotland. In the commander in chief's Ops Room annex, from which all top-secret calls were made, Douglas rang the duke, asking without preamble: "Do you know Hess?"

The duke, sounding puzzled, asked if the fighter chief meant Rudolf Hess, if so, he couldn't actually claim to know him. He had shaken hands with him once at the Olympic Games in 1936. How did the question arise?

Douglas, who had a boyish sense of humor, replied: "Well, he's come to see you or says he has. They've got him at the Central Police Station in Glasgow. You'd better pop over there and have a look at him."

"To see me at this hour?" said the duke, still puzzled. But he agreed that he'd get over there right away.

As Douglas recalled the phone chat, it was a strangely British conversation, almost as if Hess, having made no appointment, had chosen to send in his card at an inconvenient hour.

The duke, on the other hand, had no memory of this call. As he remembers it, his first intimation that something had gone awry was a midnight summons from his sector controller which brought him hastening from bed to the Control Room. The news perturbed him. The German pilot of the plane that had crashed near Eaglesham had asked for the duke by name.

At this time, the duke was positive, he had never met Rudolf Hess, either at the Olympic Games or anywhere else. Instead, while studying the German Air Force he had talked with Albrecht Haushofer, a leading Nazi theorist, who had been anxious to engineer a meeting between Hess and the duke in Lisbon. But the meeting had not taken place.

Next morning, together with Flight Lieutenant Benson, the RAF interrogating officer for South Scotland, the duke looked in on the prisoner, now transferred to Maryhill Military Hospital, Glasgow. When the German asked if the junior officer could withdraw, the duke gave consent. It could be that the prisoner had priority military information of value to Britain.

Once alone the German led off: "I was sorry to have missed you in Lisbon." Then, quite simply, seeing the duke's puzzled look, "I am Rudolf Hess." And he went confidently on. He was as close to Hitler as any man alive. He had plans for a negotiated peace with England which he knew Hitler would regard as a basis for discussion.

The duke, playing for time, said: "If it's a question of peace plans, I think I should return with an interpreter." His one idea was to get out of the hospital as fast as might be, saying nothing to anyone until he had made personal contact with Sir Alexander Cadogan, permanent under secretary to the Foreign Office.

Still closeted in his private annex, Douglas had rung both the Air Ministry and the Foreign Office—the latter would have to pass the news on to Winston Churchill. Meanwhile, Douglas recalls that he hugged the news tightly: instinct told him that this was a high-level sensation which must not leak out. In fact, the secret was well kept: as the night wore on everyone at Fighter Command prickled with the news that something strange was afoot, men exchanged meaning glances, but nobody knew why. Minister of Home Security Herbert Morrison heard nothing at the Home Office until well after dawn.

Even one of the first Germans in on the secret had refused to
believe it. A few minutes before 6 P.M. on the Saturday night
Oberstleutnant Adolph Galland, the air ace commanding
Fighter Group 26 at Wissant, near St. Omer, had Reichsmar-
schall Hermann Goering calling from Berlin in a state of frenzy.
Galland's entire fighter group were to take off at once.

Galland tried to reason with his chief. It was already getting
dark, many of his planes were still on night exercise, he had no
report of any aircraft flying in.

"Flying in? What do you mean, flying in? You are supposed
to stop an aircraft flying out. The deputy fuehrer has gone mad
and is flying to England in a Messerschmitt 110. He must be
brought down."

The drawback was that Galland didn't believe a word of it.
Instead, after hanging up, he tried to reason out who *had* gone
mad—Hess, Goering, or himself. For the first time the thought
crossed his mind: it was Goering. He toyed with the idea of
forgetting it, then duty won; you didn't buck an order from
the chief of the Luftwaffe. But Goering had given no details
except the likely course, probably didn't have any. So how
would Galland's fighters, when airborne, know which plane
Hess flew?

Like many a subordinate before and since, Galland merely
went through the motions. Ringing his five wing commanders,
he told them each to dispatch a couple of planes on immediate
patrol. He gave no reasons; it was plain that his subordinates,
too, thought the chief was suffering from overstrain.

Things went the way he had hoped. By 7.30 P.M.—just five
hours before Sholto Douglas received the staggering news—the
planes had touched down with nothing to report. So Galland
had rung Goering to admit failure, at the same time beseeching
the Reichsmarschall not to worry. The distance between Augs-
burg and England was 830 miles; he doubted that any Messerschmitt could make it. And if Hess did achieve the impossible—
well, the Spitfires would finish what the Messerschmitts had
begun.

But Hess *had* achieved the impossible, and no man was more overjoyed than Winston Spencer Churchill. At Ditchley Park, Oxfordshire, his weekend routine had been much as usual: dinner with the customary pint of champagne, hours of good talk over brandy and cigars with a few close advisers—General Sir Hastings (now Lord) Ismay, Professor Frederick Lindemann (now Lord Cherwell), Minister of Information Brendan Bracken. Twice, after the raid started, The Old Man called Home Security War Room to ask details of damage. Each time he came back strangely wistful, knowing the worst.

Toward midnight, as always, the lights were dimmed in the vast baronial hall; a mixed company of sixty or more settled down with Churchill to enjoy the inevitable film show. Tonight it was "The Marx Brothers Go West" and almost the only person who wasn't watching was Miss Mary Shearburn. As duty secretary she was boxed up in the small office at the rear of the hall, just left of the age-blackened oak front door.

Suddenly the private scrambler line from 10 Downing Street rang. An urgent message for the Prime Minister: "Rudolf Hess has arrived in Scotland." Miss Shearburn's first reaction was: "Who's Hess?" But, as always with Cabinet-level messages, she typed it out on a slip of paper; even among the select few top-secret messages were not delivered verbally. Threading her way through the darkened hall, she asked the Prime Minister to step outside.

In a minute he came—black silk dressing gown embroidered with gold pheasants over the baby-blue siren suit he called "my rompers." As he read the message, chomping on an unlit cigar, his face puckered with incredulous joy. He looked like a schoolboy about to dance a jig. When his advisers, with personal Private Secretary Leslie Rowan, gathered near, an immortal phrase ground out of him: "The worm is in the apple."

Still Miss Shearburn couldn't fathom the jubilation. In her own words: "So many other more exciting things were happening then I couldn't make out what the fuss was about."

But now an argument arose. From the rear of the hall

Churchill's bodyguard, Detective Inspector Walter Thompson, began wondering what all the noise was about. More and more people seemed to be ducking surreptitiously from their seats, slipping toward the annex. Stabbing with his cigar, Churchill was strenuously resisting Bracken's point that the Prime Minister should see Hess personally.

It made a memorable picture—the owls dipping like moths in the moonlit park, the great stone hall cloaked in darkness, Churchill arguing with his advisers, his lurid dressing gown spotlighted by the glare from the annex, while Groucho loped and wisecracked across the screen.

Drawing near, Thompson heard his master explode: "No, he'll be put inside—he'll be interned. The audacity of the man! He'll be interned like anyone else."

Here, again, there is confusion. Both Thompson and Miss Shearburn were trained observers, close to Churchill, yet both Churchill's and the Duke of Hamilton's versions differ on salient details. The duke is positive that he himself was the first to break this news to Churchill, after a frustrating non-stop day in which, having failed to contact Sir Alexander Cadogan, he finally did establish liaison with one of Churchill's aides, who was visiting the Foreign Office. After stressing that he had "something interesting" to tell the premier, the duke got swift leave of absence, flew by Hurricane to Northolt airfield, London, eventually reaching Ditchley Park late on the Sunday night.

He recalled, too, his meeting in camera—with both Churchill and Sir Archibald Sinclair, then secretary of state for Air, incredulous at the news. "Do you mean we have got the deputy fuehrer of the Third Reich in our hands?" Churchill asked with sonorous relish.

Churchill, on the other hand, was later under the impression that he had no contact with the duke at all until late on the Sunday night. Then, since a phone call from the duke, in Scotland, was interrupting the screening of the Marx Brothers' film, he left it to Brendan Bracken to make all arrangements. The duke's recollection is that this film actually followed his meeting with Churchill, although, bone-tired after a grueling day, he slept through the entire show.

The exact truth probably lies somewhere between all these versions. One thing, in any case, is certain: Hess had eluded pursuit all the way and arrived safely. But the crux of the matter was: why had he come at all? To seek peace? To present an ultimatum? To bring a personal message from Hitler? As the minutes ticked by at Fighter Command, Sholto Douglas in his private annex didn't know what to think.

But Douglas had other things than higher politics on his mind in the cold, still hours of this spring Sunday. At 12.30 it was hard to know how the battle of the full moon was going: whether it was a success, a failure, or a stalemate.

There were now exactly 40 day and night fighters ranging the target, trying their luck; so far they had claimed fourteen "kills" between them. Good shooting, if the claims were accurate; better still if the Germans had sent only 300 planes.

Not that Sholto Douglas had much doubt that his single-engined fighters could inflict punishing losses. As a member of the Air Staff, Douglas had clashed on this score with his predecessor, Sir Hugh Dowding, who believed that without airborne radar fighters would find only "an occasional fortunate encounter." To Dowding the whole fighter night conception was "haphazard," but Douglas had won the day.

Only a short while before Douglas had declared: "I would rather shoot down 50 of the enemy when they have bombed their target than ten forward of it." And again: "It does not matter where the enemy is shot down so long as he is shot down in large numbers."

The men in the sky felt much the same, but it wasn't that easy. Confident and unafraid, they were still feeling their way—some had never flown a "fighter night" until six weeks previously. Over the Thames, north of Dagenham, Squadron Leader Whitney Straight spotted two licking blue exhaust flames three quarters of a mile away—it looked like a Junkers

88—and heading direct for the coast. At 300 m.p.h. Straight began to lose height rapidly, but the Junkers was as fast: an average 295 m.p.h. without bomb load. Once he lost it for minutes on end, then that squirting blue exhaust again. Straight was at 350 m.p.h. now, losing height fast, the frozen wind hammering past his face. Over Eastbourne he was down to 1,000 feet, still losing height, and convinced that the Junkers had seen him. Suddenly the thought jolted home: supposing it's a Beaufighter?

One moment of doubt, and the plane, whatever it was, just vanished. Straight turned for home still wondering; he would have had to open fire at 200 feet. And positive identification wasn't easy in a few fleeting seconds.

Thirty miles west of Eastbourne, over the spit of land called Selsey Bill, Wing Commander Tom Pike, chief of 219 Nightfighter Squadron, had his own problems. At the controls of a British Beaufight, the young wing commander was in theory one of the favored few. His plane was fitted out with a A.I., the new air-to-ground radar; his navigator, Sergeant Sydney Austin, was in minute-by-minute touch with the new G.C.I. (Ground Controlled Interception) Station at Durrington, Sussex. With luck Austin might get a hostile contact tonight, then before any vector had even come from Control, Pike stiffened. He had seen the impish twinkle of four faint stars a mile out to sea. A Heinkel heading for London all right, and at 18,000 feet.

Carefully, at a steady 250 m.p.h., keeping well beneath, Pike stalked him. Attacking from above you risked the chance of overshooting. The moon was a white incandescent ball over the water, right in the German tail gunner's eyes. Good that— he couldn't see to fire. But the Heinkel had suddenly spotted Pike and now the chase was on, the bomber desperately weaving and twisting inland to the northeast. All in vain. In eight minutes Pike was close enough. The Heinkel narrowed to a slim pencil quivering in his gunsight.

As the four lethal cannon shattered out, the Beaufighter shook all over; long jets of flame curled from its ports. The plane glowed as if on fire, and the air reeked of acrid smoke. White stars pinpricked the length of the Heinkel's fuselage. Then with a tremedous explosion it blew up.

For a moment Pike was almost blinded and deafened. Oil slashed like rain at his windshield; chunks of flying metal struck his fuselage. Then the aircraft was spinning out of sight over Cranleigh, Surrey.

It was a costly victory. Within minutes Austin, from the hull, had signaled complications; no matter how he wrestled with the tuning control the cathode-ray tubes of the A.I. set remained obstinately blank. In this time of teething troubles even the juddering of the guns could often put a set out of commission. Reluctantly Pike signaled to Durrington G.C.I. the code phrase used when a set went wrong: "Weapon bent." Then he set course for Tangmere airfield—one of the few fighters equipped with radar, yet already out of the battle.

Back at Eastbourne, over Beachy Head, Flight Lieutenant A. H. Dottridge could hardly believe his luck—not one Heinkel but two, and actually flying in formation. One, obviously by mistake, even had its navigation lights switched on. No wonder Dottridge, a massive, barrel-chested man with bristling fighter-pilot mustaches, exultantly broke radio silence: "I've got two dirty great Huns in my sights!" The temptation was too great; from dead astern he opened fire on them both, hosing them with angry shells. But at once the Heinkels banked sharply to starboard and after a breathless ten-minute chase Dottridge realized he had lost them both in the haze over Guildford.

At the Durrington G.C.I. Station, on the chalk cliffs near Worthing, Squadron Leader Howson Devitt, the controller, had chuckled over Dottridge's exultant cry. It was almost his only cheering news that night. For two hours he had sat with his eyes glued to the small nine-inch radar screen, divided into grids, which outlined his whole sector—the 120 coastal miles between Beachy Head and the Isle of Wight.

And for two hours the screen had swarmed with darting

white blips that Devitt couldn't identify; a day fighter not equipped with radar was indistinguishable from a Heinkel or a Junkers 88. Earlier he had spent half an hour maneuvering one of his night fighters to the focal point just a mile from the "enemy aircraft." Now word had come back it was a Spitfire.

No lover of fighter nights, Controller Devitt sat sullenly on, destined to make only three contacts that night.

But the day fighters were making their mark. For two hours they had kept the bomber crews wary, never knowing where danger might strike—a tense, dry-mouthed business that limited talk over the target strictly to essentials. As Pilot Richard Furthmann turned the Heinkel south from Wandsworth, Observer Albert Hufenreuter had warned the crew yet again: "Keep your eyes peeled for night fighters."

Muttered grunts of assent came from Gunner Eggert Weber and Mechanic Josef Berzback. But they didn't really need telling; to see a fighter before he saw you was largely a matter of luck. At 12.25 on this calm, clear night Hufenreuter realized that their luck was out.

They were at 9,000 feet, flying due south; Hufenreuter's plan was to strike the Channel above Brighton, crossing the coast at 6,000 feet, sacrificing height for speed. He had made all these points to Furthmann, and the young pilot seemed to understand; now Hufenreuter, at the port side of the cockpit, was looking back over London. Briefly the sky was studded with millions of gold sparks as the barrage pounded, then a tremendous flash much closer at hand. Angry red tracer was chopping past the port engine too low to score a hit, Hufenreuter thought, near enough to be unhealthy.

"Dive," he shouted to Furthmann.

But it was too late. Furthmann bore down on the stick, but not hard or fast enough—a too-slow, too-cautious dive. Simultaneously all the dials on the instrument panel dropped at once. The temperature of the water soared to 160°. The port engine was out of control.

"Dive steeply," Hufenreuter shouted. "And fly bends. We can shake him if you only try." The tracer was flaring by but still too short—just ahead of the starboard engine or just below it. At 12.30 Hufenreuter decided they must take a chance: "Take her down as far as you dare. We'll shake him that way."

Hufenreuter knew from experience that if you sank almost to 2,000 feet regardless of anti-aircraft fire or barrage balloons, you were almost invisible against the ground. Furthmann obeyed; the Heinkel zoomed steeply. Now they were perilously close to the dark, rushing earth. But the fighter had gone.

Hufenreuter calculated fast. Everything depended now on whether the starboard engine could hold out until they reached the French coast. And the chance could vary from engine to engine, from plane to plane. Some engines were now so heavily armored that the plating alone put a colossal strain on them. Much, too, depended on the pilot; the sheer, savage will to win through that he could summon up.

At 12.35, as the Channel at Brighton came in sight, Furthmann said: "I can't make it."

"What, then?"

"I dare not risk putting her down in the sea with one engine. I'll have to take her east as far as Dover. We might stand a chance then."

Hufenreuter said nothing. For himself he would have wrestled, win or lose, to force every ounce of power from the failing engine. Now he felt powerless, impotent, realizing for the first time that a man cannot stand alone. All along he had tried to will Furthmann to do things he was incapable of doing. Furthmann was a good enough pilot; it just wasn't in him to make this supreme final effort.

With sinking heart he watched the Channel recede as Furthmann turned the plane to the east.

No word came from Weber or Berzbach in the rear turret. They depended dumbly on pilot and observer to keep them airborne.

Now they were down to less than a thousand feet. As the nose of the Heinkel sank lower, the face of England became plain under the moonlight—white level fields, black clumps of bushes, gray curving ribbons of roads. Hufenreuter could see that the stick seemed to wobble loosely in Furthmann's grip— there was almost no power left. Face foremost, he crawled on his belly into the nose, suddenly howling a warning: "Get her up! Get her up! It's a tree!"

As the Heinkel jolted painfully upward he felt hot sickness burst in his throat.

He couldn't see Furthmann but he could sense the strain in his voice beneath the outward calm. At 12.40 the pilot called to him: "We go down." Again Hufenreuter, eyes glued to the earth, shouted: "Up, get her up! It's a house."

The ground was whirling past at a furious rate: the landscape, no longer a flat, unreal relief, was alive with cottages, tall clumps of elms, theatrically black and silver under the moon. Quickly Hufenreuter scrambled back into the nose, grasping the inter-com. "Take up stations for landing." He saw that Furthmann's seat belt was already fastened and fumbled to fasten his own. Then, in a high, unreal voice, Furthmann cried: "Captain, I can't hold her."

Hufenreuter, about to test the escape hatch, saw there was no time—no time even to sit. He had a sudden feeling dangerous to a man fighting an air war: he accepted with "a kind of serenity" that he was about to die.

The earth came slanting up toward them very fast, trees, houses, barns, tearing by underneath, and in a few fleeting seconds he saw, like a drowning man, all his life pass before him: his first landing, eight years back at Fuhlsbuttel airfield, Hamburg; his grandmother lying on her deathbed; the pale gray line of the Harz Mountains beyond Quedlinburg. He balled up in the cockpit like an animal, hugging his head. The Heinkel tore into the soft Kentish pasture in a violent slewing pancake landing, and a hundred yards away the trees came racing at them. There was a monstrous roaring, shuddering, jolting like "a giant hand pounding you against the walls of some tunnel." The last thing Hufenreuter remembered was a feeling of unutterable helplessness.

At Fighter Command the ops room logged the crash—another bomber gone. But how many were left? The trouble was that at 12.45 A.M. nobody knew. Every radar station reported a mass plot, and the planes flew too high for visual checks, even in bright moonlight.

The Royal Observer Corps report centers used "gallows"—steel uprights with crossbeams, signifying ten-plus planes—but the system could fall down. Even before midnight Controller Arthur Collins at the ROC Center, Bromley, Kent, had 40 gallows up and no more available.

Deptford Warden Albert Churchman found even his private yardstick, based on the frequency of local bus services, didn't help: a No. 1 raid meant a wave of bombers every fifteen minutes, a No. 47 was a wave every ten minutes. But tonight this had fallen down; the high-pitched, whining cadence of the engines never ceased.

And at Orpington, Kent, Observer Stanley Gardner kept up a steady chant: "Another one in out, another one out, a lost coming in now . . ." It was as good a method as any. Like 300 other observers, Gardner trusted his ears to distinguish the number, to pick out friend from foe.

CHAPTER EIGHT

"I Wouldn't Have Joined if I'd Known"
12.45—1.30 A.M.

THE same sense of helplessness that overwhelmed Hauptmann Hufenreuter had momentarily gripped Post Warden Stanley Barlow and his team in St. Marylebone. At 12.30 it had all been so quiet—a game of darts going on in one corner of the post, a hand of cards in another. Only the rumble of gunfire in the hills, like surf beating against a reef, made them wonder what was happening to the rest of London.

This was the true climate of disaster: any raid when the bombs were not hailing on your own doorstep was a quiet night.

Tailoress Winnie Dorow asked trim, fair-haired Annie Hill, "How do you do it? I swear I'll never be brave enough." Not yet an officially qualified warden, it was Mrs. Dorow's first night on duty. So now Annie Hill tried to comfort her; she, too, had plotted the doorways that gave shrapnel shelter and the sprinting time between each.

Just then Barlow cut in: lull or no, he wanted the post area, less than half a mile square, patrolled once an hour. He told Winnie Dorow to make the first patrol with Mechanic Charlie Lee. A slack night would give her a chance to know the area better.

Around 12.25 Winnie Dorow and Lee set off, only their footfalls breaking the silence along the dimly-lit streets. Back in the post time dragged. Nigerian "Sam" Ekpenyon was chuckling about superstition—some shelterers reckoned his dark skin lucky, wouldn't bed down for the night until he had looked in on them. Barlow was preparing to do a round of his shelter marshals. He deputed his close friend, handsome Eileen Sloane, to take charge of the post.

At 12.36 the whole building shook as if an earthquake had struck it.

"What in hell . . . ?" Barlow muttered. All evening he had felt some kind of presentiment, and his first thought was: Can this have been why? Suddenly Warden Johnnie Noble came running. "That was Titchfield Street. They got Winnie and Charlie Lee."

Barlow pelted to the scene but already it was too late. The narrow canyon of Great Titchfield Street was like a battlefield. Yellow plaster dust mushroomed above a crater 40 feet deep; the "Bay Moulton" pub and the rest center next door were burning furiously; the top floors of three houses had been sheared clean away. Screams and cries from the trapped jarred horribly with the chorus of "Oh, Johnny, How You Can Love" rising from the pub cellar. Incongruously, Barlow thought of the beer Lee and Winnie Dorow had left for him on the bar of the pub only an hour and a half back. Now the street was blocked by a vast slag heap of rubble. Lee and Winnie Dorow must have been racing for shelter when they vanished somewhere beneath it.

Actually, Lee had been luckier; hearing something nearer to "a soft breath" than a whistle, he had ducked his head aside. The 1,000-pounder burst only twelve yards away, but there was no sound, no light—only a feeling like "a monstrous hairbrush" passing over his head. For a second he was sailing through the air, level with the first-floor windows, then the blast set him down thirty yards away as gently as if he were getting into bed. He was on the doorstep of a first-aid post, so he walked in.

Winnie Dorow was not buried, either, but as Barlow espied her through the cyclone of dust he knew that she was lying too still. Approaching almost on tiptoe, he very gently laid a blanket over her.

Within twenty minutes rescue parties and firemen had taken over at the "Bay Moulton" and Barlow was walking dazedly back to the post. One thought obsessed him: Could he get through this night and still stay sane? It made no sense. Winnie Dorow had been scared, too, but she admitted her fear, she tried to laugh herself out of it. When the raid began she was scared, but she was alive, enjoying a drink and a joke. And he kept thinking: Why Winnie Dorow and why Great Titchfield Street? He didn't think of Euston Station, half a mile northwest, twelve seconds' flying time for a fast-moving Heinkel.

As the raid grew, the same thought obsessed others: the bomber pilots had them marked out like a cat crouched over a mousehole. At Peek Frean's Biscuit Factory, Bermondsey, which was also turning out tank parts, Fire Watcher Alfred Elms was with four others in the main yard when an incendiary bomb fell neatly behind each man. Sick and shaken, they put them out; it was as if the bomber had meant to do that. In Elvaston Place, Kensington, diplomat Edward Penrose-Fitzgerald heard a bomb drop and dashed out to help, throwing coat over pajamas. Without warning he reeled back; a hot yellow light flashed across his eyes. He didn't know that fire had ignited the broken chunk of a 1,000-pounder in the basement next door, exploding and killing nineteen men, injuring eleven others. He didn't even know London Region Headquarters, the nerve center of all Civil Defense, was only two streets away. As he staggered back, Penrose-Fitzgerald thought only: Why us? Why Elvaston Place?

It wasn't surprising that fear was abroad in the city. At 12.30 the raid was suddenly too immense, too overwhelming for any previous standards to hold good.

Mrs. Isabel Penrose-Fitzgerald took one look at her husband's face pouring with blood and began to repeat like a litany: "Disinfectant, where did I put it? I know it's somewhere, where *did* I put it?" Some went completely to pieces. In blazing Baker Street Ambulance Officer Eileen Young fought silently to overpower a shrieking woman, a Pomeranian dog yapping in shrill circles around their feet.

118

"I Wouldn't Have Joined if I'd Known"

It hit the professionals, too. Near Liverpool Street Station a quaking warden told Ticket Collector William Kidd, "I wouldn't have joined if I'd known what it would be like." Dr. Barbara Morton, of Bermondsey Medical Mission Hospital, crouched in terror over her patients, trying to hide her fear, praying all the time. At the National Temperance Hospital, St. Pancras, Miss Frances Thirlby, the catering supervisor, stood rigid and voiceless in the crowded corridor, her palms slippery with sweat. She glanced so often at her watch that finally a sister seized and shook her. "You're not fit to come back. Matron shouldn't have let you."

Miss Thirlby couldn't answer. She had been bombed only recently and she knew that now even the porter was in hiding and it was the Irish sisters who carried the heavy stretchers laden with the dead and the dying.

Some tried to brazen it out. In Stoke Newington a man he'd ordered to take cover told Major Creswick-Atkinson cockily: "I've paid for these fireworks. I'm going to see them." Perched on a wall in the City of London, struggling to hold a bucking hose steady, Auxiliary Fireman Harry Weinstock just had to keep singing, everything from "Sons of the Sea" to "I'll Walk Beside You." As the flames crept nearer, Weinstock joked: "I'll die a hero. The hell with it."

At the War Office, Whitehall, as a bomb burst in the courtyard, Percy Fearnley, the duty officer, was chatting to a young A.D.C. Fearnley felt "that tremendous grasping at the air that seems to tug the guts out of you and go on and on." Then he saw the A.D.C. rise stiffly from his armchair like a man made of wood, walk robot wise across the room, and disappear. Fearnley saw no more of him that night.

Few could hold on to a thought as coherently as diplomat Edward Penrose-Fitzgerald. "It's true, then, you don't hear the bomb that hits you."

Whether you heard it or not, one woman saw it. At Poplar Hospital, East India Docks, Sister Phyllis Ward was moving quietly among her patients when the bomb that sliced the hospital in two plowed clean through the ceiling from above, ripping through the floor to explode in the ward below; killing six; shaving the front six beds off every ward; burying patient after patient under a choking torrent of masonry. In the false darkness, among the cries of men in pain, people felt bewildered, stripped of comfort, here, too. Father George Coupe had held the non-denominational service earlier, had stayed only because the raid grew heavy. Brisk, methodical Sister Ward got him out, along with eighteen others, but later the surgeons amputated his right leg. Dick Craze, a homeless fever patient, had pleaded all day to be discharged; understandably the hospital had restrained him. Before he died he had ten minutes to ponder this.

At other hospitals the picture was a little brighter, but not much. At St. Luke's, Chelsea, the bomb fell a little after midnight, smashing the receiving ward, the doctors' quarters, the main theater, yet killing only two doctors and one patient. The Medical Superintendent Dr. Taylor's belief that the raid wasn't bad enough to move the patients below had saved 140 lives: the basement was wiped out.

Even Clerical Officer Edward Glading, who pitched four flights down the shattered staircase to the basement, was shocked rather than hurt—his clutching fingermarks were imprinted on the walls for four stories. And others knew moments of pure terror—a porter trapped in a chair when the blast folded its steel arms around him; Sister Horton pinned against scalding hot-water pipes; Porter Jack Bickle blown clean into the bomb crater.

Certainly the Germans hadn't aimed for the hospital, didn't even know it existed; it was just sited too near the Albert Bridge spanning the Thames. It was an ugly quirk of fate shown time and again this night—every London hospital stood near a military target.

It was small comfort to the hospital staffs as they worked to calm their patients. In the bitter-cold hours of this Sunday morning it was grueling work. At St. Luke's Porter William

Lester and others had to shin four stories up the water pipes to the hospital wards; both staircases had gone. Then the patients had to be wrapped in warm blankets ready for evacuation; some lifted gingerly on to stretchers; there were the old folk to be reassured and wailing children quieted. At Poplar Assistant Surgeon John McLauchlan was still helping to extricate the wounded when casualties from the borough began to flood in. As usual McLauchlan gave first priority to men with hand burns: in this water-front area all a man's earning power lay in his two hands.

As Lambeth Hospital blazed, nurses and porters moved all the adult patients on stretchers to the maternity block; soon, as the flames advanced, they had to move all the children in the hospital there, too. Sometimes patients had never seemed so contrary. One old man refused to budge until a fireman had dashed through the flames to rescue his false teeth and his best suit.

It was a night of merciless priority—hospitals and any building touching the war effort first, private dwellings a long way behind. On the riverside at Lambeth Station Officer Charles Davis had one engine at work on the blazing roof of St. Thomas's Hospital when a verger came running from Lambeth Palace: the roof was on fire. Almost before contacting Fire Headquarters Davis knew the answer: no engines to spare.

The verger persisted, "You'll have to do something. The Archbishop of Canterbury is in residence."

"I can't help the archbishop; the hospital is my first concern."

Angrily the verger threatened to report him and dashed off to try his luck elsewhere—seemingly with success. Soon after, as Superintendent William Henry Thompson drove by, a man ran from the palace and flagged his staff car to a halt. "We've only two trailer pumps at work on the palace."

"Two at work?" Thompson turned to his driver, Fireman Leslie Horton. "Move one of them out, Horton—there are places of greater national importance tonight."

The tragedy was that without knowledge of how universally

bad things were, men expected miracles of the firemen and then grew angry when these weren't forthcoming. Near Victoria Station a man grabbed Superintendent George Bennison by the sleeve. "Can't you do anything to save our home? It's only just caught."

"I'm sorry. There's nothing."

"But you're the Fire Service. You ought to do something."

"Look, the war effort doesn't recognize private property. The only thing is to get your furniture out and pray."

Sometimes the interchanges were tougher. As Sub Officer Norman Cottee's fire engine rocketed down burning Brixton Hill householders ran screaming across the street to form a cordon. As the driver trod hard on the accelerator the people scattered with only inches to spare.

It was hard for anyone to understand, and especially hard for Jimmie Sexton. It had been bad enough just before midnight when that first message passed from basement control to roof—the mains outside the factory broken, no water to fight any fires that might break out. Still, with unquenchable Cockney optimism Sexton had told himself the raid might pass over.

But when Sexton walked a few yards across the roof to the parapet, he saw something that stopped him dead: the glass roof of the Toilet Mill, where the soaps and shaving sticks were made, was alive with a soft rosy glow. Close at hand Fire Watcher Albert Fey was once again reporting to the basement. Suddenly he saw Sexton come plunging toward him. "Fire—fire in the Toilet Mill."

Fey was calling this news down the handset telephone when there was a faint click. The line had gone dead.

As Fey asked Sexton how bad it was, he got a shock: he had never seen the little man look so distressed. Shakily, Sexton stammered that he thought things were very bad indeed. Fey decided that Control could never have got that message. "We'll have to get down and tell them."

It was all so urgent, yet so unreal, that Sexton could hardly believe it was happening. First, slipping and sliding, they scrambled down the iron escape to the soap powder floor. Here vast sacks of filmy flakes were piled to the ceiling. Suddenly there was a tremendous concussion; they were hurled with such force against the sacks that Sexton felt all the breath slammed from his body. Finally they reached the yard, ducked under an archway for shelter.

They could see the Toilet Mill burning now and stacked on the paving stones only twenty yards from it were vats of paraffin wax. Fey spoke for the first time in minutes: "Looks as if this place has had it." Sexton, he still recalls, said nothing.

Jimmie Sexton couldn't. He felt sick and helpless and frightened—that same sense of impotence, driving out anger that Hauptmann Hufenreuter and Stanley Barlow had felt. First he thought of the little flat near Tower Bridge, of how he had worked for the flowered print curtains, the leather armchairs, and the tomato-colored rugs. Next he thought of how it had looked the morning after the bomb had hit it—young Jim's cot smashed to matchwood, the china cabinet in cruel, glinting fragments, just one armchair still shiny and undamaged. Of how he had smashed at the leather with a lump of concrete, sobbing, "We've had the other bastards, we'll have the lot," until a fireman had led him gently away.

Last he thought that Fields' factory which had meant security and home for nine years was doomed as well.

From now on all was business. Both Sexton and Fey made a dash for the north building, whose basement housed the Fire Guard Control. One flight down they met three anxious men on their way to see things at firsthand—Fire Chief Bill Wilks, Bill Westaway, the boiler man, Fire Watcher Bob Armstrong. A hasty conference and Wilks decided they would try to subdue the fire in the Toilet Mill with chemical extinguishers. If that didn't work, they would isolate it—force the iron doors of the mill shut. They were three inches thick, well oiled, on sliding hinges; there seemed a chance they might do the trick. Bob Armstrong was sent at a run for the Fire Service.

In a body they raced to the Toilet Mill, but it was hopeless even to attempt an entry. The whole building, its shelves stacked with cardboard cartons of soap and packing-case shavings, was one mighty yellow flame; they couldn't even hear the hiss of the extinguishers. Above the din Sexton heard Wilks shout, "Doors—the doors!"

Sweating and panting, the heat scorching their eyes, blistering their palms, they began to slide the iron doors shut—first one, then doubling round the building to another, up the iron stairway to the second floor, working until every door was tight closed. Gradually, in ones and twos, they staggered back exhausted to the paved yard. The north building, thirty yards away, was still untouched.

Suddenly, with a roar, the pent-up heat blew the cast-iron doors. A hot whirlwind of blast took Jimmie Sexton skimming across the paved yard. When he picked himself up, the fire was bellowing through the buckled doors, licking at the walls of the Steerine Department close by. The building was packed with animal fats, candle grease, inflammable palm oil. Sexton thought that only the Fire Service could save the factory now.

As Wilks and the others ran for the north building, Sexton doubled back around the mill to the works entrance nearest the railway lines. His assignment was to see the Fire Service in. At the works entrance he found only Gatekeeper Bill May—he looked nervous, distracted. Suddenly the phone rang in the gatekeeper's lodge, and Sexton, answering, heard a truck driver's voice: "Any orders for Monday?"

It was so off-beat that Sexton couldn't resist wisecracking: "Yes, go to the works manager and get your cards—if he can find them!" As he hung up there was a strident jangling and a fire engine came abreast. One look at the mounting wall of flame across the yard seemed enough. "Too big—we'll find another one." Again the bell jangled as the engine raced off.

Angry and disgusted, Sexton doubled back, round the south building, past the blazing Toilet Mill, then pulled up short. Across the courtyard incendiaries had ignited the roof of the north building, where Wilks and the others had taken shelter.

"I Wouldn't Have Joined if I'd Known"

The candle molders' department, two stories given up to candles and night lights, was on fire. A sluggish, stinking river of grease 30 yards wide flowed gently down the side of the building.

Sexton's first thought was: They'll be trapped alive down there. As he pelted for the basement, he thought: The Fire Service left us to burn.

Again it was a grim question of priorities—hard for any man trapped by a raging wall of fire to view philosophically, yet it made sense. Well before the factory sent out its fire call Superintendent William Henry Thompson had driven up in his staff car. Even then, Fireman Leslie Horton recalls, the factory gates glowed white hot, like newly-forged steel.

District Officer George Earl, along for the ride, was rocked. "What on earth have they got in there to make it go like that?"

Thompson had to do the best he could. Fields' was an island site; the fire was unlikely to spread to other property; it didn't rate as a front-line factory. When he signaled back to Lambeth Control: "Make pumps five at Fields'," he expected three engines at the most. Minutes passed, but nothing came. Thompson drove on to Waterloo Station: word had come that the underground vaults were alight. There, with Staff Officer Edward Bawdrey, Thompson signaled: "Make pumps ten at Waterloo."

Still no engines. As they sat on the pavement, waiting helplessly, Thompson burst out: "We'll never get the bloody pumps, and even if we do there's no water."

If seasoned professionals like Thompson felt despair, it was only natural that civilians were completely at sea. Few had even embraced the one tenet that could help tonight: nothing was immune.

At the Alexandra Hotel, Knightsbridge, things had settled down as uneventfully as always: Mark North's staff had seen to that. Prompt on eleven, when the siren sounded, Head Night Porter Charles Mattock had sent Porters Frederick Willis and Frank Dearlove on a round of the six-story hotel, which was built as a rectangle around an inner courtyard. Tonight there were some 90 guests in residence and Mattock wanted them knocked up discreetly and coaxed down to the lounge.

In Room 14, on the first floor, Rear Admiral Martin Bennett climbed out of bed, slipped a lounge suit over his pajamas, padded down to the main hall in carpet slippers. Farther along the corridor, in Room 101, Allen Bathurst, a retired solicitor's managing clerk, hurried to do the same.

Mr. Andrew Verdie was already below, killing time in the main hall. A sound sleeper, the ebullient old Scot found these discreet nightly rappings on the door of Room 302 far more vexing than the Hyde Park guns—he could at least sleep through those. So tonight Verdie planned to have his usual chat with Porter Willis over a cup of tea, then slip upstairs like a guilty schoolboy for a good night's rest.

A few preferred the basement to the lounge, although Mattock, a grave, impassive man like a Hollywood butler, usually advised against it. Tonight, though, there was no shaking Mr. and Mrs. James Murdoch of the piano family. Along with Mrs. Elizabeth Tuchmann, a well-to-do widow, and about a dozen others, they trailed down.

Some weren't coming down at all. General Josepha Hallera and his wife had their self-contained flat. Why trade in a comfortable bed for a restless night in an armchair? On the fourth floor Mr. T. Blake Butler, one of the Ormondes of Kilkenny, had kindred feelings. As he came out of the lift on his way to bed, a woman he knew by sight hailed him: "I'm going to the basement. I think there'll be trouble tonight."

Butler laughed. "I'd rather stop up and come down with it than have it fall on me," he replied. As always, however, he climbed into bed fully clothed—you never knew.

Gradually in ones and twos people were drifting into the lounge, some wearing bathrobes over day dresses, a few men in sports clothes but more in lounge suits, standing and sitting, clustering in little knots, wondering what sort of night *this* would be. Mrs. Alice Woods chose a comfortable armchair. The Percy Strauses settled in an alcove.

Checking over his charges, Head Night Porter Charles Mattock reckoned about 30 in the lounge, with another dozen or so in the basement; as usual about half the residents were taking a chance upstairs. A few weren't yet in—the keys for Rooms 212 and 314 were still on the hook in the main hall. Mrs. Frances Morgan and her daughter Daphne, visiting the Caledonian Club around the corner, had probably stayed late with friends.

At 12.25 the lounge, which was to the left of the main foyer, overlooking the street, was in semi-darkness—only a blue pilot light burned dimly as the residents stirred uneasily in armchairs, a few groups still on their feet talking in undertones. The hall, too, was half-dark, lit only by another pilot light in Mattock's box to the rear of the hall, on the right.

Andrew Verdie was now in the main hall, near the telephone kiosks, standing midway between the glass swing doors fronting on the street and the swing doors of the dining room, which directly faced them. He was chatting to Night Porter Frederick Willis and awaiting that cup of tea. Almost everybody liked "Bismarck" Willis, and he, in turn, was the kind of man who nursed the residents along. That night he had deliberately stayed late on duty knowing that Mr. Verdie liked a chat and the company.

Outside in Knightsbridge the sound of women's voices singing carried a long way in the still night: Mrs. Morgan and Daphne were returning from the Caledonian Club in light-hearted mood. On the corner by St. George's Hospital they stopped to chat with the policeman on duty. He had a soft spot for handsome gray-haired Mrs. Morgan, whom he called "My lovely lady."

At this moment Warden Jack Smith was literally far above them. With the Reverend Robert Moline, part-time warden and vicar of St. Paul's, Knightsbridge, he was on the top floor back of the Alexandra Hotel conducting his usual nightly survey from the point where the stone service stairway met the roof. The barrage was beating against the sky, and the horizon glowed with the driven fires. As the red markers broke above them, they heard no plane.

"We're in for it," Smith cried. As the green marker broke they were clattering away down the service stairs.

In the main foyer of the Alexandra Andrew Verdie chatted on to Porter Willis, to be joined now by Head Night Porter Charles Mattock. Mattock was a shade uneasy; the barrage was getting heavier, and out of the corner of his eye he could see people starting to wander. Mrs. Frances Morgan and Daphne had collected their keys and started upstairs. Allen Bathurst, too, was on his way up—in his hurry to obey the summons he'd forgotten his book. Mrs. Tuchmann had drifted up from the basement; now, in company with a man named Ullmann, she had wandered back again.

And it looked as if even Andrew Verdie was in restless mood. A man he knew passed through the hall. "Are you coming up, Andrew?" Mr. Verdie had to admit it. "I'll be with you in a second."

Just then Porter Frank Dearlove emerged from the dining room with a tray of tea—a cup for Andrew Verdie, one apiece for Porters Willis and Mattock. He told Mattock, "I've put our dinners under the grill." Now he was on his way to the top floor to roust young George Alfry, one of the kitchen porters, out of bed. There had been talk of an incendiary earlier on and Dearlove wanted to make sure it had been dealt with.

"Use the stairs," Mattock advised. "You know they have warned us not to use the lift when a raid is on." But Dearlove only chuckled. Six flights was a long way to climb. The passenger lift stood just left of the main staircase, facing manageress Paula D'Hondt's office. He stepped in, thumbed the sixth-floor button.

Jack Smith and the Reverend Robert Moline had just pelted into Old Barrack Yard, the mews at the rear of the hotel, when they heard the bombs above them—a crowding, whining shud-

Above. The Temple. *Mirrorpic*. *Below*. Toppling buildings, like this one in Queen Victoria Street, blocked almost 8,000 streets after the May 10 blitz. *Imperial War Museum*

Firemen at work on the buildings in Ludgate Hill. St. Paul's Cathedral is in the background. *Radio Times Hulton Picture Library*

dering like an express train flashing from a tunnel. As they reached the shelter in the mews, the bombs seemed to burst inside their eardrums. Close at hand a girl screamed hysterically; Smith lashed out to quiet her. Then, groping through a blinding fog of dust and ash, he stumbled toward the warden's post in Belgrave Square.

Inside the hotel no one had heard a thing; the bombs had struck almost as one. Glassware was breaking somewhere above. The blue pilot light glowed brighter, then went out. Close to Rear Admiral Bennett a woman cried, "Oh, where are you, George?"

The air shook with a volcanic rumbling. The darkness thickened with a cloud of dust. In the main lounge a marble pillar snapped like a tree trunk and toppled with a crack that rocked the room, missing old Mrs. Alice Woods by inches, wedging her in her armchair. The Percy Strauses, groping cautiously from their alcove, found it blocked by a smoking feet-high mass of timber and bricks.

Rear Admiral Bennett was still upright on his feet. After seeing the whole far end of the lounge collapse, he was shocked and bleached with dust, but miraculously alive. Somewhere under the debris he heard a woman cry out; her legs were broken. But in the pitch darkness it was impossible for him to see or to help.

In the maelstrom of dust, tumbling masonry, and splintering woodwork it was hard to know what was happening. Charles Mattock was pitched across the foyer, clean through the swing doors of the dining room, landing unconscious in a tangle of linen and cutlery. The blast didn't catch "Bismarck" Willis or Mr. Verdie, but within seconds they were lost to view beneath a tumbling, blustering niagara of flotsam—plaster dust, wardrobes, planking, tables, chairs.

While the first bomb had exploded on the third floor, the second and worst had hit the lift shaft, bringing the lift, the the stair well, and the best part of five floors down with it. Porter Dearlove never stood a chance.

The City That Would Not Die

The walls seemed to burst apart, raining light brackets, mirrors, clocks, chunks of ceiling. As the ground floor split open and the debris thundered to the basement, one terrible cry came up from the shelterers beneath.

Then silence, an aching, empty silence broken only by small sounds: the rustle of broken water pipes, the slow trickle of plaster dust, a faint whimpering as if a child had bad dreams.

Gradually people began to take stock. On the first floor General Josepha Hallera and his wife found, bemusedly, that they were unhurt; though the french windows of their suite had come in on the teeth of a whirlwind, heavy velvet curtains had staved off the ugly shards of glass. The general's instinct as an old campaigner was to get out and reconnoiter. Halfway to the corridor he had inexplicable second thoughts: he went back to fetch his gas mask.

It might have made sense. Outside, a vortex of smoke and oily fumes seemed to suck him into its midst. Glass gave with an ugly snapping sound underfoot. Reaching the head of the stairs, the old general trod cautiously forward, then recoiled. The stairs had gone. He was stepping forward into space.

At the rear of the hotel he struck luckier—most of the rooms, including Andrew Verdie's, were untouched, even to the pajamas folded neatly on the pillow. The steel emergency stairs running down the outside wall were warped and twisted, but from third floor to ground level they seemed to hold. Only above the third floor were they unrecognizably bent—a writhing skein of steel winding absurdly out into space.

Thus General Hallera was able to make the ground floor without too much trouble. The first thing that hit him forcibly on entering the lounge by the front hall was the number of people milling around. The second was the spectacle of a woman he knew well by sight: every evening she sat on a sofa in the lounge, smiling placidly, her husband beside her. Tonight she was again on the sofa, white with leprous patches of dust, but still smiling fixedly. Her husband was beside her, stone dead.

"I Wouldn't Have Joined if I'd Known"

Neither then nor at any time was the general in any way surprised by the proceedings. Instead, he went back the way he had come to take a bulletin to his wife. He held the intriguing if improbable theory that the fate of the Alexandra—indeed the raid—was all linked with the "French" officers who so mysteriously invaded the conference room with their air-flight chart.

True or not, the hotel was a scene of horror. From the upper floors now came the steady drumming of fists on door panels, the trailing cries of the frightened and trapped. In stray shafts of moonlight the dead lay carelessly, in grotesque doll-like attitudes, sprawled across corridors, looped over broken balustrades.

Some couldn't even move. On the fourth floor Mr. T. Blake Butler awoke soon after the bombs had fallen, to hear a stealthy crackling and feel a vast weight pressing down on his legs. Finding he could move his hands, he switched on his bedside torch and a chill like ice shot through him. He could see nothing. He was blind. Trapped by the legs, he would be slowly charred to death.

The truth was more consoling. The blindness was real enough —though it lasted only days—but never at any time was the hotel on fire. It was merely that the blast had blown away all the outer walls of the fourth-floor front; the bedrooms stood wide open to the moonlit park. Most probably the crackling Mr. Butler heard, borne like a zephyr on the spring night, was the sound of Mayfair burning.

At Westminster's Post 12 Headquarters, Belgrave Square, the old town house of Lady Bathurst, all this fell into the lap of Herbert S. Mills, a dark, impassive man who had been deputy post warden since his job as chauffeur to Sir Geoffrey Duveen folded at the outbreak of war. As the bombs split the Alexandra apart, Mills and his assistant, Nat Williams, who kept the local cigar store, had been standing outside the post. "Bit noisy tonight," said Mills judicially, although the bombs seemed some way away.

The City That Would Not Die

The chauffeur's first instinct was to move swiftly toward the sound of the explosion, then he checked it firmly. If it *was* in their post area, one of his wardens would be near enough to make a quick reconnaissance. That done, the man would dash to the post and report—what had been hit, the type of damage done, whether or not people were trapped. The firsthand report would save Westminster Control endless trouble when ordering out emergency services; tonight, like every other borough, Westminster needed to hold back all the reserves they could. So it was common sense for Mills to stay where the warden reporting would expect to find him.

Calm, methodical, diligent, Mills applied common sense in life as coolly as he had once applied his capable fingers to spinning a Rolls-Royce through traffic. He was the ideal Civil Defense warden.

Three minutes passed—five minutes—ten. Deliberately unhurried, Mills chatted on to Nat Williams. Suddenly Warden Jack Smith, his denims as white as a miller's smock, almost collapsed on top of them. He gulped out, "Alexandra Hotel."

It was enough, but as Mills grabbed up two blue road lanterns, the only tackle he needed, and started off, he felt a faint qualm. After all, less than three years ago he had never bothered with this kind of thing; he had been content in the pretty little mews flat, gay with water colors, where he still lived with his wife Minnie, the cars all polished in the garage beneath and ready to go whenever the boss called, winters spent in Biarritz or Monte Carlo, according to the family's whim. It was a neighbor calling at the time of the Munich scare, suggesting it was up to everyone to do their bit in case of trouble, that had started all this off.

Mills had agreed, although without much enthusiasm; neither of them fancied the Fire Service, so they opted for Civil Defense. To Mills the memory held its own irony: though he completed the course, his neighbor never turned up to one lecture.

And a stranger irony that, two and a half years later, the greatest responsibility he had ever shouldered had hit this normally quiet post area. The blue lanterns, the blue steel helmet he wore, stamped Mills as one of the new incident officers —wardens especially trained to avert too-frequent chaos by assuming supreme control over every service on the spot. Tonight every decision, right or wrong, would have to be his.

Already things were moving. At Belgrave Square Jack Smith stammered out a hasty report to the post telephonist. By 12.47, in the white toneless lighting of Westminster's Control Room, Message Supervisor Elsie Ferguson was reading:

> 00.40. Post 12. H. E. Alexandra Hotel,
> Knightsbridge. Casualties many. Roads
> blocked. End of message.

Though bald enough, it was a start—it gave Controller Sir Parker Morris and his staff plenty to do. They must send ambulances, stretcher-bearers, rescue parties, to begin with. In case of leakages or short circuits, the local gas and electricity boards would have to know. Roads blocked meant diverting busses, so they must ring London Passenger Transport Board. Someone else must call Kensington telephone exchange.

The wires hummed busily, taking the news to all points across the City of Westminster. Soon help would come. But for twenty critical minutes the whole weight of the disaster rested squarely on the shoulders of Herbert Mills, just then stepping across the Alexandra's splintered threshold into a gray dust fog that seemed without end.

Hauptmann Albert Hufenreuter felt oddly lightheaded. He was conscious of surprise, too; he wasn't dead, after all. Although he had pitched clean forward into the nose of the plane at the moment the Heinkel crashed, he didn't even seem to be hurt.

Clambering back into the cockpit, he saw that Richard Furthmann was still alive, though obviously badly shocked. He was slumped against the maroon-colored leather of the pilot's seat, mumbling disconnectedly, like a man talking in his sleep. Hufenreuter unstrapped him, but he couldn't lift the youngster bodily from the plane or stop the uncontrolled twitching of his wrists. He realized that in his delirium Furthmann was still trying to keep the Heinkel aloft.

As Hufenreuter lowered himself gingerly on to the edge of the cockpit, poised above the grass, he noticed that his left leg swung as loosely as a shutter. Almost idly he saw that a bone had skewered clean through his flying suit and was poking through his rubber boot. He must have walked back into the cockpit on his stump, but the shock had been so great he felt no pain at all.

A man came panting across the pasture and Hufenreuter hailed him. "Where are we?" Puzzled, the man called back, "In England." Hufenreuter's reply was almost English in its understatement. "Oh, damn!" he groaned.

More specifically, the Heinkel had pancaked on a meadow called "The Camp," above the tiny Kentish village of Kennington, near Ashford. Only a windbreak of stout hawthorn bushes snagging the starboard wing had stopped it from exploding nose first against a screen of oak trees. The first man to reach the scene, Ambulance Worker Frederick Huckstepp, who lived nearby, had thought a British plane was in trouble.

Soon more villagers had scampered to the scene—butcher Edward Ward and his wife Ann who were sure the plane was going to land in their back garden; Charles Peters, with his daughters Joan and Joyce. Yet with droves of Heinkels still winging their way north to pound London, it was hard for the villagers to know which note to strike—whether to accept the Germans as human beings in distress or to repel them as a ruthless enemy. Many, still clad in their night clothes, just stood staring, as if space men had crashlanded their sleepy Kentish village.

But some were more positive. The Peters sisters doubled back to the cottage to fetch blankets and pillows. With difficulty Huckstepp lifted Pilot Furthmann from the cockpit and laid him tenderly on the grass, while Joan Peters wrapped an eiderdown around him; they found later that his spine was fractured. Others helped lift Gunner Weber, who had both legs broken, out of the turret; Gerhardt and Berzbach, though only shocked, were both unconscious. Someone else phoned for an ambulance and a doctor. As Joan Peters coaxed Furthmann to drink a little water, an artillery captain arrived to take charge, steel helmeted, with a pistol belt strapped over his pajamas. Hufenreuter asked him if he wouldn't mind looking in the cockpit and retrieving his forage cap. The captain obliged without demur.

Now Hufenreuter was lying on the frosty grass with his neck against a cushion. One of the women kept saying, "Soon going ambulance," spacing out the words carefully so that he should understand. He felt grateful, but he felt an overwhelming disgust, too—they had been within an ace of home and now this.

He understood the woman's English well enough; his father, back in Quedlinburg, was the local schoolmaster. By degrees it dawned on him that he might now have some years to perfect this language.

At Fire Brigade Headquarters, about this time, Major Frank Jackson sent for his staff officer, District Officer Edward Kirrage. "Well, it's time to move."

"Which way do you want to go, sir?"

"Let's go up Queen Victoria Street."

Now Jackson had seen the disposal of his forces on the big mobilizing boards and maps; the pattern of the raid had developed. And the largest fire areas were plain, too—the northern bank of the Thames in the mile between Blackfriars and Tower Bridge, spreading a mile inland. This area alone had five conflagrations, and Queen Victoria Street was the main approach road from Blackfriars Bridge to the square mile of the City of London.

It had been Jackson's area long ago, as a young divisional

officer—the peaceful years when, as a lonely widower, he had still found time to indulge in his favorite sport of salmon fishing.

The black Armstrong-Siddeley made good time toward the City—only once did Jackson halt it to put down the hood: "We'll have this back, then we can see where we're going." As they drove, thousands of red eddying sparks drifted at them on the still-windless air. At Queen Victoria Street they pulled up dead.

From end to end the street was alight; the gas mains were white pillars, lancing 50 feet, with a terrible rasping sound, to the red sky. The gutters were choked with idle pumps, coils of empty hose. Firemen huddled in cold, dispirited groups, doing nothing, or hung on to branches whose nozzles only dribbled water like tea spouting from a pot.

At the northern end, toward Mansion House, even the roof of the fire station was alight. Suddenly Jackson broke silence. "My God, Kirrage, what a sight!"

It was agonizing to watch—and not in Queen Victoria Street alone. Above the City for a hundred square miles the London sky pulsed like a blast furnace—red, angry, frighteningly alive. Slow-rolling columns of yellow-gray smoke bannered across the buildings and the river; and the piled clouds gave back the molten glare to the earth. It glowed on the black wasteful puddles of water, on the firemen's boots and oilskins. It glowed on buildings already alight on every floor, their office windows lit up like showrooms.

A thousand tiny red embers drifted in the air, lodging painfully in the eyelids. As the heat dried out a man's skin, the smoke peppered his lungs and nostrils, parched his lips; time and again the firemen sucked at the tiny draught of cold air that hovers around the water jet. Down in Stepney professional Fireman John H. Good felt for his cigarette lighter, then stood staring—his uniform was intact yet the heat had peeled away the aluminum shell in dry, crumbling flakes.

Never had men been so hot—and yet never so cold. As the jets fountained through the stone canyons of the streets, the breath of the fire drove back the water; every man was drenched to the skin with a fine spray like Irish rain. In a temperature one degree below freezing—the coldest May night in British records—firemen hugged their branches, wet and bewildered, wondering how long *their* water would last out, or if it would ever come.

In some districts it seemed as if the noise would never stop. In Theobalds Road, leading Fireman Morrie Zwaig, an auxiliary, was petrified by the throb of planes, the savage pummeling of the guns; the steady droning of the pumps' engine; the nerve-tearing scream of bombs. And only a mile away all might be silent—the quivering orange light; the dry crackle of the flames; far away a fire engine tolling like a passing bell. By the burning Temple Church Journalist Alexander Werth was one man with time to *listen* and hear a vast ring of fire breathing rhythmically, like a living thing. He thought: For once Wagner was right.

There had never been a bonfire like it—molten lead at the Farmiloe's Paint Works, Battersea; 250,000 books at the British Museum; bonded brandy and cigars at Waterloo Station; butter and York hams by Tower Bridge; 6,000,000 Red Cross flags and 10,000 collecting tins; the Royal College of Surgeons with the army's collection of plaster wounds; the skeletons of kangaroos brought back by Captain Cooke; and the skeletons of Mosquito aircraft in Bethnal Green; chocolate and raspberry jam in Poplar; cable and wireless headquarters in Moorgate; 10,000 pairs of shoes in Freeman, Hardy and Willis's store; Fields' Candle Factory; all Mr. Alvah Clatworthy's lace doilies; £100,000 worth of Gordon's gin in the City Road.

And still the fires were leaping—a barge called *The Silver Wedding*; six acres of rubber and anchovy sauce at Hammersmith; Lambeth Palace; McDougall's flour mills; a two-acre waste-paper dump; gyro compasses for night fighters in Hatton Garden; Salvation Army Headquarters; £60,000 worth of railwaymen's uniforms; the Clubland Boys' Club; the roof of the House of Commons.

The City That Would Not Die

By 1 A.M. Jackson had ordered "Emergency Working"—and this alone showed how desperate things had become. The London Fire Service's 1,270 fire appliances were already in action. Now the 1,242 appliances from the outer London borders must move in without delay—and many more were needed.

All over the City people huddled on rooftops, silent, speechless. Behind Westminster Abbey John Hodgkinson and Diana Riviere watched the glowing skeleton of St. John's Church—"Queen Anne's footstool"—and remembered the opera *Don Giovanni*, when Don Juan descends to the fires of hell. Artist Kathleen Brooks watching black spires and turrets etched against red from a Knightsbridge roof understood better the words of G. K. Chesterton: "Some moment when the moon was blood . . ."

On the fire ground it was different. What struck District Officer Kirrage in Victoria Street was the lack of organization—even if the sixteen-inch water main *had* gone the firemen weren't making intelligent use of what little water remained. At one point some firemen were laboring with two 500-gallon Coventry Climax pumps and two lines of hose. Kirrage urged: "Look, knock out one line, boys—that way you'll get a real jet." It was the same all along the street.

It was a heartrending sight—especially so to men like Jackson and Kirrage. Under normal conditions Jackson's Brigade was a tough, highly disciplined force, capable of tackling and mastering any fire. Its members prided themselves on being "smoke-eating firemen"; they shared the same tradition of hard work, off-duty pints of "old and mild," warehouse fires that had flickered out twenty years back. Most of them had lived all their lives in married quarters—"born under the hose cart," they liked to say. Their wives shared recipes and tea-party gossip, knew the pros and the cons of every station—this flat didn't catch the morning sun, that flat needed its plumbing fixed. They were true professionals, stuffed with tales of when things had been tougher, of supers whose oaths were fiercer than any flame.

Since the blitz, though, this small, exclusive world was breaking up. The hard core of 2,800 professional firemen had been swelled by a wartime influx of 28,000 auxiliaries, some volunteers, some conscripts—courageous and keen enough but lacking the years of training that went to make the professional. They all added up to a force of 30,000 strong, but among them only one man in forty was a peacetime officer who could sum up a fire situation in an instant.

On this night old hands like Kirrage wasted precious time exhorting and chivvying. At the City end of Queen Victoria Street the harassed district officer found another knot of firemen staring at a doorway blaze no bigger than a coal fire. "What's the trouble here, boys?"

"No water, sir."

It was no time for words. As Kirrage waded in to stamp it out the auxiliaries followed suit. They weren't scrimshanking; the idea had only now occurred to them.

Other professionals found the same—the auxiliaries didn't seem to understand. In Holborn Superintendent Joe Ansell found only one fireman with a line of hose, training a weak jet on a burning department store—already a solid sheet of flame. Ansell stepped in. "Look, swing your branch to the left, son—give the Shoe Lane corner a drink. This one's a write-off—you can only stop it spreading." When Ansell came back five minutes later the auxiliary had the branch back in the old position—a spurting dribble against the impenetrable flame.

Finally Ansell swung the branch himself, to show how the brickwork on Shoe Lane corner steamed as the jet hit it. "That way you're cooling it down—you're stopping the fire from spreading." Even then the auxiliary didn't seem to catch on.

It wasn't really surprising—few auxiliaries had experienced even a sizable peacetime fire. At the City end of Upper Thames Street, above the river, Temporary Fireman John French had a seven-story rubber warehouse on his hands—and two years' experience. Farther down the same street Station Officer Robert Stepney, who had "never even had experience of a decent peacetime fire," had a whole block alight. Leading Fireman Morrie Zwaig, in charge of a pump crew at the Theobalds Road conflagration, had two years' service. The same for Leading Fireman Joseph Cotterell, who took over the *News Chronicle* Building in Fleet Street. His crew was made up of a furniture salesman, a fun fair attendant, a plumber, and an ice-cream tricyclist.

In peacetime the chief officer of the brigade and all his senior staff would have been present on these fire calls—with pumps surrounding the building.

As things stood, even experience couldn't help much. At Upper Thames Street French had a four-man crew and one pump. He knew that he wanted at least ten pumps, but he compromised, summoning five. He got nothing, and the building burned down. In Theobalds Road there was no water; a bomb had smashed the mains in Red Lion Street. Fireman Zwaig did the best he could, smashing a manhole cover and pumping water from the sewers, but the filters kept clogging up; anguished minutes of waiting while they picked them clean.

In their eagerness some took risks that would have turned an old-timer cold. In the *News Chronicle* Building, several flights up, Leading Fireman Cotterell had one jet and a flaming insulated cable. He remembered the training-school precept —never put a jet on an active cable, you'll get a high-voltage shock back through the water. Then he turned to his mate. "What about it?"

"Come on, let's have a go."

Luckily the cable wasn't live, and Cotterell survived to shudder at the memory.

Even the seasoned hands were finding it hard going. At the junction of Mark Lane and Great Tower Street Station Officer James Ellis had an almost impossible assignment: to stop the fires spreading farther east and engulfing the Tower of London. Some pumps promised from Kent hadn't yet arrived

—meanwhile, with the mains gone, they needed a hose-laying lorry to relay water from the river 200 yards away.

Stumbling west along Great Tower Street, Ellis found one finally, but the driver wasn't keen to budge; he swore the street was impassable. So Ellis jumped on the running board and guided him—through potholes, over piles of broken brick, with flames fanning across the street, the driver almost blinded by drifting dust and the shimmering red reflection. Smeared with soot, his eyes streaming, choking with the acrid smoke, Ellis got the lorry back to the Control point.

"Where did you go for that?" Superintendent Joe Ayling, Ellis' chief, asked curiously.

"To hell and back," Ellis replied.

And to the man on the spot, Lambeth Control—the "underground firemen"—sometimes seemed quite a bottleneck. Assistant Divisional Officer Kenneth Hoare, a monocled former naval officer, was perched on a green baize card table at the corner of Old Street and City Road when he saw the flames fanning north from Holborn Viaduct—the railway station and the bridge were alight from end to end. Hoare rang Lambeth to let them know—the fire was marching to an area where they had ordered twenty pumps to rendezvous.

"They'll have to proceed as directed," a curiously calm voice told him.

"I don't think it's wise. The fire is spreading north. They stand every chance of being marooned."

The voice begged to differ. They had no reports of fires north of the viaduct. Hoare persisted: the mobilizing order was an hour old, the situation changed. The voice acknowledged his report. Nothing more was said.

A little later Hoare had word that the pumps' crews had escaped but the machines had gone. Boxed in by debris in the narrow streets, their petrol had caught; the intense heat had reduced them to a dripping, molten mass. Between twenty and thirty pumps were lost.

In any case, there was nothing Hoare could have done.

Despatch riders were hard to come by, walkie-talkies non-existent. And he was a mile from the scene of the flare-up, with no men to spare.

Down at the Elephant and Castle Superintendent George Adams was at his wit's end. Within five minutes of his urgent call to Control the first of his pumps had arrived. The problem now was to hem in the vast circle of fire, stop it from spreading outward. He sent the first six pumps that reported to the farthest points on the outer perimeter a quarter of a mile away—to Walworth Road and New Kent Road in the south, to Newington Butts in the west, and Newington Causeway in the east, to London Road and St. George's Road, which ran north and northwest of the Elephant.

At 12.40 more pumps arrived. They began opening up the first of the hydrants at the Elephant junction. Dry, every one.

A tough, hoary old fireman with a bulldog jaw and a parade-ground invective, George Adams wasn't giving up. Ordering on two water units, he set one of his trailer pumps into the 5,000-gallon dam by Spurgeon's Tabernacle, now burning as brightly as a birthday candle. In five minutes the hose went limp. The dam was bone-dry.

Bombs were still falling, rumbling and thundering between the blazing cliffs of houses; somewhere above a day fighter buzz-sawed, machine-gunning a parachute mine; it exploded, veining the air with yellow light. In this din it was hard for a man to make himself heard, let alone think. But Adams was keeping his head. He sent two more pumps to Manor Place Baths, an emergency supply of 125,000 gallons sited down Walworth Road. Three more to the basement of the old Surrey Music Hall, 600 yards northwest by St. George's Circus. There were 200,000 gallons there, and Adams would need every drop of it.

Meanwhile, grim news was trickling back from the outer perimeter. Vital water mains had already gone, fractured by the incessant pounding of the bombs—the twenty-inch main in the Old Kent Road; the twelve-inch, high-pressure in the New

Kent Road; the twelve-inch in Newington Butts; and more were going. Station Officer Sydney Boulter and his men tried twenty hydrants before they found one half a mile away that would help.

If part of the answer was emergency water supplies, this plan, too, had gone awry. The steel dams and concrete basins scattered over 100 square miles of London held a little more than ten million gallons. Later the Home Office was to re-estimate the need at four million gallons per square mile—for most of the metropolis about forty times the quantity available on this Saturday night.

So Adams knew the main hope was water relays from the Thames and from the Surrey Canal by Camberwell Road, a mile away. Special hose lorries, like the one James Ellis had rescued at Mark Lane, carried a mile of coupled hose, stowed so that it would snake from the tailboard in a continuous line. In theory a mile of hose could be laid within minutes—with special pumps set in to it at intervals to keep the water moving. Along the route lynx-eyed operators had to watch the compound and pressure gauges to avoid burst lengths ahead or overtaking the amount of water delivered by the pump behind them.

Adams didn't think the method entirely trustworthy, but without emergency water it was the best available. Now he signaled Lambeth Headquarters: "Make pumps fifty."

A new arrival on the scene was Assistant Divisional Officer Geoffrey Vaughan Blackstone. A six-foot-plus Rugby football enthusiast, Blackstone had no illusions about the dangers piling up. One of Jackson's principal officers and deputy chief of the Southern Division, he had for months urged the need for on-the-spot emergency supplies. But somehow neither the Treasury, who fixed the costing, nor the Architect's Department of the London County Council, who carried out the work, could muster much enthusiasm. They swore by a few big reservoirs—where the cost per gallon was less—rather than small ones scattered through unblitzed property.

Ironically, the Surrey Music Hall reservoir, the one big supply on which the Elephant now depended, was partly Blackstone's doing. He and his chief, Lieutenant Commander John Fordham, had seen the need for the site months before, had cemented it up using Fire Service labor without waiting for L.C.C. authority. At the time a report dubbed this "unconstitutional."

Four lines of two-and-a-half-inch hose from this "unconstitutional" supply had just been laid when Blackstone arrived at the Elephant. Adams had set up a scaffold dam holding 5,000 gallons by Burton's, the Fifty Shilling Tailors, and water was just coming through.

Still Blackstone didn't like the look of things. Manor Place Baths were now reported dry—within the hour they were on fire. Although George Adams had laid on a relay from the Thames at London Bridge, the hose lorry had a mile and a half to go through the shivered streets. The total of broken mains was creeping up—more than thirty within a mile radius. At 1.00 A.M. one thing was plain to Blackstone—the Surrey Music Hall reservoir was momentarily all that stood between the Elephant and annihilation.

Over the river, in Farrington Street, City of London, water wasn't the only thing lacking. As Superintendent Ted Overton watched his firemen use their razor-edged axes on locked office doors, he burst out, "Why in hell do they have to padlock them? Don't they want us to save their property?"

Overton had cause to grumble. With District Officer Walter Hall he had spent precious time driving up and down Holborn, breaking into building after building to douse incendiaries. In Cannon Street Police Sergeant Fred Scaife and his team had no axes but they used their truncheons joyously on every window that was still intact.

Farther east, in Fenchurch Street, Fire Watcher Thomas J. Burling, a shipping agent, shrugged as the flames fanned up through a tailor's shop two blocks away. "What can you expect? There hasn't been a fire watcher there in months."

In any case, short of a battering ram Burling and his team had no means of entry. The firms always took the keys with them.

The government's policy on emergency water was not the only factor hampering the Fire Service. Almost as frustrating was Herbert Morrison's Fire Precaution and Business Premises Order of January 15. Drafted to insure that men between sixteen and sixty registered for forty-eight hours' fire-watching duty a month, it offered so many loopholes that claims for exemption totaled 75 per cent of registrations. Again Morrison had been unwilling to resort to autocracy if there was any other way out.

In Bishopsgate, by Liverpool Street Station, Fire Watcher Claude Evans saw a bomb fall on an adjoining roof. Evans blew a cutting blast on his whistle; although he had not seen them on the roof all evening, he knew that the building housed four full-time fire watchers. When a policeman in the street heard the noise, Evans shouted down details. The policeman ran into the building to rustle up the fire watchers. Within five minutes he was up on the roof with them, neutralizing the bomb.

From the parapet Evans cursed them like the Middle Ages, but the men turned away sulkily, saying nothing.

Twenty minutes later two more bombs hit the roof. Again no fire watchers. Evans blew his whistle for two minutes until the policeman shouted up—he was busy but he would alert the fire watchers. When they finally did come, they huddled in the rooftop doorway, unwilling to advance farther. Evans had to shout directions, pinpointing the bombs, before they dashed out to tackle them.

Later the policeman told him that each time he had found the team sheltering on the ground floor.

It was the same story time and again. Four times Evans saw incendiaries plow through the roofs of warehouses in Hounsditch, a few hundred yards away. Dancing up and down on the roof, shouting and tooting on his whistle, he thought he had attracted attention, but no one appeared on the roofs to tackle them. Three of the warehouses were locked and deserted; the fire watchers had bolted from the fourth.

Soon all the fires had merged into one battering sheet of flame, and by then nothing could have stopped them.

To Temporary Fireman John French, on a warehouse in Upper Thames Street, the fires seemed to start almost innocuously—like upended candles flickering gently downward. Within thirty minutes the outlines of a building were gone; there was nothing but a soaring shaft of yellow flame.

Some did their best. As Clubland burned, the Reverend Jimmy Butterworth's teenagers defied death on the blazing parapets until the police broke the nozzles on their hand pumps to compel them to come down. In parts of St. Marylebone people trooped from the shelters to stamp on the incendiaries, leaping and singing. Looking back on it, Warden R. B. Kingham was reminded of a square dance. And at Kennington Station Officer Bunday stopped short for a strange sight: a deserted street; a shower of incendiaries; every front door opening as one and householders, silent and purposeful, whisking out to deal with them; men, women, small children, armed with sand, buckets of water. Then every front door shutting again like clockwork and not a word exchanged—"like something out of Disney."

But for every householder and business firm pulling their weight there must have been three who weren't. Police Sergeant Fred Scaife reckoned that in the whole City of London fire watching was no more than 10 per cent effective. In Chelsea and the Belgravia district of Victoria whole streets of empty pillared mansions glowed with neglected fires—Bernard Shaw's Heartbreak Houses whose owners had quit London when the bombing began. At one Chelsea house Architect Arthur Butler and his team just lost their tempers, stamping out incendiaries and sloshing water about like naughty children. "You might as well put up a notice 'Do come and burn me!'" Butler snarled.

Even by the Elephant young Bill Sherrington had to let

some houses in Pastor Street burn down; the owners had locked up and quit, leaving no key. In Battersea south of the river Warden Alec Woolfe was shocked: on St. John's Hill, by Clapham Railway Junction, street fire guards had to hack their way into building after building, shops, houses—even factories. And householders weren't the only offenders. At the Council's depot, where the furniture of the homeless was temporarily stored, not one fire watcher turned up for duty that night. At one Battersea wharf the fire watchers got bored with the job, went home to see how things were going. Most of the wharf was gutted.

And when men clung doggedly to orthodox channels and outmoded procedure it made things harder still. Temporary Fireman John French needed access to a burning bonded warehouse in Upper Thames Street, but first he had to parley with police and customs officials; they wanted an assurance that nothing would be moved outside the premises. In Fleet Street Basil P. Bothamley, manager of Lloyd's Bank, saw incendiaries strike the east end of the ancient Temple Church, where the Crusaders were blessed before going on their pilgrimages. But the local warden's post pooh-poohed his offer of help; the Temple had its own fire brigade, which would arrive in due time. Sergeant's Inn, too, had caught, but the caretaker had locked up for the weekend and taken the keys. Soon both were burning implacably with a luminous yellow fire.

The organization fell down almost everywhere. Just after midnight Jackson's deputy, Principal Officer Clement M. Kerr, had a fire call to Buckingham Palace. Outside the gilded iron gates he found pumps and water but no means of entry; King George and his family were at Windsor, the palace dark and silent. The police on duty had merely locked up and gone to ground. For the first time in history the London Fire Service had to enter Buckingham Palace by scaling the high railings.

Yet no one came to challenge them as they searched the roof and upper rooms. They found a corner of the roof where

147

something had smoldered, but no bomb. Kerr never knew who made the call.

At 12.50 Kerr had word that disastrous roof fires had broken out at the Palace of Westminster—the site embracing the House of Commons, the House of Lords, and the centuries-old Westminster Hall, with just on five miles of narrow stone corridors. As his staff car winged along the Mall, a shot crackled past Kerr's head. The driver stopped to find the Home Guard was warning them to keep out. Kerr's frustration began to mount. No one had warned the Fire Service that St. James's Park was temporarily closed to traffic.

At the House of Commons more confusion. Kerr found pumps and crews, but the men on the spot were sullen; they claimed that a busybody custodian had tried to keep them out on the grounds that they didn't enjoy parliamentary privileges. Kerr couldn't nail the rumor down, and it certainly wasn't set policy; the main problem was that without hard-and-fast compulsion even the Palace of Westminster had to rely on twelve policemen, who were only on loan, to keep fire watch on the palace's 1,000 rooms. At times certain doors, like St. Stephen's Portal, were locked, and it took time to find the right man with the right key.

As the Temple, Sergeant's Inn and Pump Court burned with a quiet, unearthly hissing, Journalist Alexander Werth recalled an old legend: the Temple had burned in 1666, too, because the authorities wouldn't countenance outsiders dealing with Temple fires. By now more bombers had moved westward, over Kensington, Paddington, St. Marylebone; to all London's consternation it was every man's raid, but tradition died hard.

CHAPTER NINE

"An Order's an Order Tonight"

1.30—2 A.M.

IT seemed, suddenly, as if the raid would never end—and it was almost as great a shock to the German pilots. At 12.38 A.M., as Leutnant Martin Reiser's Heinkel had swung away above the smoke drifts of the Millwall Outer Docks, Reiser had instructed Wireless Operator Leo Schuderer: "Contact home base—say mission completed."

Neither the Bavarian nor his crew were sorry. As the Heinkel droned steadily south for the English coast, each mile seemed an eternity. Never had Reiser so longed to see Villacoublay airfield again. Never before had he consciously thought of a mission: "Well, we lived through that."

Reiser must have been worrying all the evening without realizing it. Normally the restaurant keeper had a robust digestion, but tonight the stale aftertaste of fried potatoes kept returning to plague him.

As the glowworms of the Villacoublay flare path loomed ahead, Reiser relaxed consciously for the first time, feeling relief seep through his whole body. He wouldn't want to live through this night again. As he climbed from the plane, mechanics were already swarming on to "B for Berta," and the armorers were standing by with their bomb trolleys, but Reiser hardly noticed them. Oberleutnant Speck had spoken of two sorties at the afternoon's briefing, but that wasn't unusual: a reserve crew would be taking Berta out again.

The crew set off to the mess hall for a snack. Reiser, instead, walked across the frosted grass to Control office, the drumming of bomber engines waking to life all around him. It was now 1.45 A.M. Two old friends, Leutnant Koch and Unteroffizier Brunner, were already at Control, reporting to the duty officer—some stranger from Group whom they didn't know.

The three exchanged greetings. Had either of them seen Speck, Reiser wanted to know. They shook their heads; he hadn't yet touched down. Reiser began to worry. Earlier that evening he had watched, alone in the darkness, as Speck's plane took off over the treetops toward the coast. But the Longbridge Steel Rolling Mills had been timed an hour earlier than London. Speck should have been back by this time.

Now it was Reiser's turn: a short, concise report to the duty officer. Yes, they had bombed—seven 250-kilo bombs released at intervals across the horsehoe of Millwall Outer Docks. Naturally they had planted them as near the fires as possible. There was a little cloud at 14,000 feet but nothing below to obscure the flashes.

As he finished, the duty officer said briskly, "Well done. Get your plane refueled, see that it's bombed up, and take off again."

For a moment Reiser was speechless. To take off again on a night like a summer's afternoon? Didn't the High Command even think about the lives of the pilots they sent out? Worse, this officer from Group Headquarters, so blithely giving the orders, was an outsider who knew nothing of the wing's problems.

"That is a crazy order, sir, if you'll forgive my saying so," Reiser protested. "It is absolute suicide to take an aircraft and a crew back over England in weather like this." His joke about being "the oldest man in the Luftwaffe" came back to him, and he thought fleetingly that now it might help. They would know he wasn't a coward, they couldn't reproach him with that, they might even reconsider . . .

But the officer was suddenly looking so sad that Reiser felt a pang of shame at his thoughts, realizing that this came from

"An Order's an Order Tonight"

Field Marshal Sperrle himself, that he was only doing his job. "I know the way it is," the man sighed, "but an order's an order tonight."

Even tired and overwrought, with the dragging pain beginning over his heart, Reiser felt a stab of remorse that he should have queried an order. He said "Yes, sir, I see," and walked very stiffly out of the Control office.

The order was, in fact, an unvarying facet of Sperrle's technique: a second and smaller sortie, timed to dovetail the start of its attack with the tail end of the last main wave. They might not achieve a vast amount of material damage but they could at least further the prevailing chaos—stoking up the fires, disrupting factory production and goods traffic, keeping the citizens awake.

All this Reiser accepted as common practice. It was just that neither he nor any of the crews shared Sperrle's passion for moonlight nights.

Now there would be no time even for a cup of tea, but in any case he felt suddenly too sick to want one. As he walked back toward "B for Berta" he wondered if anyone would ever remember his protest. Out of the corner of his eye he saw a truck jolting across the airfield, packed with NCO's; one of them seemed to lose his balance and somersaulted backward on to the grass.

Still Reiser felt a strange detachment, as if all this was happening to someone else. He hoisted himself into the plane, and shortly Pilot Adolf Schied and Mechanic Lorenz Huber joined him. Watching Schied initial the bomb manifest and hand it down to the chief armorer, Reiser suddenly realized: Wireless Operator Leo Schuderer was missing.

Schied said he thought he'd be along. The sturdy little wireless operator had fallen off a truck and hurt his hand: he was getting medical attention.

Despite the frightening knowledge they all shared, he still addressed Reiser formally as "Herr Leutnant," referring to the wireless operator as "Überfeldwebel Schuderer." The procedure never varied, even in times of stress: ranks were used while on the ground, Christian names as soon as they were airborne.

At a time like this a man clutches at small straws. Reiser thought: We can't fly without a wireless operator—there probably isn't a reserve man on the field at this hour—maybe we still won't go. But at two o'clock, there was no hope for it; Schuderer clambered into the plane, grumbling that the doctor hadn't bandaged his thumb properly, that now he'd have to get it fixed when they got back. He seemed disproportionately ashamed of the accident, begging them all to support him in his story that he'd fallen down a flight of stairs. The youngster seemed to feel that the humiliation of being jounced off a moving truck was not for public consumption.

As Reiser gave his promise he thought how strangely unimportant all of it was. He felt quite powerless in the grip of circumstances. He surrendered suddenly to the belief he had fought to keep at bay: Speck was already dead. At 2.04, as the green signal light showed for take-off, he knew they, too, were going to die.

Few men were so sure. As always, in the midst of great disasters, most continued to behave as if immortality was their portion.

Since the raid began Albert Henley, mayor of Bermondsey, was no exception. Henley had spoken confidently enough of going to the shelters to talk to people about War Weapons Week, but tonight there had been no time. By 1 A.M. Deputy Controller Joe Blake and his staff knew that for London in general and the dockside borough in particular there never had been such a raid.

For two grueling hours Henley had been in the thick of it. Just after 1 A.M. he and his chauffeur, Eddie Taylor, had returned from a wrecked house where he had helped to hoist a piano off a trapped man. First, a hasty journey to the Control

Room to make sure that Gladys was all right. As usual, she was busy about the basement making tea for burly Joe Blake and his staff.

As Mrs. Henley saw Taylor and her husband slip upstairs again, she wasn't too worried. Although the underground room shuddered time and again as the bombs came howling from the sky, so that it seemed as if anyone would be lucky to come through this night alive, she thought that Albert was usually one of the lucky ones.

Groping through the darkness of the courtyard behind the Town Hall, Henley and Taylor had parted—Taylor to put out incendiaries on the roof of the Municipal Buildings, Henley climbing a ladder to the flat roof of the electricity substation. Incendiaries had burned the tarpaulin covering so that the rafters lay bare like wooden ribs under the moon. Presently Henley was joined by his brother Percy, one of the borough's incident officers.

The brothers chatted for a moment; Albert Henley suddenly slipped; he fell heavily with one leg on either side of a rafter. He was moaning a little as Percy lifted him, complaining that he had hurt his ankle. He thought that if he lay propped against the gutter for a short while he would feel better.

It was time for Percy Henley to return to Control for fresh orders. Before he left he cautioned his brother against descending to the yard via the outside ladder propped against the wall. He thought the chances of Albert heeding his advice were very slim indeed.

There had been a time, early in the blitz, when Percy, in charge of an incident, had sent Albert scurrying off on some errand—all the incident officers did the same. The chief warden, shocked, had said, "Do you know who you are speaking to?" And Percy Henley had answered, "Yes—my brother. He came and asked to help and I gave him a job. Now he's happy."

Thus Percy Henley had little hope that his younger brother would do what he was told. If an incident broke within the next few minutes, Albert would pick the shortest possible route to get there. He never forgot that he had been an able seaman, twice torpedoed, in World War I. He still took a stubborn pride in doing things the hard way: scaling ladders, playing football even though it gave him cramps.

In the Control Room Percy Henley had word that Peek Frean's Biscuit Factory, by the railway line south of London Bridge, was ablaze, and that all telephone links were cut off. At just after 1.15 he set off.

Around 1.30 drivers George Blake and Jack Hart got an emergency call in their rest room below the municipal buildings—the Peek Frean's fire was so serious that the dead had to be evacuated right away. As they tumbled up into the yard they were surprised to see Albert Henley silhouetted against the parapet of the electricity station. With surprising agility for a heavily-built man, in spite of a hurt ankle, the mayor shinned down a stackpipe to join them.

"This is a bad night," Henley said. "Where are you going?"

George Blake was making for one of the two green-painted mortuary vans. "We're evacuating Peek Frean's."

"I've just put out one or two incendiaries on that roof," Henley said. "I'll come and help."

They were, characteristically, the last words he ever spoke. Above them in the sky Blake heard a thin, high rending like tearing silk; as he flung himself forward he shouted to Henley: "Dive, Bert." All three men were scrabbling for some kind of cover when the bomb burst, piercing Jack Hart's chest with a fragment of shrapnel; puncturing George Blake's eardrum with its percussion; killing Henley outright.

Half a mile away, in a phone kiosk near the Peek Frean Factory, Percy Henley was reporting to the Town Hall. The bomb that killed his brother was a faint echo, like the dying note of a gong, up the wire.

Not that Percy Henley—or those on the spot—realized it then. In the resultant chaos, with a thick yellow haze of dust seething over the courtyard, those who ran from the basement found only Hart, moaning in agony, and George Blake dizzy with shock. Chauffeur Eddie Taylor, who dashed from the roof within minutes, had no idea that Albert Henley was lying within feet of him. He was convinced that the mayor had set off hotfoot, as he often did, in search of some incident. Taking the black-and-green Austin 24, he started out on a pathetic all-night round of post after post in search of his beloved guv'nor.

Meanwhile, in the Control Room, incidents were piling up. It was some time before one of Controller Joe Blake's officers stumbled on Henley's body lying in the yard, within twenty minutes according to Joe Blake, as long as an hour and a half according to George Blake, his brother.

A forceful, muscular man, Controller Joe Blake was faced with a fearful decision. As he received the whispered message, Gladys Henley was only a few feet away, doling out the latest brew of tea. Percy Henley had just arrived back for fresh orders. As Henley's nearest relatives, they had a right to know, and now.

On the other hand, Blake had to consider the fury of the bombardment. Even the great docks raid of September 7 had not surpassed it. One incautious word now, and the news would go the rounds of every shelter; there would be incredulous grief, perhaps even panic. Blake had no need to conduct a poll to know that 40,000 Bermondseyites were bearing up to this night better because they believed that Albert Henley—*their* mayor—was out in it as he always was, working like ten men.

So Blake said nothing—not to his staff, to Gladys Henley, or the borough at large. Only Percy Henley knew a vague disquiet. Usually incident officers took it in turns; now he was told that a parachute mine had landed on the Metallic Capsule Company's factory by Surrey Docks, and hustled off within minutes.

Despite the cold night, Joe Blake found himself sweating as he sat on with his secret, waiting for dawn. In Westminster, where they grieved for their own mayor, Councillor Leonard Eaton-Smith, they would have known how he felt.

There is no doubting that Blake took the right decision. At 1.30 A.M. the truth about Albert Henley's death was almost the only rumor that wasn't passing from mouth to mouth along an invisible grapevine.

Bethnal Green's Chief Operations Officer Arthur Caldwell heard that Goering was over the target in person, directing the bombing. (He wasn't, or indeed on any other night.) Near Paddington Station Warden Anne Kingham had an identical buzz running through her shelters—with Hitler as the master bomber. In Hampstead Warden George Titcombe's aides knew well enough why so many incendiaries were not igniting: they had been sabotaged by the Polish Underground. Camberwell shelterers had expected the raid all day—they believed implicitly the scurrilous untruth that every broadcast by the American jazz pianist Charlie Kunz was a signal for attack.

At St. Mary's Hospital, Paddington, the staff were on pins all night; Paddington Station had been hit, just as "Lord Haw Haw" had predicted. Yet the traitor's broadcast, which many still swear they heard that night, was only a five-minute fill-in, without any mention of the station.

With the pandemonium of crumbling buildings blotting out all sound, a man could give credence to anything. In Ebury Street, near Victoria Station, Superintendent George Bennison was spun backward on his heels by blast to find himself slowly and horribly choking to death. Fighting and clawing for life, Bennison had no doubt what it was: Hitler's secret weapon that all had been warned to expect.

It must be a gas more deadly than phosgene. Then, near to blacking out, Bennison relaxed and began to laugh weakly. The chin strap of his steel helmet had hooked over some iron railings and he was in the process of throttling himself.

On such a night it was easy to believe the worst. In Fighter Command's operations room Captain Clifford Mollison, Home Forces liaison officer, was doing his best to sort out a report for his chief, Field Marshal Sir Alan Brooke. Suddenly a hysterical Observer Corps man was on the line: "There are 10,000 planes

over the target." Mollison roared his disbelief and five minutes later the man was back: "Sorry, a thousand."

Even then Mollison couldn't credit it. The board showed no
more than 300 German bombers at the most.

The confusion was understandable. Toward 2 A.M. many
men and women had seen sights which had never been seen before on land or sea.

Most Londoners could say with Shakespeare's Casca: "Never
till now did I go through a tempest dropping fire." But there
were worse things than fire. In Stepney Mrs. Esther Prisant,
a greengrocer's wife, found herself packed in a shelter with
several hundred terrified people and a black-draped coffin
brought on a handcart by a Jewish funeral party. All night,
as the barrage thundered, the candles flickered; the mourners
uttered their shrill, wailing cries and rent their clothes. Herself a Jewess, it was still to Mrs. Prisant "worse than anything
from Edgar Allan Poe."

North, at Stoke Newington, two land mines hit a cemetery,
scattered the newly dead and fragments of granite impartially
over acres of red-brick streets. Rescue Chief John Frisby and
his men were so shaken that as creaking boots echoed a long
way off in the stillness every man was silent, holding on to
sanity. Suddenly an outraged Londoner loomed from the darkness—bowler hat, topcoat over candy-striped pajamas, a coffin
lid balanced on his shoulder. He accosted them without ceremony: "I was in bed with my missus when this bloody thing
came through the window. What do I do with it?"

Frisby and all of them collapsed into wild laughter, offer-
ing suggestions.

Some sights made the spine crawl with a nameless terror.
By Surrey Docks Fire Watcher Alec Watt saw a blazing
barge upside down, literally flying for one split second across
the sky. Near Brixton Hill a house stood like a giant spider's
web fashioned from lead: it had shaken loose all its timber and
bricks and only the pipes remained. At the Elephant and
Castle a bomb struck an underground shelter to leave an un-

forgettable sight—the forms of humans imprinted on a neigh-boring wall like a travesty of Pompeii.

For some the ugliness dawned by degrees. Superintendent Bill Norwood followed the trail of an unexploded bomb down flight after flight of the Victoria Tower at the House of Commons, finally ran it to earth in a basement. As he sized up the danger he wondered why water was dripping on his hand from above, then realized that it wasn't water. The bomb had plunged through the ceiling after killing an official in the room above.

For others it was a night of harrowing sound—the fevered jangling of burglar alarms set off by impact; the doomsday knell across the City of London as St. Swithin's Bell ricocheted down the tunnel of its steeple; the terrified screeching of the gibbons in the Regent's Park zoo; the clip-clop of hoofbeats down Piccadilly as a woman rode on a horse through the drifting smoke.

Almost any sensation seemed bearable—if it had roots in normality. As a parachute mine struck near the Mayfair Hotel, Pianist Freddie Aspinall felt the piano surge like a breaking wave beneath his fingers. But he kept playing so the revelers kept dancing. P. C. George Wharton, off duty and asleep in City of London Police Headquarters, woke at 3 A.M. to see the whole street alight from end to end and a fireman sitting on his window sill with a jet in play. Wharton thought things were in capable hands: he went to sleep again.

But any deviation from the normal triggered fear. Mrs. Kathleen Sales, returning from a dance during a brief lull in the raid, heard a soft, sinister rustling and dived for the ditch—then realized it was the first time she'd been able to hear her white taffeta dress. In Camberwell Warden Percy Lovett and two policemen were in search of an unexploded parachute mine. As they spotted it in a back garden, the silk of the parachute rustled. A cock struggled to the edge of the mine and crowed to the paling sky.

When Lovett recovered from his shock, the policemen had

gone. They had taken to their heels like two-year-olds; he never saw them again.

It was worse for some. For them the horrors were not fleeting; they worked all night in their company. At 1.45 on the Sunday morning Caretaker Frederick Haafe, stumbling from the basement of No. 43 York Terrace, Regent's Park, was the first intimation Wardens Eric Wills and James Ireland had that the Group for Sacrifice and Service, 99 strong, were worshiping the moon beneath a naked glass roof.

Both Wills and Ireland were men who knew the world—one a former public schoolboy and former dancing master, the other a rich man's chef. But they had never seen a sight so bizarre—a bewildering mixture of rich and poor; women with chased-silver, diamond-studded brooches; men in shabby, unpressed suits; the secretary, an elegant, imposing woman explaining that she could identify many of the dead by the rings and brooches which established their place in the hierarchy.

While Rescue Chief Andy Sutherland and his team worked by arc lights to free 60 people trapped on the ground floor, Wills and Ireland were viewing unbelievable sights: an etching of Christ still intact on a shattered wall, a running buffet in full progress in the main hall, a prayer chart detailing the hours of meditation.

And more surprises were to come. According to Wills some of the dead wore the white albs of priests, now patched black with blood; as they were laid out beside the porch on the graveled carriage sweep, the moonlight sparked fitfully from the birthstones they wore. The dead archbishop, Dr. Bertha Orton, a well-known London ocultist, wore no jewels —only a solid-gold cross studded with diamonds around her neck.

Close at hand lay the body of Dr. T. Mawby Cole, the Harrogate businessman who had predicted "something staggering" would happen on May 11.

It was all part of a macabre picture from which neither wardens nor rescue men could extract much sense. What were the moon worshipers, the British branch of a Californian sect, doing in the house at all? Once it had belonged to Lady Wyndham, formerly Mary Moore, the actress; as a young man about town Wills had danced in the painted ballroom. Now, according to the records, it stood deserted. And neither Wills nor the borough of St. Marylebone ever did succeed in penetrating the mystery. When Wills went to make inquiries of the survivors they were chatting animatedly in a drawing room set aside for the purpose. From a chaise longue a portly woman called, "Warden, I'd be grateful if you would get me a car."

James Ireland was having even more of a problem with Frederick Haafe. The caretaker, rummaging in the rubble, kept stressing that the altar must not be defiled "by pagan hands." Ireland, steeling himself for something that would "do credit to eternal Rome," gulped when Haafe salvaged the top of a scrubbed deal kitchen table. But the caretaker would allow no one to touch it, insisting it must be burned right away.

To top it all, a sudden argument arose about cremation, Haafe insisting that none of the sect must be cremated until three days after death, for fear the silver cord linking body and soul might be sundered. Goaded, Ireland burst out, "Does it matter?"

He meant that it was no time for niceties. On the other score, Ireland and everyone else found unity. Hundreds of men, women, and children were already dead. Hundreds more might die before morning came. But meanwhile everything was dedicated to the proposition that life was sacred—that no effort was too great if one man, woman, or child could be saved.

And by 2 A.M. the situation could hardly have been worse. Across London rescue men were already at work on more than one hundred and fifty incidents where people lay trapped. In some boroughs the situation had been critical an hour earlier: with thirteen major incidents logged in two hours, Paddington Rescue Chief Sidney Smith split his four-man teams into two for the first time in the blitz.

Every qualm the wardens felt earlier that night had been

justified. The people had written the blitz off too early; now
for many of them it would always be too late.

Among those who toiled, Deputy Post Warden Herbert
Mills somehow emerges as symbolic. Within minutes of first
arriving at the Alexandra Hotel, the dark, impassive former
chauffeur had felt the same fleeting despair that engulfed
Superintendent George Adams at the Elephant and Castle: the
job was too big, the confusion too great. Then it was gone, and
Mills was again the perfect employee, realizing that only he
and practical men like him could restore order from chaos. He
felt no contempt, no patronage—merely an awareness that
the kind of people the Alexandra housed were part of a world
too civilized, too remote, to cope with the horror that had be-
fallen them.

He was right. Inside the Alexandra a gray luminous pall of
dust still wavered like a curtain. Hundreds of people—though
there scarcely can have been more than sixty—seemed to be
milling excitedly about, grabbing the first person they could.
Mills saw one thing: unless the uninjured were got out of the
way and fast they were going to prove quite an obstacle.

Outside in Knightsbridge more welcome sounds became
audible above the cracking of the Hyde Park guns: the clangor
of bells and the crescendo of approaching engines as the ambulances and sitting-case cars came jolting and crunching over
the strewn rubble. Half the upper stories of the hotel had cas-
caded like a landslide across the road.

The rules laid down that stretcher-party cars must be used
only by those who couldn't walk, but Mills saw no chance of
restoring order that way. Rear Admiral Bennett seemed fit
enough to go to the Underground nearby; he was soon out of
the hotel, escorting a Mr. and Mrs. Waterfield, with about
twenty others tagging along. Next Mills had the cars backed
up to the curb. He gave crisp instructions: the uninjured were
to be driven to the Ormonde Court Hotel nearby. The slightly
injured to Kingston House Civil Defense Depot, which had
a first-aid post in its basement.

Then he started off on a quick reconnaissance with Assistant Nat Williams. As they trod up the main stairway they stopped short; a woman with a Red Cross cap on her head was spread-eagled across the first flight. The face, wide open from scalp to chin, had no connection with anything they had ever seen.

Beyond this point the stairs vanished into the sky, shorn clear away.

Now, Mills in the lead, they doubled around to the rear of the hotel, up the stone service staircase. The corridors were flooded with rubble, blocking access to many of the bedrooms, but it was no longer difficult to sum the position up. And Mills felt a sudden prickle of horror.

With the central portion of the hotel gone from top to bottom, every floor quaked like the sagging shelves of a cupboard. A few seconds of silence followed each salvo from the guns. Then the building gave out a stealthy crackling like the first warnings of an avalanche.

Mills said: "My God, Nat, the place is alive."

The problem was hideously simple. There were people trapped, many of them injured, on the upper floors. There were people trapped in the basement. All of them were blocked off by rubble, and it would be necessary to cut through several rooms to get at them. Meanwhile, one bomb falling too close, one lively salvo—even the right brick dislodged at the wrong time—and the whole trembling shell would topple like a chimney in a gale.

Worse, Mills didn't even know who was in the hotel—how many were staying there, how many were trapped aloft, how many in the basement. The Alexandra should have phoned in its total of residents to Mills's post in Belgrave Square, but somehow they hadn't. The register had vanished beneath the debris—it never was found. And the manageress, Paula D'hondt, who could have given firsthand detail, was locked up in Hyde Park Underground; the police would let survivors in but while the raid was on they wouldn't let anyone out.

Mills had never even heard of the one man who could have

helped him. Head Night Porter Charles Mattock was still unconscious and unremarked in the ruins of the dining room.

Impassive, unhurried, Mills set up a table, his blue lamp glowing beside it, on the pavement outside the hotel. From now on this would be the control point for every aspect of the rescue. As the stretcher-bearers struggled from the hotel with their burdens, he and Nat Williams tried to get everyone's name, a note of just where they were going. This could save endless trouble with the relatives of survivors.

A squad of Guardsmen came doubling up, an officer in charge asking if they could help. Mills swept a hand over the drifts of debris that virtually blocked Knightsbridge off: "You could clear that away for a start." They looked a shade surprised, but they waded in.

More consultation, this time with Rescue Chief Albert Marotta, a film stunt man, who had brought a tough, six-strong team along with him—Marotta settled every argument arising on a job with judo. Tonight his peacetime background came in useful: Mills wanted a reconnaissance of those parts of the upper floors starting nearest to the demolished stair well. As Marotta began his gingerly climb, he found the spiral stone stairway had been snapped back to the stubs, cantilevered out from the wall.

Beyond the second floor they began to crumble. There was a sudden gush of plaster. Marotta could save himself only by clinging like a fly to the wall and the remnants of the balustrade.

But the lift cables still held intact, and Mills decided these could be used to lower some of the worst stretcher cases from up above to the front hall. The sooner these were cleared the better. He set ambulance men and a few of Marotta's team to work.

The worst problem was the basement. As faint cries filtered up through massed debris, Mills realized that some of the shelterers were still alive. Using wicker skips to pile the rubble, working with hand shovels and even bare hands, Marotta and his crew began to terrier away.

Every so often they stopped, ears cocked, eyes straining upward in the eerie half-light. The building had given another ominous rumble, as if it were shifting slowly on its foundations.

Standing there, only a few feet above them, Mills felt suddenly too tall, sensing that somewhere beneath the bodies of people who wanted to live were being pressed and stifled beneath the crushing weight. At 1.40 he knew that whatever the danger he was not going to give up, that no one else working under him was going to give up either. There were lives to be saved.

To do them justice, nobody gave it a thought. At the rear of the hotel Police Constable Reginald Oakes, a fair-haired young water-polo champion, was at that moment walking a plank as confidently as he had ever sprinted along a diving board.

The difference was that the plank, twelve feet by nine inches wide, was perched precariously above a dark abyss 45 feet deep which ended on the concrete floor of the inner courtyard. Its outer end rested flimsily on a window ledge opposite and was being held steady by P. C. John McKenning and another constable. The inner end rested on a crumbling ledge a few inches wide which jutted five feet below the windows of the fourth-floor rooms.

Oakes, also under Mills's directions, was attempting a near-impossible rescue feat. A boot manufacturer named Davies, his wife, and two daughters were trapped in their fourth-floor room overlooking the courtyard. There was no other way to get them out.

Oakes's one consolation was that it was too dark to see clearly. He had no conception of the drop involved; he was too preoccupied with the fact that he had broken his police lantern by diving too hard for cover when the bomb fell. They might stop it out of his pay . . .

But Oakes decided that on his own he could do little about shepherding the Davies to safety. He called, and P. C. McKenning, a slow-spoken Scot, trod warily across the plank to join him. Oakes then hoisted himself up, sat astride the window sill, grasping each member of the family in turn by the waist. Exerting all his strength, he managed to lower them bodily down to McKenning. The Scot had one foot just resting on the plank, one on the narrow ledge supporting it, with his left shoulder pressed against the angle of the wall.

To Oakes it didn't always seem that the family appreciated the gravity of the situation. As the elder Miss Davies was entrusted to McKenning's grip she screamed shrilly: her night-dress had ridden up beneath the pressure of Oakes's hands. Gently her sister reminded her: "We're getting out alive. We needn't be *too* demure."

First the daughters, then Mrs. Davies, one by one, with Mc-Kenning's arms encircling them from the rear, they teetered giddily across the narrow plank. But at the last, when Mr. Davies refused to be parted from his brief case, Oakes lost his temper. "Look, don't be silly, will you? You're getting out of this, aren't you? I'll bring it with me when I come."

As they staggered across Oakes thought for one moment that the boot manufacturer's executive-sized bulk would topple them smashing to the floor of the yard. But they made it finally, and from then on it was a routine trip along rubble-choked corridors to the service stairway.

As they stumbled into the street, Mr. Davies tapped Oakes on the shoulder; he wanted a note of his name. But Oakes was feeling sour; there would be trouble enough explaining the filth on his uniform and the shattered lantern. Now, because he had spoken sharply, this man would report him for insolence. "Never mind my name," he answered roughly. "If you've anything to say about me, I'm P.C. 369 B."

The rest of the night he spent drafting a report to try to smooth things over. The fact that the family's account earned him the George Medal strikes Police Sergeant Oakes as inexplicable even today.

But the same spirit of dedication had seized others. Down

The City That Would Not Die

by Battersea Power Station—which the bombers never did hit —rescue workers Jack Searle and George Smith delved to reach a trapped family in a tunnel no higher than a footstool, tons of rubble creaking perilously above them. At one point Smith had to lie as still as a rock for two hours holding a woman's head while Searle chiseled away the concrete and woodwork encircling it. Even then Smith would accept no relief; Ambulance Chief H. M. Westgate had to haul him out by the scruff of his neck.

Some achieved miracles of improvisation. In Stepney the Reverend J. Newton Sykes, chancing on a man with a broken leg, quietly fashioned splints from wood wreckage with bombs dropping 30 yards away. Among the blazing acres of the Elephant and Castle an unknown man appeared from nowhere with a bottle of whisky for four people trapped under a kitchen table. When Warden Arthur Knight sent him for tea he vanished into the flames, returned minutes later with a large jug—"hot with plenty of sugar."

In Islington Warden Rob Connell took all the weight of a heavy wooden beam on one arm and shoulder, using the other hand to scrabble away bricks that had trapped a couple in bed. Streets away rescue men under Warden Nat Sharpe dismantled a tottering wall brick by brick for fear it collapse on a bedridden woman.

Sometimes the ends hardly justified the means. At the Royal College of Surgeons' fire, Lincoln's Inn, the astonished post warden, Victor Wootten, heard rescue men report a heavy casualty list—then realized they were saving specimens in pickle. As a fireman smashed into Woolworth's store, blazing in Bethnal Green, Sub Officer Sam Cheveau held his breath, then saw the man stagger out disgusted. He was risking his life for a wax dummy.

And a few, just to make things harder, didn't want rescuing. Warden Jack Blaine, arriving to evacuate a Free French billet in St. Pancras, found General de Gaulle's men propped up phlegmatically in rubble-strewn beds refusing to move—

a civilian had no right to give orders to soldiers of the Republic. Even Blaine's query as to how many should be on the spot was poorly received: was it law that a man should sleep in his own bed on Saturday night? A friendship was cemented finally over the least palatable early-morning snack Blaine had ever eaten—oily tinned sardines, French bread, raw red wine.

No such problems beset Warden Stanley Barlow. Not long after 1 A.M. all his conflicts and doubts were resolved at one stroke.

As usual, Barlow wasn't taking it easy at Post Headquarters. Although the death of Winnie Dorow, the tailoress, had left him cold and dazed, he was forcing himself to go on as if nothing had happened. Barlow thought that few of his wardens would understand why; they had even thought him callous when he had driven a girl warden sick with shock out to patrol again. It had been the same in the early days, when panic broke out in an underground shelter and people clawed hysterically for the entrance; in another minute they would have stampeded blindly through the streets. Barlow had blocked the shelter entrance, swinging at every male chin within reach. Brutally efficient, it had stilled the panic like a pail of cold water.

Barlow understood fear precisely because the seeds had sprouted inside him. It was an enemy, he knew, that could be allowed no quarter.

Tonight, though, he was patrolling with one of the few who did understand—trim, fair-haired Annie Hill. Once Barlow showed razor-sharp presence of mind when they had gone to watch a blitz from a roof and blast slammed the door on a spring lock, blocking their exit. Without hesitation Barlow scrambled down one and a half stories to a lower roof, then caught her in his arms as she jumped. Miss Hill knew that Barlow was often afraid, but she admired him as a man who fought his fear as another man might fight a craving.

As they rounded the corner of Hallam Street, which ran at right angles to Portland Place where the post was sited, Barlow saw a light shining at the very top of the great Gothic syna-

167

gogue which stood on the Hallam Street-Great Portland Street corner. Inwardly he cursed; some careless worker had left an electric light burning.

A closer look, and he began to run. The synagogue roof was a furnace of blue-white incandescent light. Barlow was unaware that a bomb had fallen on the northwest tower, setting the gas pipes in the gallery alight. The gas, as he had so often stressed, should have been turned off at the main, but tonight someone had neglected to do this.

Meticulous, painstaking, Barlow knew every inch of the rabbit warren of basements and cubbyholes that ran beneath the synagogue and the two connecting buildings. He knew who sheltered there, too; in his notebook every name had been carefully entered up in the tiny accountant's handwriting. A quick mental check—there must be 14 in all.

Both he and Annie Hill ran for the synagogue: farther down the street a woman with a dust-smeared face leaned against a wall, giggling hysterically. Barlow turned to Miss Hill, ordering, "Get her up to the hospital." Again the knowledge of what fear could do prompted his order. If people ventured from below ground and espied a half-crazy woman, the panic would spread faster than fire.

Alone Barlow ran on to the synagogue. Now he could only hope that an incident report would get back to the Post and quickly. Again he couldn't know it, but the teachings of eighteen months were paying off. Warden "Sam" Ekpenyon had been the first to see the synagogue take fire as he left the basement of Yalding House, a tenement standing opposite. He had an Express Report back to the Post in seconds. Now Barlow's words came back to him: "Wherever you are, stay there and take charge."

The blast from the bomb had roused the shelterers in Yalding House. Within seconds scores of people were surging for the entrance. Suddenly at the head of the basement steps the brawny Nigerian towered above them. "Man, see *me* excited? See *me* worried?" As he launched into a heartstirring Negro

spiritual, the fear began to evaporate. Ekpenyon sang on, doing what Barlow would have expected him to do.

At the entrance to the synagogue basement Barlow had
paused. The stairway down was blocked by a gigantic tumble
of masonry, six solid feet of it. Impossible to claw at it with
his hands—he needed leverage.

Without thinking the young accountant whipped off his tin
hat, bent almost double, scooping away at the debris for dear
life. It seemed hours before enough of it rolled aside to reveal
a faint light beyond—a funnel large enough for him to ease
forward on his belly and tumble headfirst into the basement.
For a moment the blizzard of plaster dust stirred; he could see
four people reeling like sleepwalkers, picking feebly at the
debris that blocked off the basement from the hall. He knew
two of them—Mr. and Mrs. Roth, the caretakers. He never did
know who the other men were.

Nor, for that matter, was he quite sure how he got them out.
But he had to make a quick decision. The three men seemed
dazed but capable of understanding; the woman was moaning,
almost paralyzed with fear. He would take the men first, then
return to tackle her on his own.

Already the heat was uncomfortable. It beat down on them
from the blazing roof, as if they were ants under a burning
glass. Yet strangely the fire was no help in guiding them. To
clamber their way over the debris they had only the milk-
water light of Barlow's pocket lantern. By the time they had
reached the street the fire had spread; every building stood out
clear and sharp in the light of the dancing flames. There was
no sign of the Fire Brigade.

Barlow told the three men to hang on outside, remarking
more confidently than he felt: "I'll be back."

Once more into the burning building. This time it was
much worse. The light of the torch seemed dimmer and for
minutes he couldn't locate the way back, groping in the black-
ness with only anonymous piles of bricks to offer clues. For
the first time fear swept over him like a wave. He thought

he would be trapped down there and slowly cremated in the hot embers.

It was a good ten minutes before he found the basement. The woman's nerve had practically gone; as Barlow slithered over the rubble, she was backing away, never taking her eyes off him. Barlow kept repeating: "It's all right, look, I'm trying to help you." He just managed to catch her as she fainted in his arms.

For the second time he began the return journey, almost by guesswork. With the woman an untidy bundle in his arms he could not focus the torch properly. Suddenly there was a smothered roar and something struck him a spine-jarring crack on the shoulder, nearly flinging him off his feet. He thought it was a coping stone, but its only effect was to make him grasp the woman tighter. He didn't know that the greater part of the roof had fallen in on him.

Nor did he realize that for a moment one warden actually saw him, silhouetted against the livid glare. Then he was lost to view in a roar of timber and a red-gold rain of sparks.

This warden ran two streets to the Post, to find only Eileen Sloane, Barlow's closest friend, and Miss Donaldson, the telephonist. Shaken, he blurted out: "I've just seen Mr. Barlow down by the synagogue carrying someone in his arms and the roof fell in on him." Then what was the man doing here, Miss Sloane wanted to know. Suddenly, losing control, she shouted, "Get down there and get him out."

In the middle of it all the phone rang; District Warden Harold Scoble had a routine query. Something in Miss Sloane's voice struck him as odd.

"Hullo, what's the matter with you?"

"I don't know. I'm just praying God it isn't true, but they say that Stanley's been trapped down by the synagogue."

Faintly she heard his shocked "My God" as he hung up. In ten minutes Scoble himself had arrived at the Post Headquarters. He seemed to think she might need relieving. "I'll be all right," Miss Sloane replied. "Heaven knows I've enough to keep me busy, but I can't even go down there to see. I've no one to send and things must go on."

Barlow's system had always been to have just one warden in charge of the post between midnight and 4 A.M.; on a heavy night the others stayed on patrol. Barlow's words came back to her: "If you're in charge of the post, you're in charge of it. You accept the responsibility. Whatever the circumstances, you don't move from it." At 1.30 Scoble realized there was no shifting her. Miss Sloane, too, was staying where Barlow would expect her to be.

To Herbert Mills, Stanley Barlow, and several million other Londoners, the blind fury of the raid made all the difference. On other nights there had always been the hope of the raid petering out after the first waves—fog might close down across the Channel, as it had done on December 29. Or again it could be the other man's raid. But by 1.30 on Sunday, May 11, it was plain that all such hopes were gone.

And most people would have agreed with Captain Clifford Mollison—Goering had lost his temper. To Alderman Leonard Styles, Southwark's Civil Defense chief, the raid was "a deliberate attempt to create terror by fire." Stepney Controller Roger Corderoy and his staff dubbed it "a pure spite raid from start to finish."

At London Region Headquarters, Kensington, Deputy Administrative Officer Julian Simpson had a truer picture. As the night wore on the teleprinter clattered out facts so grim they needed no embellishment.

One by one the railway terminals were going; St. Pancras and Cannon Street by 12.15; at 1.00 Euston and King's Cross, the alternative routes to the north; at 1.25 Victoria out, with four unexploded bombs; Paddington at 1.15 with an appalling casualty list; Liverpool Street, the main-line terminal for the east soon after. All three southern terminals—Charing Cross,

London Bridge, Waterloo—were out, too. Only Marylebone remained.

And this was only the beginning—every river bridge between Lambeth and the Tower of London was blocked or cratered. Twenty-nine miles of the underground railways were out; six telephone exchanges already gone in the City of London alone; all power including the high tension cut off in the South West Indian Docks; Beckton Gas Works, the largest in the world, blown sky-high, and 700 gas mains fractured across the City; thousands of streets impassable with fallen buildings.

As key point after key point was knocked out, London Region's experts began to see it as a raid executed with the deadly precision of a hammer driving home nails.

But the ferocity had one effect: it stirred Londoners to action. At 2 A.M. the mood that swept the City was to save something from the wreckage—whether it was a life or merely property.

The things people gave priority showed the way they felt. In Lewisham a baker came bounding out of his bombed shop, carefully laid a mammoth slab of butter on the pavement. Mrs. Monica Pitman, a Hampstead housewife, risked her life to rescue a gray tailor made. Near Norwood Junction Mrs. Henrietta Cartwright saw a man walking vacantly along a street stripped as naked as a battlefield clutching two coat hangers. In Theobalds Road, Holborn, a man nipped in and out of a blazing shop piling sewing machines on the pavement. Hours later he appeared with a wheelbarrow, trudged off with all the heads leaving the stands. At the Gordon's Gin distillery in City Road Production Manager Walter Greaves and his staff labored in choking smoke to salvage twenty precious tons of juniper berries.

Some had less luck. Miss Esme Glynn raced in to a block of luxury flats in St. James's to save her fur coat; in her confusion she grabbed only a handful of bills. Near Leicester Square a streetwalker raved and screamed outside a burning tenement; her fur coat was burning on the top floor. Beside her, her fancy man kept assuring her that he'd buy her another on Monday, but it didn't help a bit; she wanted *that* one. At Westminster Abbey, where the deanery and all the cloisters were blazing, an assistant verger realized that he had left his Home Guard uniform in the deanery—and tomorrow, for the first time, the volunteer force were to mount guard at Buckingham Palace. But after a heroic tussle the flames beat him back; he saved only a rifle and a pet canary.

Inevitably, some found time to covet souvenirs. As Station Officer Leslie Sinden made the rounds of his firemen at Druce's blazing department store, he found one of them trying to wrench up Baker Street with a hammer and chisel. An incendiary had printed its German serial number neatly into a paving stone; the man wanted to take it home. In Stoke Newington Major Charlie Creswick-Atkinson found a girl trying to dismantle the green-silk folds of a parachute looped over a garden wall. When the major explained that an unexploded mine was lodged the other side, she fainted clean away.

A few, by sheer chance, saved their own lives. Old-age Pensioner John Meggs, a Boer War veteran, had a heart attack just before the raid started; for two hours he lay gasping and alone in his Islington tenement room. When the attack passed, the old soldier applied the remedy that he always did, raid or no raid: he went for a walk. As he stepped briskly along the burning streets, like a man savoring the sun in the park, a bomb tore the house to pieces.

Chance favored Lord Donegall, too. He was just leaving the Colony Club in Berkeley Square after that dinner with George Ronus when the Dorchester Hotel's manager realized he had lost his keys. The two men went back and found them beside the table. But in the street the car was now a tangle of smoking metal. Lord Donegall would have been pressing the self-starter at the moment the bomb went clean through the hood.

Camberwell Ambulance Officer William Harrison had a premonition: he was on his way to pay a duty call on a sick driver when "someone" grabbed him by the shoulder. He spun around but there was no one there. So Harrison decided against it—went back, instead, to the depot. Two anti-aircraft shells sliced into the pavement outside the driver's house five minutes later, the time he was due to arrive.

In the hospitals, the one thing that counted was the lives of others: at St. George's Hospital, by the Alexandra, the blood transfusions went on for thirty hours non-stop. On no other night had the casualty lists in some boroughs mounted as they did now—the white-tiled foyer of St. Mary's Paddington ran red with blood. Theater Sister Margery Vickers walked into her ground-floor office at Mile End Hospital to find someone had laid six dead bodies neatly on the floor, but she stayed on duty without flinching all through the Sunday. Even for traumatic surgery, the conditions were primitive; when the emergency lighting packed up at the National Temperance Hospital, St. Pancras, the surgeons had to work on by torchnight. And the pre-operative treatment alone took hours: morphia shots to ease the pain, shots of anti-tetanus serum to nullify infection, blood counts to gauge the extent of secondary shock, the thick yellow patina of plaster dust to be scrubbed from naked flesh.

It hardly seemed a night to make medical history, yet Police Constable John Dickie did just that. Five minutes after the Alexandra Hotel collapsed, the young constable was carried into St. George's Hospital near to death. A third bomb had exploded simultaneously in Rotten Row, fragments of it tearing into Dickie's side, rupturing the lung and diaphragm, lodging in the spleen.

By a stroke of luck one of the duty surgeons was a gynaecologist, with more experience than many of infinitely delicate surgery. Although it was nowhere in the book, he took what seemed the safest, most sensible course—removed the spleen through the punctured lung, then stitched the lung up again, leaving the abdomen intact. The clock in the operating theater at St. George's Hospital showed 2.45 when the first transpleural splenectomy in medical history was successfully performed.

"An Order's an Order Tonight"

And still the bombers were coming, the hell's chorus of their engines drowning out all other sound. Householder Ernest Maidwell, nursing a splitting headache in Dagenham, Essex, calculated that not once in three hours had the night been silent. From the roof of St. Pancras Hospital District Officer Edward Baker, London Fire Service, watched the planes calmly flying in line abreast against the moon, seeming to bomb at a given signal.

Steadily, without hindrance, they moved back and forth across the City like tractors plowing a field. And at 2 A.M. Leutnant Martin Reiser and almost two hundred more had not yet reached the coast of France.

CHAPTER TEN

"Don't Let Them Drop Any More"

2.00—3.20 A.M.

At Fighter Command, though, the mood was one of buoyant optimism. By 2 A.M. more good news was through: Flying Officer Norvak of 306 (Polish) Squadron had sighted a bomber near Camden Town, tailed it as far as Brighton, watched the flames black out as the Channel waters closed over the flaming Heinkel.

As Squadron Leader Reginald Tate, Air Ministry liaison officer, passed on the news, a subdued murmur of approval arose from the officers around the control gallery and was echoed by the WAAFs on the plotting board. Squadron Leader Cyril Leman and all of them felt better; they were really showing the Germans this time.

If the casualties were mounting so, too, were the claims, and Air Ministry was making sure the world knew. In the Savoy Press Room Quentin Reynolds and the others were munching "Tich Specials"—three-decker sandwiches of bacon and scrambled eggs made up by the barman, "Tich" Massara—when Jamie MacDonald of the New York *Times* hastened in: there were 400 planes over, 14 already shot down. At the Royal Observer Corps, Bromley, Kent, Controller Arthur Collins noted a friendly tip from the Kenley, Surrey, fighter sector that might have given the newsmen food for thought: Kenley's stations alone had bagged fourteen.

"Don't Let Them Drop Any More"

Air Marshal Sholto Douglas was more than satisfied. Steadily the claims were coming in: at least ten bombers claimed as destroyed, six more lethally damaged, four claimed as probable.

No wonder Douglas felt moved to remark: "We should soon have been inflicting such casualties on the enemy's night bombers that the continuance of his night offensive on a similar scale would have been impossible."

To date some 50 day fighters and 30 night fighters had taken part in this spectacular sweep, and more than twenty were due to be airborne within the next hour.

At Wittering airfield the scene was perhaps more typically English than most. As the moon swam up above the Lincolnshire countryside, a dozen or so pilots sprawled on bunks or mattresses in a converted gamekeeper's cottage on the airfield perimeter, awaiting the take-off signal.

Pilot Officer Andrew Humphrey, the youngest there, was outwardly relaxed, inwardly alert. He knew exactly what to do: the commanding officer of 266 Squadron, Squadron Leader Pat Jameson, had briefed them as soon as the "fighter night" was laid on. At 2 A.M., five minutes after Jameson and Squadron Leader "Barney" Beresford were airborne, Humphrey and three others would take off.

First he had to climb to 18,000 feet; as the youngest he had inevitably drawn the highest "layer" on the Southend-Ramford patrol line. He was to keep this up for an hour or more, eyes straining all the time in the hope of sighting an enemy, then return to base.

Humphrey, who had shot down his first Heinkel two nights earlier, at 21,000 feet, over Nottingham, felt his chances were very small indeed.

This was typical of Humphrey, a dark, lean, good-looking youngster of twenty; his pleasantly diffident manner might have led harder, more assertive types, like Hauptmann Hufenreuter, to underestimate him. But Humphrey was deceptive. Away from the drome he enjoyed driving fast about the countryside in his high-powered (and almost brakeless) Talbot 105;

recently he had arrived back with the remains of a level cross-ing adorning his bonnet. But he also knew and cared about a surprising number of other things: church architecture, good food, above all flying. As a boy he had made model aircraft, like other youngsters, but unlike the others, he worried about the power-weight ratio when they came to grief. Cool, enthu-siastic, analytical, he had been a star pupil at the RAF College, Cranwell, when war broke out.

At this hour on a Sunday morning nobody felt much like talking. The lighting in the cramped little cottage was kept purposely dim to aid the pilots' night vision. If it hadn't been for the knowledge that his parachute was already stowed in the Spitfire, ready for action, Humphrey could have drifted off to sleep. Already he had done three hours' practice flying since breakfast on Saturday.

Just before 2 A.M. the telephone cut the silence and Jameson answered. "Time to go, fellows." Half-a-dozen pilots climbed leisurely from their beds, set off along the moonlit lane to the grass airfield where the planes were drawn up yards away.

As he swung into the cockpit, patting the toy fur rabbit he kept there for luck, Humphrey thought about the others. They were a mixed bunch, but he felt they knew the answers to problems he hadn't even begun to formulate. Pat Jameson, a wiry New Zealander and an old 46 Squadron man, had operated off pure ice in Norway, was torpedoed on H.M.S. *Glorious*, flew all through the battle of Britain. "Barney" Beresford, a devil-may-care Irishman, seemed to bear a charmed life.

And Pilot Officer Richard Stevens, still awaiting the "scramble" at dispersal, had a cold, deadly flair that was almost frightening. After a German bomb had wiped out his family in Manchester, Stevens, a lean, aloof man in his thirties, seemed to develop a sixth sense; he would even break radio silence to call up the Gun Ops rooms and direct their field of fire. On nights when no one else could spot a Heinkel Stevens could do it, and once he had spotted it there was no hope for it.

The chances were that Stevens, Jameson, and Beresford

would all find their targets tonight and Humphrey, who had less than a year on Ops, wouldn't. To Humphrey it seemed as logical as that.

At 2 A.M. they took off, climbing into the pale sky, Jameson hugging his Spitfire at a level 14,000, Humphrey, 4,000 feet above him, the others spread evenly in layers 500 feet apart. A long way off the City glowed gently, evenly, like hundreds of campfires fanned by a bellows: even the hard-bitten Jameson felt himself growing angry at the sight. But the earth itself was almost invisible—only faint gradations of shadow, like a relief map seen in twilight. In twenty minutes the flying contours would grow lighter, then Humphrey and all of them would know they were over the sea.

Despite his fur-lined Irvin jacket and fur-lined trousers, Humphrey was bitterly cold; although the Spitfire had been designed to fly with the hood shut he always kept it open. It was something else he had worried out in six weeks of "fighter night" experience—an open hood aided the night vision.

The paler gray of the sea showed ahead, and Humphrey's mind ticked over points. Speed was all right—115 m.p.h. maximum. He was learning fast; already he knew that the greater your speed the less chance you had of even spotting a raider. Over Nottingham he had closed up so fast that he overshot his man. The bomber hadn't seen him so he had just waited for it to catch up, but luck might not favor him again.

Already Andrew Humphrey had learned certain tricks. He nursed his night vision in dimly-lit rooms, flew with his hood open, kept his windscreen highly polished, searched for the enemy with the corner of his eye instead of staring dead ahead. But it was the problem of temperament that worried him more. By day a fighter pilot had to shoot well and quickly, judging from angles of deflection. At night you were a different man. Even at 100 yards dead astern you could hardly miss, but you had to be cautious, methodical, and take a lot of time judging your position.

And tonight was no exception. The icy air that cut like

barbed wire; the moon a milky trail across the water; ten miles out across the North Sea beyond Southend, then the slow turn back to face London. Suddenly he stiffened: an aircraft's tail-light had winked several thousand feet up but almost dead ahead. Alert for battle, Humphrey hurled in, speed mounting from 120 close to 200 m.p.h. Suddenly he throttled back, easing off in a long, slow curve to port. He was chasing a star.

He flew on. In a moment the Thames estuary lay ahead under the dead glare of the moon. To patrol the northern bank as far as Ramford, Essex, twelve miles east of the City of London, would take just ten minutes. Suddenly, about 2,000 feet above, a vapor trail spread its thin ribbon across the sky. It was following a steady course of 080 degrees, toward Ostend—a raider and probably a "returned empty," one who had delivered his bombs and was going home.

The last thing Humphrey wanted to do was to get far out to sea. But it seemed there wasn't much choice. By the time he had brought the Spitfire around in a starboard turn the aircraft was out of sight. Now he would have to follow and make sure, which meant closing to 400 yards. The young pilot cursed aloud: "Damn it, another wild-goose chase."

Reluctantly, without hope, he started off in pursuit. The minutes ticked by . . . five . . . ten . . . fifteen . . . by now he must be near the opposite coast, and still no sign of the plane. The moon was over his right shoulder, which made it hard to see. Time to turn back. He had lost it now.

At this moment Humphrey saw the aircraft again. It was heading down moon, just beginning to climb. Without hesitation he dived, sensing, at the same time, that the tail gunner had seen him, too. The aircraft was streaking for home base.

He slammed the throttle back, the air screaming past his head as he dived steeply away; 15,000 . . . 12,000. At 10,000 feet it was dead level and ahead, near enough to see the characteristic four sets of exhausts, the two-in-line engine. A Heinkel right enough, and diving fast.

Nine thousand . . . 5,000 . . . 3,000 . . . at this moment Humphrey didn't even realize that he was well over the coast, only a few thousand feet above enemy-held Belgium. He didn't even wish the German crew, as such, any harm. Instead, it had become an absorbing technical problem—could he catch it before it hugged the earth and vanished from sight?

Suddenly it was now or never. He had closed so rapidly that the Heinkel was now only 100 yards ahead, bulking enormously in his windscreen. He fired. With sudden and terrifying impact the Heinkel exploded.

For a minute Humphrey could see nothing. Somehow he kept hold of the stick, but the searing glare had washed clean across his eyeballs. Instinctively he reefed away in the tightest turn ever, missing the tidal wave of flame by a second, but unable even to focus his instruments. He had the ugly feeling of being quite lost.

Around this time Leutnant Martin Reiser was actually landing on enemy soil with that same feeling. His premonition had been all too accurate. They had scarcely bombed Millwall Docks for the second time when from nowhere a fighter got them fair and square in the port engine. After this Reiser was never too clear what happened. Pilot Adolf Schied had been badly wounded, he knew, the rest of the crew either dead or knocked senseless. But as Reiser tried to struggle through to the rear to see to them the plane dived like a comet. Smoke that reeked like burning castor oil came pumping through. Reiser realized that Schied had baled out; there was nothing he could do now for either crew or aircraft. He, too, baled out.

Minutes later he hit the damp Sussex grass face first, tumbling over and over with the drift of the parachute. Suddenly the night seemed too silent for comfort. Far away he could see the red London sky, and for the first time impersonality gave place to faint regret. He thought: "I had a hand in that." The next thought was more prosaic: his feet were cold and wet. He must have lost his boots as he baled out; he had landed in England in his socks.

As the first contingent of soldiers, armed with rifles, came doubling across the meadow, Reiser's eyes turned again to the skyline. He felt tremendously alone, wondering what these men would do to him. Their bitterness and vengeance, he thought, could be a fearful thing. He had hurt his back, but although they supported him from either side no one said a word as they tramped across the frosty pasture over a ditch; toward some kind of encampment where army trucks were drawn up by a huddle of tents.

As they motioned him to take off his cap and flying jacket, starting methodically to search his pockets, Reiser could still see the burning City through the tent flap. Still no one spoke a word. The Bavarian felt a mounting unease. They must see that skyline, too. What kind of torture would they inflict on him?

Suddenly, without affectation, one of the soldiers handed him a cigarette.

As he lit it, drawing down a ravenous lungful of smoke, Reiser was stammering out incredulous thanks. The man achieved a cautious smile. One of the other soldiers went away, returned with a blanket.

A long time seemed to pass. Reiser thought of Leo Schuderer and how they had all promised to say nothing about the way he had sprained his thumb. It would never matter now. He sat on, smoking with the two soldiers, all three sometimes smiling timidly, not speaking. Presently a truck drew up outside and Reiser was led out. Now, for the first time, he sensed constraint, a constraint mingled with sympathy. It was as if, like the doctors, the soldiers had only bad news about his heart but could not find the words to tell him. Almost diffidently they motioned to him to climb over the truck's tailboard; one shone a small pocket torch to aid him. For the first time he saw he was sharing the truck with another aviator.

The man was lying on his back, staring at the moonlight, and as Reiser scrambled alongside he almost cried out. Although Pilot Adolf Schied had his eyes open, he somehow didn't seem to focus his observer at all.

But some animal instinct held Reiser back from touching him. He knelt, keeping his distance, asking, "Adolf, what's the matter?" Again he said, "Adolf, why don't you answer me?" It was the first time he had ever used the Christian name when they were not actually airborne. Finally he summoned courage to take the pilot's hand in his own, and then he knew why Schied had not answered him.

The treatment accorded Leutnant Reiser and Hauptmann Hufenreuter stood in marked contrast to the way the Home Guard handled the Baron Von Siber. But there were other reasons than the difference in location. Between the baron's capture and Reiser's exactly three hours had elapsed. On Sunday, May 11, three hours was time enough for a man to do a lot of thinking.

If cold, remorseless anger was to follow, it played no part while the raid was at its height. Instead, most men and women found every facet of the raid too overwhelming for any emotion as simple as hatred. It was as if a fury had been unleashed that even the Germans had no power to control.

It was hard for the mind even to focus on disaster. As District Officer Thomas Goodman arrived at the Elephant and Castle he wasn't conscious that he and 500 other firemen were ringed by five acres of fire. He only noted that the block housing his dentist was burning with the rest and thought, "Thank heaven, I shan't have to go on Tuesday."

To the firemen it seemed that whatever they did they couldn't win. If they had the appliances, they hadn't the water. In other districts where the water held out there wasn't an appliance to be seen. But no one bothered to reason out just which authority had let them down or how badly. There was time only to act.

"I think we're holding it at last," Assistant Divisional Officer Geoffrey Blackstone shouted to Superintendent George Adams. Blackstone had cause to be jubilant. At 2.20 the four lines of hose leading down from his provident supply at the Surrey Music Hall had jerked taut. Water was gushing through to the canvas dam.

Two minutes later the great knot of firemen by the Elephant crossroads looked apprehensive. Above the blowtorch roar of the flames had come an explosion that seemed to tear the earth apart. Near Blackstone someone said: "I think that's where our pumps are." At the same time Blackstone had the eerie impression that the water had crawled back into the hose.

Jumping into his car, he raced off to the Surrey Music Hall. Although it was hard to peer closely through the teeming dust, he could see enough to make his stomach knot up: the jaunty red of fire engines strewn callously like discarded toys across vast hillocks of masonry. The engine of one fire pump, blasted from its chassis, had gone clean through the wall of the Salvation Army Hostel, skimming over the heads of 300 down-and-outs, fetching up against the opposite wall.

Twelve men lay cut to pieces in the rubble and all access to the vital water supply was cut off.

And it seemed as bad everywhere. Minutes later, shaken by the carnage, Station Officer Ronald Thorn phoned Southwark Mortuary: "Send a van to the Surrey Music Hall, St. George's Circus." An angry attendant screamed back, "You send a pump to us! The whole bloody mortuary's on fire."

Back at the Elephant Blackstone went into a quick huddle with his chief, Lieutenant Commander John Fordham, the lively red-haired former naval officer who had fought so valiantly for nationalization. There were other alternative supplies but they would take time. A fire barge had been ordered to the Surrey Canal to start a water relay, but that was a mile away. Other lines were coming from Westminster Bridge and Waterloo Bridge in the north, but both were a mile and a half from the fire ground and the firemen would have that thick black mud to contend with, too.

The one immediate hope was the three-and-a-half inch relay lines, now arriving from London Bridge. As Fordham and Blackstone chewed things over, water was pumping steadily into the dam.

George Adams now ordered some of the firemen to get their jets to work. They had scarcely begun before the water again died away.

Station Officer Sydney Boulter came running to explain why. A burning building had slumped clean across Newington Causeway, scoring through the lines from London Bridge and burying them in a mound of red-hot bricks. Simultaneously, on all sides, the fires seemed to get away. They gusted so hard across the narrow streets that the flames seemed to join like stretching hands far up in the sky; old Superintendent George Halley, off Newington Causeway, watched them romping down Rockingham Street faster even than a man could walk. Never would he forget the feeling of despair—"sick with the loss of pride that for the first time in thirty-two years a fire was beating me and there was nothing I could do about it."

It was time for emergency measures. In surrounding streets men slapped frantically at their clothes, where the flames had caught them. The heat was suddenly so great that the paint on the control cars was blistering. Showers of sparks drifted like red-hot hail across the street; to Blackstone it was "like holding your face to an infrared grill." He ordered the Control cars moved due north of the Elephant, into London Road. That done, he sent a priority message to Control: "Make pumps 100" before hurrying back to Fire Brigade Headquarters for a conference with Major Jackson.

It was no time to stand on ceremony. As Blackstone burst into the Control room, District Officer Ernest Thomas never forgot his first words: "Look here, sir, our bloody relay's gone for a burton."

But Jackson knew what he must do if any of London was to

be saved. He contacted Regional Fire Officer Sir Aylmer Firebrace's staff. The problem now was passed to Minister of Home Security Herbert Morrison.

In the basement of the Home Office, Whitehall, Morrison was shocked to hear the news. A South London policeman's son, the Elephant and Castle was to him a cherished symbol. He, too, racked his brains to think of some untapped emergency supply, suggesting "Try Lavington Street Baths." He could remember attending Labor party dances there as a young man. But Lavington Street Baths were dry, used up in minutes in an attempt to stem the fires around London Bridge.

So it seemed there was only one solution. Morrison ordered Firebrace's staff: "Lay on the steel piping." A new kind of emergency main, made up in twenty-foot lengths, the steel piping was virtually impervious to both high explosives and red-hot bricks. As with nationalization, the idea was scarcely new; the Home Office fire adviser had first advocated it back in 1932. The Home Office had placed the first orders three months back, in February 1941.

Given men who knew their job, a mile of this six-inch piping could be laid along the gutters in fifty minutes. By the beginning of April more than two miles of it had been received by the London Fire Service. Curiously, no instructions had been given to lay it in preparation for an emergency.

Mulling over the reports of the shattered mains, Jackson could see they would need piping from outside London, too— four and a half miles in all. They would need a mile of it from Bankside, Southwark, to the Elephant. And there were other sites; half a mile to cover the stretch between London Bridge and Queen Victoria Street, by St. Paul's; another half mile from Tower Bridge to Aldgate.

It wasn't at the Elephant alone that things were critical. In Whitechapel, where the office blocks of the City of London met the slums of the East End, District Officer Cyril Tobias had his problems, too. At 1.20 he had been confident the water problem could be solved. By the time he had emptied Goulston Street Swimming Baths of its 60,000 gallons, his relay would be nicely through from Tower Pier, three quarters of a mile away on London River.

At 2 A.M., with the water in the swimming bath sinking fast toward the tiled bottom, Tobias knew he had been too optimistic. A bomb had fallen on Tower Pier, spinning the fire pumps into the river, blasting two firemen to pieces. The naval patrol depot, H.M.S. *Tower*, a 100-ton hulk moored alongside, was sinking fast, her decks awash with blood and oil, strewn with wounded men.

All around Tobias the little tailors' shops and garment factories that make up Whitechapel burned like cardboard houses. And there was nothing he could do; again it meant taking time on a night when there was no time. Laboriously his men began to manhandle what trailer pumps they had back toward the river, to try to connect up again with the old lines and feed water back to Whitechapel.

It would be a two-hour job at least, and Tobias wondered how much of Whitechapel would be left by then.

As building after building caught, the heat became unendurable. In Stepney, not far from where Tobias fought the Whitechapel fires, Warden Louis Squersky saw a lamppost wilting backward like a grass stem in a bonfire. In many streets the paint streamed like water down the walls. All the way from Cannon Street Station to Fleet Street the wooden blocks of the roadway were alight with a merry glare. As Superintendent Joe Ansell watched, a line of charged hose hissed into a cloud of steam, shriveling to nothing.

Even behind closed doors and windows the fires glowed like a blinding sun—in the words of scores of witnesses "light enough to read a newspaper by." Most were too busy to try, although Basil P. Bothamley, seeking an errant office boy from his Lloyd's Bank fire-watching team, eventually ran him to earth on the bank's roof. Completely unperturbed, the twelve-year-old was sprawled flat on his stomach, writing a letter by the light of the Temple fires.

Fire Watcher Claude Evans, in Bishopsgate, was sickened by the smell of scorching polish; the office furniture was as hot as a stove lid. In St. Marylebone Mrs. Helga Feiling, 500 yards from Druce's Department Store, felt pain knife across her eyes; her lashes had frizzled with the heat.

The smoke crept under doors, squeezed through cracks in windowpanes. In his flat close to Druce's Journalist Charles Graves kept rinsing his mouth with soda water, noting clinically that his saliva had turned black.

And a strange illusion arose. Most men, recalling this night, speak of the lively wind. Driver Leslie Stainer, crouching on Cannon Street Bridge, recalled "the strong wind blowing up the Thames." To Geoffrey Blackstone, down by the Elephant, it was "a brisk, warm wind, like you get in a tunnel after a train's passed through." A few streets away Chief Superintendent Frank Dann noted "a hot whirling turbulence." It struck an eerie note with Chief Superintendent Frank Bitten in the City. In the warm wind shop signs stirred to and fro, metal screeching gently on metal.

Until almost the moment the raid began the northeast wind had been Force 3—enough to stir a flag on a pole, not enough to fan an inferno. Yet by midnight although a Force 3 easterly wind blew gently up the river, elsewhere it had dropped to zero, so that in these critical hours men sensed a wind where there was no wind at all.

What had happened? At Druce's Department Store in Baker Street Superintendent George Bennison thought he knew. The whole building was one ungovernable tempest of heat, and as Bennison watched, the firemen clinging to the branches seemed to be literally sucked toward the fire "like a handkerchief up a chimney flue."

Beside him District Officer Thomas Hesketh felt the same tremendous force, as if something, against his will, were tugging him forward.

At once Bennison shouted to District Officer Victor Botten,

"Don't Let Them Drop Any More"

"Get those men back across the street. We'll have a fire storm if we don't look out."

There is no doubt that Bennison was right. In some streets the heat was so intense that it ballooned in vast, egg-shaped bodies to the sky, setting up a monstrous vacuum that gulped greedily for air around its perimeter. By a stroke of providence it sprang up almost exclusively on island sites that formed natural firebreaks, so that no fire hurricane actually arose to bluster through the narrow streets, carrying trees, houses, even men in its wake.

Even close to it was beyond most men's imaginations. In Fenchurch Street, City of London, Fire Watcher Thomas J. Burling and his team heard that two women were trapped in a burning building. Frantic to help, they dashed to the scene, armed with a tube of burn salve, to find they couldn't even approach the building. With proof positive that the women had been there the City's medical officer, Dr. Charles White, couldn't afterward discover one trace of their presence.

Although it was like fighting a tornado, the firemen wouldn't give up—more through a sheer determination to stick it than from any belief they could hold the fires. Standing on the roof of St. Thomas's Hospital, all water cut off, Station Officer Charles Davis felt as if he were on a raft in a sea of swelling fire.

"Good God," he burst out finally. "What the hell's the use?"

The little auxiliary fireman beside him was irrepressible. "Yes, but we aren't going to give up, guv, are we?"

After that Davis somehow couldn't. By a miracle he saw a fire float sailing up the Thames and managed to use his lamp to flash them in Morse that he had no water. After a dry half-hour it started to come through.

In truth, the hospital was lucky: fire after fire got no attendance at all. At Shadwell Fire Station, by the Pool of London, Fireman John H. Good saw the pink slips that detailed fire calls pile steadily up in the watchroom unregarded. As he waited, a message came through: "Make pumps two at the

Library." Fifteen minutes later: "Make pumps five at the Library." Shortly: "Make pumps ten."

Although there wasn't a pump to be had, Good became intrigued; the Public Library, run by Stepney Council, was only a quarter of a mile away in Cable Street, the heart of dockland. Jumping into a staff car, he set off there. The main double doors from the street were standing open. He mounted the stone stairs and went in.

Suddenly the strangeness of it all swept over him. The fire, which had started in the roof, was burning downward, so that the leaf edges of the books, stacked on the shelves, were catching and crinkling first—while even those books still untouched by the fire were scorched red-hot, sending up tiny spirals of smoke and sullen flame. To Good it was like an unexpected peep into Aladdin's cave.

After a few moments he left. And still the street stood as lonely as a desert: not a soul in sight, no pumps in view, no clue as to who had made those weird, persistent calls.

To the firemen the true death traps of the night were the old stone shrines beloved of millions—built for gentle, dust-smelling meditation, they only impeded desperate action. The men who finally got to work at Lambeth Palace had to haul their hoses around and around a spiral staircase; coming down was like a helter-skelter, and molten lead from the old roof kept dripping on their faces and hands. At Westminster Abbey, with the fire dancing 130 feet out of reach in the turrets, Chief Officer Arthur Johnstone needed all his ingenuity. First he decided to sling a light pump on lines, haul it up to a convenient balcony, and boost the water up. But first everything movable inside the Abbey had to be shifted in case it took fire—lecterns, chairs, pews. Meanwhile, Superintendent Henry Davies was using similar ingenuity to stop the fire from spreading—shanghaing a dozen soldiers and sailors from an all-night canteen and using them to form a bucket chain on the roof above Poets' Corner; training all the jets he could on the south entrance to stop the fire spreading north to the Treforium, the wide corridor 60 feet up that girdled the interior of the Abbey.

High up on the ancient lantern, silhouetted against the sky, other firemen worked with their sharp-bladed axes to chop away burning timbers. Just after 3 A.M., as Johnstone's pump at last got to work, the whole roof of the Abbey fell in with a roar.

But the worst was over. As firemen, vergers, clergymen flooded in across the stone flags, trampling out embers, wielding buckets, Johnstone heard a sigh of relief. From Ditchley Park the Prime Minister had sent an impressive order: "The Abbey must be saved at all costs." Johnstone liked his job; he had no wish to cross swords with Winston Churchill.

Across the street, at the Palace of Westminster, Chief Superintendent Charles McDuell had received an identical message: at all costs, too, the House of Commons must be saved. But McDuell faced a fearful problem. The Debating Chamber of the House of Commons was already an unquenchable ball of fire, fanned fiercely by the old-fashioned heating system that fed the Chamber through grilles set in the floor. But across the narrow courtyard the oak beams and soaring arches of Westminster Hall—begun by William Rufus in 1097 and the largest in the world—were only just alight.

Yet the door at the north end of the hall, from which the firemen could attack most effectively, was locked, and McDuell was reluctant to have them batter the ancient oak door with their axes. Colonel Walter Elliott, M.P. for Glasgow, Kelvinside, hastening to the scene from his house nearby, found them dithering, irresolute. So Elliott seized an ax: "As a privy councilor, I have the authority to do it myself."

As he chopped away, he said later, he "understood, in a kind of ecstasy, the mentality of all iconoclasts."

The die was cast. For the next hour McDuell was concentrating the bulk of his fifty pumps on the rafters of Westminster Hall, the water rising so fast on the stone flags that Fireman Conrad Sanders and his crew were soon almost waist deep in water.

As they directed the jets vertically at the wooden roof, Elliott kept exhorting them from the side lines: "Remember the building is a thousand years old. It must be saved." In the pitch darkness, with water, burning timbers, and debris raining down on them, the firemen were in no mood for a history lesson. Sub Officer Joe Edmunds growled: "Never mind if it is a thousand years old, don't risk your bloody necks if it gets dangerous."

Even here it wasn't easy—the static supplies were soon exhausted; firemen had to manhandle a trailer pump down the steps of Westminster Pier to the river; the turntable ladder that Principal Officer Clement Kerr had set up to tackle the roof kept sinking into the soft turf. For the firemen on the job it was a wretched, sodden night they would long remember. After half an hour, when the roof was almost under control, Fireman Sanders and his mates were relieved by a fresh crew. Going out, Sanders stumbled over a stack of leaded lights and went clean under the water. Later a chunk of Big Ben landed at his feet, but he cheered up when the old clock boomed the half-hour.

At the House of Commons, across the courtyard, it was still touch-and-go. To Sub Officer Herbert Rous and his crew, tackling the fire from inside the old stone building, the water seemed to damage them more than the fire; the jets were breaking up into a fine rain that drifted back long before the water hit the 350-foot roof. As Rous sent back word to the pumps to increase pressure to 120 pounds per square inch, he worried afresh: would the hoses, with a working nozzle only one and an eighth inch wide, be able to stand it? The hose began to whip and thrash so savagely that four men at once had to grapple it; as they wrestled, cannon balls of masonry were crashing into powder at their feet. Beside Rous an auxiliary who had spent his life big-game hunting grunted appreciatively: "Damned nearly as good as a safari."

Outside London no one seemed to understand. At Home Office Fire Control Chief Superintendent Augustus May still clung exhausted to the phone: at long last the relief crews were coming but with agonizing slowness. At intervals May checked through to London's five fire-brigade districts: "What's your position now? Have any pumps arrived?"

At 3 A.M., in some cases, the first provincial crews had checked in, but Southwark badly needed more pumps, nothing had reported as yet in the Baker Street area. Whitechapel still awaited pumps from Ipswich, 70 miles away.

May assured each station: "I'll see if I can let you have more later, but I'm down to bare poles." A fireman talking to firemen, May knew that the old-time slang for a fire station without appliances would strike home.

The few already booked in could scarcely work to advantage. In Montagu Square, at the Bayswater end of St. Marylebone, Mrs. Helga Feiling, the post warden, found a crew from Reading helplessly lost; her post area had logged 97 fires in just on two hours, but the firemen had no idea where to report or where the hydrants were. A crew reporting from Bristol to London Wall had the wrong couplings; while London standpipe threads had a right-hand thread, most British towns used a left-hand pattern. It was a problem normally solved by adaptors, but in the burning, ravaged streets each journey back to the station to rummage through scores of different adaptors was a hazard in itself.

At the Mark Lane conflagration, City of London, Station Officer James Ellis and his men had checked the fire from spreading toward the Tower of London when the promised crew from Kent finally arrived; soon after they got to work on Mark Lane the water died away. Ellis went to investigate, found that their lifting pump wasn't using its maximum length of suction. Unused to working with tidal rivers, the crew had hauled up their suction to add another length. The tide had dropped in the meantime.

With the confusion of uniforms and rank badges it was often hard to tell who was in charge of any fire. Near the Elephant and Castle District Officer Thomas Goodman saw a station officer, a seasoned veteran, jump smartly to attention in search of orders from a band of country firemen. It was understandable—all of them were wearing the double epaulets of a district officer and above.

Hastily Goodman found a small paint factory alight, got them all to work out of harm's way.

Whatever the provincials lacked, it wasn't courage. One engine from the Hertfordshire corn belt brought the hay knife used for rick fires in its locker, but soon it was chugging away alongside the London pumps, delivering its steady 500 gallons a minute, oblivious to the crash of bombs. In Bethnal Green Chief Operations Officer Arthur Caldwell found a fire pump from Bishop's Stortford, Hertfordshire, throbbing away steadily in a deserted street close to an unexploded parachute mine. Caldwell intervened: the vibration of the pump might set the mine off.

The firemen debated—there was only one water point and it was coming through nicely. As Caldwell waited they went into a huddle, then reported back: "We've decided to carry on."

"And if the mine goes up?"

"Well, then, it's the last fire we go on."

Over a hundred square miles fire after fire was completely out of control. It was plain now that acres of London would have to burn. The only thing the firemen, or anyone else, could do was to try to stop them spreading.

In the midst of such a holocaust a man might have been forgiven for wondering if any effort was worth the trouble, yet despite that the human spirit seemed indomitable. In the wet littered streets, which glowed with a red phosphorescent light, people forgot their own problems to help others regardless of their own safety.

Off Mile End Road Warden Merion Davies slithered down into a bomb crater, scooped up bucketfuls of loose earth, used it to smother a nearby fire with his bare hands. In Leytonstone Police Constable Horace Rutter, jumping from a tottering

194

building with a six-year-old boy in his arms, landed heavily on a four-inch nail which drove clean through his foot. Still holding the youngster, Rutter struggled on until two of his mates appeared to relieve him.

On the Thames Embankment a war-reserve constable erected a rope barrier around an unexploded bomb, chalking a "Road Closed" notice, puffing placidly all the while at his pipe.

Poplar Warden Dan Russell, a dock laborer, saw a parachute mine drifting as slowly as a seed across the sky to tangle with the parapet of a block of flats. He decided that it wouldn't explode, was running to warn anyone out of shelter when the mine went off. Russell found himself still running but backward, as if he were jet propelled, finally skimming full length along the pavement like a man on an ice floe.

His uniform and buttocks were ripped to shreds; he only learned later that there was no one in the tenement.

At Poplar Hospital, a few streets away, there was the same spirit. Along with the others, House Governor David Lindsay worked on in the ruins, ignoring the occasional twinge below his breastbone; only after a game of golf did he realize he'd broken two ribs. And the urge to carry on went deeper than conscious thought. At the Alexandra Hotel, Knightsbridge, Head Night Porter Charles Mattock woke up shivering, struggled blindly out of the dining room, across the ruined hall, past Herbert Mills and his rescue workers, out to the rear of the hotel. When the police found him he had collapsed after trying to turn off water and gas, vomiting tar and plaster from deep inside him without any knowledge of being there at all.

The bomb that shattered Tower Pier, cutting off White-chapel's water relay, had also fractured the skull of Lieutenant John Woodburne, R.N.V.R., and blown in his eardrums, yet automatically Woodburne hobbled to the edge of the wrecked pier and tipped one surviving drum of petrol into the river for fear it caught light.

More knew what they were doing—but still accepted the risk. At the House of Commons the roof of the 350-foot Victoria Tower blazed as brightly as a box of matches. It seemed a perfect beacon for the German bombers, yet when Police Sergeant Andrew Forbes ran to the base of the tower he found the door locked. Without hesitation he grasped at the tubular scaffolding that workmen had left surrounding the Tower and began to climb. As he reached the turret, the dark river spinning dizzily beneath, two firemen helped him over the parapet. They had been luckier in their search for a key.

Near Aldersgate, City of London, Police Sergeant Edmund Bartlett saw a woman wandering down a deserted street, heard a bomb coming. As he hurled her to the pavement, covering her with his body, his steel helmet tilted forward, and a flying fragment pierced the base of his skull. He lay where he had fallen, not moving.

The night was full of such chivalry. If the raid could lay bare the ugly side of human nature with a scalpel's precision, it had a unique power to show the best in it, too. Sometimes, as with Pilot Officer Andrew Humphrey, it was less conscious courage than curiosity, ingrained deep in the character, canceling out fear, driving a man on to see how many liberties he could take with fate.

About the same time as his first victim plunged like a torch to the earth Humphrey recovered his night vision and his self-confidence. Suddenly he saw below what he took to be the approach lights of an airfield. Again the analytical approach that made the youngster fly with his hood back and puzzle out each new problem took him down to investigate.

The airfield lay hard to port, spread like a dimly-lit railway junction across the moonlit earth. In leisurely fashion Humphrey began to circle it on a left-hand pattern. Just then, about a thousand feet above the ground, he saw another bomber clearing the runway—one more of the second sortie on which Leutnant Martin Reiser had already left. Its red and green navigation lights were clearly visible.

"Don't Let Them Drop Any More"

Tonight Humphrey's curiosity was almost fatal. He came down hard and fast, traveling at 200 m.p.h. just above the German runway. At 250 yards he was dead astern of the Heinkel, opening fire and closing all the time. For fifteen seconds the red tracer split the night apart, then with a roar Humphrey shot clean underneath the bomber, slugging tracer home at its belly. At that moment the Heinkel went into a dive.

He sensed that it was coming clean on top of him, and in the same analytical way his brain registered: "This is a day fighter's mistake. A day fighter's instinct is to break away downward."

For one second the bomber was a black rushing shape, boring down on him as the tracer went on striking home. Humphrey judged there was less than 50 feet between the planes, and a fearful vertigo overtook him. He slewed the Spitfire violently to port. The Heinkel passed over him like a rushing wind, flames blossoming out of it as it smashed violently into the ground to starboard.

But Humphrey's troubles weren't over. He was now only 50 feet above the ground, likely to slice into a tree any second, and from the far side of the airfield the light flak suddenly opened up. White ribbons of tracer flung at him in slow motion, curving away very fast behind.

He put on full power, swerving in a quick spiral climb until he had topped 2,000 feet. It was then, just below him, that he saw the Messerschmitt 110. It seemed quite oblivious of him, on routine patrol, but Humphrey couldn't resist it. He peeled away to port, attacking from above, guns chattering, then abruptly, as the first twinkling flashes showed on the Me's fuselage, the sinister hiss of compressed air through his breech blocks. His ammunition was finished.

Humphrey was suddenly shocked into realization of his position. He counted himself lucky that the Messerschmitt had reefed away out of sight; without ammunition he felt naked and foolish, wondering what he was doing here at all. It was definitely time to be getting home to bacon and eggs and the

197

crate of bottled beer that was always left ready in the mess after a "fighter night." Not only was his ammunition finished; he was perilously low on fuel, too.

Nor was he at all sure where he was, and he had brought no map to guide him. Despite the icy wind he began to sweat a little. He started to climb fast on a northwesterly heading, keeping a sharp eye open for German fighters. But the earth and the sky lay sleeping. The whole crazy split-second battle might never have happened at all.

Toward 3 A.M. he was over the North Sea, close enough to call up Wittering and ask for a homing. The sector controller sounded puzzled; assuming Humphrey was between Southend and Romford, he hardly bargained to find him over Belgium. The young pilot, a little dazed, didn't know where he was relative to the aerodrome, explaining, "I only know I'm heading southwest—and I think I've shot down two Heinkels." He was slightly shocked to hear himself say it: a man could get himself killed taking risks like that.

No one in London wanted to die, either—yet no one could feel quite comfortable unless this blitz had somehow touched them. By Regent's Park Mrs. Monica Pitman thought of cricketers relaxing in the pavilion after an innings; with shrapnel spattering and the sky as light as noon, people from her bombed block of flats were strolling unconcernedly up and down the pavement. "Ah, well," said someone contentedly nearby. "We've had *our* bomb."

Others felt the need to be in the thick of it. Mrs. Olive Smith, a mobile canteen driver, felt even at 3 A.M., with her house full of acrid smoke, that she should be on duty. From her Bayswater home she phoned the Relionus Car Hire Company, who promised to do their best. An urbane voice cautioned: "In the circumstances, madam, I'm sure you'll understand there may be a certain amount of unpredictable delay."

Farther north, by Hampstead Heath, the bombs had been few enough, yet Miss Ann Flax, at an all-night card party, suddenly threw down her hand. "I do feel a rat." There was nothing she could have done back home in Bethnal Green; she just felt she ought to be there.

At 3 A.M. the feeling was universal. Those who'd experienced something were satisfied. Those who hadn't, wanted to get into it somehow.

At 48 Turney Road, Dulwich, it seemed plain to Marguerita Stahli that nothing would happen to her area tonight. To the north and south, over Lambeth and Croydon, the raid was like a nightmare. But tonight Turney Road was much as it always was—an isolated suburban pocket of red-brick villas and privet hedges.

It was plain, though, that Windsor couldn't risk cycling home to Croydon on a night like this. Now Marguerita suggested: "Look, I know Aunt Maud wouldn't mind—you'd better have my room and stay on until the all-clear." The young airman seemed almost too tired to argue; the six hours' journey and the long, fruitless patrol up and down the avenue had brought him to the point where he couldn't stay awake.

But it seemed politic not to undress. In Aunt Maud's old-fashioned bedroom Marguerita threw off her raincoat, lay down on the heavy feather mattress in her thin cotton frock, and pulled the eiderdown over her for greater warmth.

Along the corridor, also fully dressed save for his greatcoat, Windsor Neck was reclining under the eiderdown on Marguerita's bed. Stretching out, he switched off the bedside lamp with the golden silk shade that had been a present to Marguerita from her brother Jack. Rex, the fox terrier, had retired to his chair in the dining room.

Except for the steady crump-crump of the barrage overhead, the nasal throbbing of the bombers, the house was quite silent, wrapped in darkness.

Lying in the darkness Marguerita wondered about Windsor. Six months since they had last seen one another. How long before the next hastily-snatched meeting? Almost nothing in war was as cruel as this: the separations, the letters, the bitter-sweet reunions. The one consolation was that tonight's meeting, coming after they had been apart so long, had taught them one thing. They were not going to wait. Ring or no ring, they would be married before the year was out. It wasn't all that they wanted by a long way, but it would be something. If the pain of parting became immeasurably greater, at least they would belong to one another in a deeper, richer way. And whatever happened, nothing could destroy that.

Without warning the house shook twice from floor to ceiling. As Marguerita Stahli started upright it was as if someone had taken the room bodily and was rattling it like a box. The floor heaved. There was a shattering blow against the bedstead. Instinctively she yanked at the eiderdown, trying to pull it over her head. Suddenly she had the sense of falling—a little like taking a lift. It was a moment before her mind registered the truth. She was buried alive.

With remarkable self-control she did not panic. First, she tried gently to move her head to left or right and was dismayed to find that she couldn't. Next she tried to wriggle her little finger, but had no luck even with that. Although she could see nothing there was always the sense of something pressing down. The air seemed to grow quickly dry and stale, like an unlived-in room; soon she could scarcely breathe. From somewhere she remembered that the more you moved, the more oxygen you used up. She decided she must keep completely still.

Anxiously she called into the darkness—perhaps somehow Windsor would be able to claw a way through. Only the dying echo of her own voice drifted back to answer her. She thought he must be stunned by the blast. No sound came from Rex, either. Perhaps he, too, was buried, wondering what had suddenly struck him, too tightly wedged even to whimper.

An orphan who had lived most of her life with relatives, Marguerita Stahli, characteristically, was not thinking much of her own plight. Through most of her twenty-five years she had thought habitually of what would trouble or what would give pleasure to others—her grandmother who had brought them up when her mother died, in the old house on Herne Hill nearby, Aunt Maud, who had taken charge of her when her father died. Her father himself—a man to remember, who had been all his life on the executive side at the Savoy Hotel. She still remembered the awe with which she crept along the blue-carpeted corridors to visit his office at holiday times.

Now the old habit prevailed. At 3.20 Marguerita Stahli decided quite calmly that it was only a matter of time before she died. Her one regret was that she should have brought her fiancé into this. If only he had taken her bicycle and gone home to Croydon, after all.

But the chances were that Windsor Neck would have walked into trouble as bad. In South Croydon Mrs. Margaret Daley, along with others at St. Augustine's Ambulance Depot, had decided it would be one more uneventful night. In two hours now it would be dawn. All night the raid had trembled, like a summer storm, to the north of the town. But there, too, the quiet suburban avenues a mile west of the main rail artery to the south had enjoyed an uneasy peace.

Mrs. Daley and Olive Ward were now engaged in a spirited game of darts with two other drivers. Mrs. Daley was feeling good, too, as the shafts plunked home: two more lucky shots and they'd have won. She thought that she and Olive were a formidable team, a match for any two men.

The dart was still poised in her hand, a fresh brew of tea was coming up, when the outer door of the long, draughty hall shattered open. They had heard no bombs, yet now a tram driver was standing there, the tears streaming down his face, repeating over and over, "My conductor's dead . . . he's dead, my conductor."

At first someone tried to soothe him: "Oh, he can't be—he's just had a shock, poor chap." But as the man went on weeping bitterly they knew it was the real thing.

As they ran for the yard at the back, Mrs. Daley was terror-stricken, her heart was knocking like a hammer in her throat. It was always like this: when things were quiet she yearned for action, but when action, however mild, came she could only hope her fear didn't show, that the others weren't feeling as bad. Both women piled into the big Chrysler and Mrs. Daley let in the clutch. As they raced down the long, tree-lined avenue, the first of a convoy of six, her old fear of being buried alive grew irrationally stronger. If they went full tilt into a crater without warning, both of them might be trapped in the suffocating darkness. To everyone that night fear wore a different guise: Mrs. Daley could not have faced the ordeal that Marguerita Stahli now endured and stayed sane.

As they drew near the main London-to-Brighton Road, an incredible sight met their eyes. The London Transport bus garage at the foot of the hill was a writhing ocean of flame. Behind it, and closer to the railway, tins of blazing varnish from a paint factory fountained like Roman candles to the sky. A blazing gas main roared upward, as high as the 30-foot sycamores lining the road.

The tram from where the driver had fled was marooned in front of the garage, slewed across the opposite side of the road, its overhead wires looped everywhere. The conductor was on the back seat, his money bag beside him, a young man with fair, curly hair. Timidly, Mrs. Daley approached; sitting as he was in profile, what she could see of his face seemed young and smooth, quite undisturbed. Suddenly she realized that the blast had struck the other way. Above the man's collar there was just nothing at all. Never in her life had she seen anything to equal this. Although she knew she should keep calm, she burst into tears and ran blindly from the tram.

By now the others were on the scene. There was no time to lose. Inside the garage the best part of 60 busses, their engines already refueled for the morning's run, burned with a fearful, thundering sound like somebody beating on sheet metal. Beneath them some of the inspection engineers were actually trapped in the pits; within minutes they would be literally barbecued by the heat. Ambulance Chief Harold Lock Kendell, plunging in, managed to save four; although the fire brigade trained their jets on him the water striking his skin seemed like the contents of a boiling kettle. And others worked as valiantly. Warden Geoffrey Green, who had never driven a bus in his life, went in after Kendell and drove out eight.

While some kept their heads, others surged here and there in a panic of fear. By now the fire had caught the busmen's Home Guard magazine, and bullets snapped and whined above the roar of flames. Nearby two sticks of bombs had blasted forty houses, killing 11 people outright, injuring 70. Now the inhabitants swarmed through the streets barefooted, running heedlessly over broken glass, through pools of blazing varnish.

Many of them, in any case, knew that the garage might blow like a gusher at any moment. Close to 80,000 gallons of petrol were bunkered below in underground tunnels.

On the outskirts of the inferno Mrs. Daley fought to regain her self-control. A faint feeling of shame mingled with her fear. After eighteen months of war this was the biggest incident her depot had known, and she had wanted to be of use—why else had she joined? Yet this first sight of violent death had almost shattered her nerve.

Suddenly a man wearing a lounge suit and brown trilby hat staggered from the garage. Mrs. Daley saw him come, thought he must have been just finishing duty when the bomb fell. After a few faltering steps the man suddenly collapsed in the gutter.

At once Mrs. Daley recovered herself. She ran across, trying gently to lift him. It was a shock case, of course; he would need a warm blanket and one of the hot-water bottles, strong sweet tea. Then she realized that the man was trembling all over from head to foot, as if an electric current ran through his body. He was trying painfully to frame some words.

Now, as it struck her that he probably had bad internal injuries, she looked around for help. But although the road was milling with people—wardens, firemen, terrified householders—it was hard to attract attention at a time like this. As a woman came screaming from a house by the garage, Mrs. Daley shouted to her to fetch a pillow.

It was doubtful whether the woman even heard her. Repeating over and over, "Must go to the shelter . . . the shelter . . . must get there," she vanished from sight.

Mrs. Daley accepted that the man was going to die, but no woman, herself least of all, could leave a man to face death, bewildered and alone, on a rubble-strewn pavement. Deftly she stripped off her overcoat, bundling it into an improvised pillow. Kneeling beside the dying man, the pillow propped on her lap, she cradled him in her arms like a little boy.

On this cold and terrible night it seemed that all her war— all the purpose of her life even—fused into this moment; that nothing in the world mattered so much as that this unknown man should not die unfriended. The man's eyes never left her face, the painful stammering never stopped; although even if he had spoken, it was unlikely that she could have heard him. As the last sortie came in to attack, the noise of the planes overhead was unbearably loud, swelling like an abscess in her brain, drowning the roar of the fire.

Now she was rigid with fear; no matter how overwhelming your own private disaster, an air raid goes cruelly, inexorably on. She began to pray aloud, whispering over and over, "Oh, Sacred Heart of Jesus, don't let them drop any more." And often, to the man she nursed at her breast, "It's all right, it's only our anti-aircraft fire." For a moment she saw wonder and contentment on his face, like a child waking to a night light and a well-loved voice. Gradually his trembling ceased, and after a little while she knew her vigil was over.

CHAPTER ELEVEN

"You Will Never See Another Sunrise"

3.20—5.50 A.M.

As the last bombers closed in, high above the tall trees and the old Georgian roofs, a strange calm fell over London. It was as if, with the realization that there was to be no respite, people faced death almost passively.

"Have you made your will yet?" called Truck Driver Edwin Wheeler to his next-door neighbor, Harvey Wittred. "You will never see another sunrise."

Sitting outside his galvanized-iron Anderson shelter in the garden at East Ham, Wheeler fully believed that the end was at hand. When an incendiary fell almost on top of him a second later he was sure of it.

All over the City, in shelters and basements, the same sense of resignation crept in. Not all of it was expressed in words. In the Elephant and Castle underground twelve-year-old John D. Allen could tell all he needed to know from the faces around him. The walls seemed to transmit every bomb, every salvo, like a depth charge through water. In the ghostly light the boy could see hundreds of pairs of eyes turned upward in silent apprehension.

It was the same in the wine cellar below Signor Giacomo Prada's restaurant. When one of the staff peeped down to see how he, Prada, was faring, he was on his feet, eyes closed, arms outstretched in prayer over his precious burgundies.

The City That Would Not Die

The shelter philosophers had a well-worn platitude—"It'll hit you if your number's on it." But could a man ever know what that number was? Driver George Irish and Fireman Joe Cheetham, shunting the few coaches that had survived at St. Pancras Station, thought they could; their engine was just moving away toward the sidings when a shunter dashed past shouting, "I'm off." Investigating, Irish and Cheetham saw a parachute hanging from the signal 12 yards away. Nearby the mine was lying on the track between Platforms One and Two. Picked out in white lettering on the black eight-foot cylinder was the number 1991.

To Irish's alarm Fireman Cheetham first sat on it, then put his ear to it. "This is a dud one, George," he reassured the driver. "It's not ticking."

Two hours later, in the engine shed, Irish was making out his time sheet when he heard a dull report. The mine had gone off. Irish felt cheated—unaware that a parachute mine only ticked just prior to the explosion, then his sense of destiny took over. Whatever his number was, it wasn't 1991.

Few knew now when the next bomb would strike or where: the pattern of the raid was too confusing. At 3.30 A.M. Paddington was still under intermittent attack; bombing was just closing down in the City: South London was due for more than most boroughs north of the river. If Poplar's blitz was finished, in Shoreditch it was at its height. The bombers cruised fitfully, stoking up fires here, hoping to start a fresh blaze there. A cabinetmaker's flaring upward in Tabernacle Street, Shoreditch, may have prompted the bomb that burst with a hammer-blow concussion outside Shoreditch Fire Station.

For Fireman Albert Edward Clarke, arriving to tackle this fire, it had been a relatively quiet night. He had come up from Hammersmith on relief; at 9 A.M. his wife was expecting him home to breakfast. It was harsh fate that the bomb killed him dropping when it did.

But everyone was now prepared for the worst that could happen. In the Savoy Hotel's shelter a handsome dowager in

206

full evening dress sipped a tall drink, said matter-of-factly to Quentin Reynolds, "I wonder how many of us will be alive by morning." Police Sergeant Alf Lucas, hugging a wall in the City of London, said aloud, "This is the last night of my life." Below Fenchurch Street in the City the petrified caretaker told Thomas J. Burling and his fire-watching team, "Only God can save us now." Somehow no one could bring himself to answer him, let alone disagree.

Near the Elephant and Castle old Mr. Matthew Hanley, fitfully roaming the streets, was surprised to find a pub open and doing a roaring trade at 4 A.M. "Drink the beer while it's here," said the licensee, drawing pints as fast as he could for his firemen customers. Outside, the light of the fires glowed ruddily on the swinging pub sign, "The World's End."

Only a few remained indifferent to the danger. Near Millwall Outer Dock Station Officer Bernard Belderson and a police sergeant met a small girl skipping unconcernedly along the road, eyes glistening with excitement, only a coat thrown over a thin nightdress. When she answered that she was just having a look around, Belderson expostulated: "But look, there's a German aeroplane up there."

"Huh," she grunted. "That's all right. That square-headed bastard couldn't hit a haystack."

In the ruins of 48 Turney Road Marguerita Stahli felt the same resignation: it was only a matter of time before she died. As she lay pinioned and helpless, hours seemed to pass in which she could hear no sound. It was oddly relaxing, as if the world of guns and bombs in which this had happened was now no more and she already inhabited a more peaceful world where such things had no place. She felt no fear, only a strange tranquillity.

But by degrees the silence assumed an ugly, brooding quality that feral instinct told her was the silence of death. There should have been some sound, some movement, to tell her that Windsor and Rex were still alive. But she was listening only to silence. A cold hand clutched her heart and she knew, as only a woman can know, that Windsor and Rex were not stunned. They were somewhere very close at hand and they were dead. All these hours, while she thought them alive, they had been dead.

In such a situation she was bound to lose all count of time—the records show that not more than fifteen minutes elapsed between the bomb's falling and rescue parties arriving. Marguerita Stahli's first knowledge of this was hearing voices some way off. They were pitched on a conversational level, like two men chatting in the next room. Mustering all her strength, she gave one tremendous yell. After a moment someone shouted back, "Where are you?"

"Here," Marguerita shouted back. She realized that this probably wasn't very helpful. But lacking precise knowledge of where she was herself it was the best she could do.

In a little while the voices came nearer. They seemed a very long way above her. Then a probing began, gentle, persistent, followed by a dry rumbling: a sudden rattle of plaster, the slam of a wooden board. Curiously, Marguerita Stahli was now terrified. The very sound of the debris shifting made it seem alive and menacing for the first time, something that really had power to harm her.

As a groping arm encountered the fingers of her right hand she clutched it tightly. "Please," she begged, "let me hold on to you. Please don't go away." Now she needed reassurance that she really was going to be saved. At this moment she could not bring herself to ask about Windsor or Rex.

Time seemed to pass with agonizing slowness. She had to fight an almost hysterical impatience with everything she knew. Above the yellow-white dunes of debris she glimpsed a white helmet; she supposed it must be a doctor. "Are you all right?" he asked gently, and she answered quite seriously, "Yes, I think so, only my neck's broken." For a moment it really felt like that; the headboard of the bed collapsing under the weight of the wall had pressed the pillow viciously into her shoulder blades, jamming her head forward.

"You Will Never See Another Sunrise"

When the rescue men began to uncover more of Miss Stahli, one cried appreciatively: "Oh, what a lovely leg." She was woman enough to take pride in this tribute and remember it: it helped sustain her through almost two hours of probing and fumbling until the rescue workers lifted her out. Naked and wrapped in a blanket, she was carried away from the vast crater that was all that was left of 48 Turney Road. Near at hand she saw the Reverend James Capron, the vicar, and it was then she found strength to say: "My fiancé's in there, too."

She had nothing left in the world now as they carried her down the quiet street to where a private car was parked in the moonlight. She said, "This seems very special," and one of the men explained that it was the worst night ever and they had run short of ambulances. They climbed in, but the car had traveled only a few yards when they had a puncture. It seemed such a strange anticlimax to a terrible adventure that Marguerita Stahli didn't know whether to laugh or cry.

One man who was determined not to die if he could help it was Jimmie Sexton.

As the night wore on, he had a yardstick of how great the danger had become. The basement of the north building of Fields' factory in which he and the other fire watchers had taken shelter grew steadily and unendurably stuffier.

When Sexton made his frantic dash for the basement steps after seeing that terrible river of molten wax flowing down the north building, the course had seemed plain. They could not save the factory now. And besides the fire watchers there were 30 civilians, mostly women and children, bedded down in the basement. They would have to make a dash for it.

But once Sexton had led Fire Guard Chief Bill Wilks and a few others to the archway abutting on the ground-floor entrance they could see that there was no chance. The raid was so heavy that the wail and crash of high explosives drowned out all sound. At 3.20, with a roar like an avalanche, the whole of the south building across the yard fell in.

It made an unforgettable picture—the silent, crouching men, unable to speak, their faces lit by the kindling glare of the flames, watching the factory that had spelled security topple in ruins.

Back in the basement a kind of stunned despair overtook the people. All of them felt frightened, alone. If they stayed down here, they stood a chance of being roasted alive. If they tried to escape, they would have to run for it through a steady rain of bombs. And the construction of the building made the bombs seem closer than they were. The lift shaft that ran from top to bottom of the four-story building brought every reverberation on top of them like a clap of doom.

Some, huddled in their blankets on the floor, still tried to sleep, but gradually the heat became too overpowering, even for that; the shaft was bringing oven wafts of heat from the blazing upper story. The children were whimpering and restless, making endless trips to the toilet. Presently a steady murmuring arose, like the noise of a crowd heard a long way off. The women were hunched in prayer.

Sitting on his camp bed, plunged in gloom, Jimmie Sexton could think of nothing useful to do. At a time like this a man abandons logic. It seemed to the born family man that if only Bill, his brother, had been fire watching with him this weekend, all this would never have happened.

Toward 5 A.M. he could stand it no longer. He wandered from the basement up a flight of stone stairs to the ground floor. And now he realized with a surge of alarm that something would have to be done. Sour-smelling brown smoke was billowing from almost every room along the ground floor. As he watched, the glass-shuttered entrance doors split vertically, like cracking ice, with the heat.

Pelting back, Sexton grabbed Fire Chief Bill Wilks. "You can't stop here another five minutes—the fire'll be down on top of you."

Wilks wrestled with the decision. "But all these people . . ."

"You Will Never See Another Sunrise"

The little man was adamant. "We can either stop here and get burned alive or make a dash for it and try to get out."

A second's silent cogitation, and Wilks agreed. He thought the best plan was to form a human chain, everyone linking hands. In that way no one could get left behind. As Wilks mounted on a chair, made the announcement, people began to stir uneasily, getting their bundles together. Jimmie Sexton was packing his small attaché case—apart from pajamas, a sweater, and toilet things, he had no chance to take more. His bicycle would have to stay and burn along with his camp bed.

Gradually the people drifted into line. As Wilks started off in the lead, he cautioned them again: above all, don't panic. Sexton was toward the front of the line. Hands clasped tightly—it wasn't easy with everyone carrying a bundle—they shuffled timidly up the stairs like children going on a picnic. But as they ducked through the gutted doors at the top of the stairs, Wilks stopped them short. The only exit to the street now was through a 25-yard-long tunnel used by the transport lorries. From where they huddled in the doorway they could see that the farther end was blocked. The candle wax dripping from above seemed to form an almost solid curtain, like giant stalactites suspended from a cave. Yellow flame came flickering and bannering out of it.

"Oh, my God," Sexton heard Wilks groan. "We're sunk."

Then an inexplicable thing happened—inexplicable because meteorological records show that at this hour, 5.30 A.M., there was still almost no wind. But all at once Sexton, Albert Fey, and several of the others gave a cry. The flames had parted and despite the hanging festoons of grease their way was now clear.

Tripping, stumbling, gasping for breath, they ran for it—women, children, old men, fire watchers. As the last survivor tumbled through into the inky gutted ruins of the street, Wilks was all business. He began to call the roll of names, was halfway through, when he realized that to one name "McBride" there was no answer.

Fire Watcher Albert Fey was so tired he wasn't even listening. The first thing he knew was that little Jimmie Sexton had turned back from the safety of the street and was running wildly into the factory—through the great veil of grease, which again blazed fiercely, vanishing out of sight up the long tunnel. Scandalized, he called: "What's up with Jim?" Someone answered: "He must have gone to fetch McBride."

Jimmie Sexton had. Without stopping to think he had dived back into the north building. By now the flames were fluttering across the ground-floor corridor, through the grille of the lift shaft. They came in short, hot bursts, like a welder's lamp, passing narrowly above his head as he clattered the twenty-two steps from ground floor to basement.

Sexton knew exactly where to find Albert McBride. The old man was sitting on a camp bed in a dark corner of the basement fumbling painstakingly to strap up an attaché case, quite oblivious of his peril. Sexton thought that the old veteran had been so long with the firm—almost forty years—that he probably believed, as the others had done, that nothing could happen to Fields'.

What was more he seemed cross, almost resented being rescued. As Sexton tugged him forward toward the stairs he voiced an old man's grievance: it wasn't natural the way young people hustled about in these days. Sexton didn't answer; with his other hand he was scooping up a black cat that had somehow got left behind. When they reached the yard and saw the flames, the cat scratched wildly, tearing itself free and bolting from sight. But Sexton got Albert McBride through the tunnel, even though they had to bend double under the dripping flames.

There was no cheering—hardly any emotion at all—as they rejoined the group. For his part Sexton had not expected that there would be. Albert Fey thought that in any case people were too stunned to take it in. They had resigned themselves to death. Now they were alive, in a dawn shot with angry fires, and for them it was all over. It was going to take time to readjust.

"You Will Never See Another Sunrise"

One woman was not resigned to die, and for Herbert Mills at the Alexandra Hotel she was the greatest single problem that night.

No sooner had Albert Marotta's rescue workers tunneled far enough into the basement to uncover her head than she began to scream voicelessly. She would not say a word, would not tell them her name—merely that appalling, nerve-edged screaming that went on and on. Big gentle Bill Garnan, a peacetime all-in wrestler, who could lift a paving stone with one hand, was more distressed than anyone. "For heaven's sake, miss," he pleaded with her, "we'll get you out." And ignoring the risk to himself, he took off his steel helmet and placed it on her head.

Mills had other reasons to worry. With rescue men and ambulance workers inching delicately from room to room to save those trapped on the upper floors, he wanted no mass alarms. He sent a messenger doubling to St. George's Hospital next door and shortly Dr. Edward Ensor, a young house physician, arrived. The only way to reach the woman was down the 15-foot shaft that Marotta's men had excavated, but the doctor didn't hesitate: he shinnied down a rope holding his morphia syringe in his teeth. He injected the standard quarter grain of morphia, then clambered painfully back to the ground floor. Suddenly there was an electric blue-white flash from the street outside.

As the whole hotel shook and rumbled with the bomb, Mills and Nat Williams glanced tensely upward: was this it? But no the building had subsided again, although they realized with bitter frustration that all the earlier work had been in vain. With a dull roar the shaft caved in.

At 3 A.M. Marotta and his men began the backbreaking work of tunneling the shaft all over again.

They had known triumphs as the night wore on: Percy Straus and his wife rescued alive, Miss Alice Woods freed from the terrible menace of that marble pillar. But they had known tragedy, too. Allen Bathurst had died en route to find that book. Mrs. Morgan and Daphne must have died at the same moment—they had just reached the first floor. It seemed unlikely now that they would ever reach Mr. and Mrs. James Murdoch in time.

Yet somehow Mills's calm, authoritative presence staved off all panic or frantic haste. Patiently, his white coat plastered with filth, Dr. Ensor agreed to stay on—he, too, was acutely conscious that one wrong move could bring the building crashing to trap them all. A long hour went by; the shaft began to take shape again. As if on cue, the woman began to scream.

Swinging back down the rope, Ensor once more plunged the hypodermic home. Afterward he thought that due to a deranged circulation the woman must have been absorbing the morphia very slowly, if at all.

About 4 A.M. Mills and Nat Williams took a breather outside in Knightsbridge. They were resigned now that it would be many days, maybe weeks, before this incident was finally closed. All the while they would have to call on reserves of the same infinite patience—dealing gently with the next of kin; checking the credentials of everyone who wanted entry; drawing up pathetic lists of personal property. They would have to live with the incident, sleep with it even, until it was part of their lives forever.

Now a strange hush had fallen on the scene. Across the park the guns were silent; the only sound was the muted blare of a gas main burning in Park Lane. The brilliant moonlight washed the shattered outline of Princess Alexandra's town mansion, silvery and unreal, like stage lighting.

Suddenly a tremendous explosion from a bomb nearby blew Mills heavily against the iron railings, bruising him across the small of the back. His first reaction, after picking himself up, was again for the hotel: would it collapse? His second reaction, when it didn't, was the goaded fury of a Londoner driven almost beyond endurance.

"Now look here," he said, as if Nat Williams were personally responsible, "I'm really fed up tonight, I don't mind telling you. I'm just about ready for it to end, aren't you?"

This understatement was the nearest Williams had ever seen Mills come to being angry.

It was the same everywhere. If many were prepared to die, they now somehow sought for the right note to strike. It was as if death would be met with the traditionally courteous reserve with which the British receive visitors in general.

Near the Alexandra, at 10 Grosvenor Crescent, Lady Palmer, wife of the biscuit magnate, was sitting on a flight of stairs, unwilling to descend farther. She explained to Warden Jack Smith that she didn't feel she ought to go downstairs for a man like Hitler. In Brixton Warden George Brown was urging a woman to vacate a burning house. She replied that the place wasn't nearly tidy enough; she'd come when she'd finished her dusting. And when Rescue Chief Sidney H. Smith crawled into a blocked basement in the Bayswater Road, the lady of the house greeted him: "I'm so glad you've come now. The kettle's just boiling."

The men were almost as bad: as if, whatever the stress, they had to react conventionally. On the third floor of the *Daily Mail* Building Journalist Alexander Werth passed the washroom, thought of a pressing physical need, then decided against it—too undignified to be killed in that position. Bishopsgate Goods Depot was ringed with fire as Yard Inspector Robert Bromley hunted through desk after desk to find the goods agents' private address. When he found it he would call and report the damage. In thirty-seven years this had been standard procedure; it never occurred to him to vary it now.

In the midst of death men still preserved the outward forms of dignity. Aboard a hospital ship in London River Lieutenant Commander Herriott, captain of the sunken H.M.S. *Tower*, seemed at the last gasp—weak from loss of blood, his arm hanging by a thread. Diffidently he entrusted his wallet to Lieutenant Frank G. Creswell: "If I peg out, you might see my wife gets this—there are enough stamps inside to cover postage." The greater the danger the greater the decorum.

Mr. Shirley Brooks was one of ten people trapped in a Paddington basement—beneath such a weight of debris that the doctor couldn't squeeze in to give morphia. One victim, a medical student, called up, "If you passed me the syringe, sir, I think I could administer it—I *am* in my second year."

Often a total disbelief in disaster lay behind it. As Deptford Warden Joseph Bellaby cut through a back garden, approaching a row of blasted houses, a furious head popped out of an Anderson shelter. "Don't you touch that ruddy trelliswork— I only put it up last Saturday." Bellaby marveled at his countryman's *sang-froid*; the front of the house had gone altogether, yet a pot of stew still simmered gently on the cooker at the back.

In St. Marylebone the bombs had thundered all night around the street shelter in Lisson Grove—it ran parallel to the marshaling yards—but by the small hours Mrs. Rose Simons was too sleepy to care. She had even forgotten that it was now officially her son John's third birthday; the little boy, in his push chair, was sleeping soundly as always. Her husband, Private Arthur Simons, was out getting a breath of air.

Suddenly he burst into the shelter. "Our house has gone."

Mrs. Simons, gazing at him sleepily, decided he was joking. "Don't be daft."

"I'm telling you, gel, the house has had it."

"I'm too sleepy for leg pulls, mate, and that's a fact."

No man can ever have found his wife so aggravating. For a time Private Simons tried to convince her, then finally gave up. He decided that soon it would be dawn, then she'd see for herself.

For Major Frank Jackson, in the City of London, it was all too easy to believe in disaster. To north, south, east, and west of St. Paul's Cathedral the fires were now burning roughly in the form of an outspread fan. To the south the quarter-mile stretch between the cathedral and the river was one steady sheet of flame. In the west the flower girls' church of St. Clement Danes, with its "Oranges and Lemons" theme song, was the beacon that marked the first break in the fires for half a mile. To the north it was worse—a square mile of fire, with the stalking columns of flame only 300 yards from the cathedral's northwest corner. It was almost as bad to the east. Scarcely a building that hadn't caught in the mile between the cathedral and Aldgate Pump.

Certainly the water was coming—but how soon and how much? The first steel-piping relay from New Fresh Wharf, London Bridge, was already on its way—that would mean up to 1,000 gallons a minute emptying into the 5,000-gallon dam by St. Paul's. From Lambeth Headquarters Station, Officer S. J. Hender had phoned the Control point to say the Metropolitan Water Board were doing their best. All the water they had was being fed to that spreading fan of fire.

There hadn't even been any need for Chief Engineer H. F. Cronin to issue special instructions. At pumping station after pumping station startled engineers had seen their sinking pressure gauges and taken action.

The trouble was that water for the East End and most of the City of London was fed from the River Lea, at West Ham, via the Crouch Hill and Maiden Lane storage reservoirs—a tortuous ten-mile journey from east to north and then south again along the worst-hit distribution system of the night. Even at the best of times a powerful twenty-four-inch main could feed only 15,000 gallons a minute, and tonight there was no means of knowing how much water was bleeding uselessly into the gutters.

Even to shut down a main at all to prevent further leakage was a primitive affair involving four men and a six-foot radius treadmill, which might take all of two hours.

Watching Jackson, District Officer Edward Kirrage could only marvel at the man. If London burned, it was Jackson who would take responsibility, despite the inadequacy of the tools he had been given for the job.

But nothing of this showed in Jackson's plump, impassive face as he moved from fire chief to fire chief in the red dawn, bustling over the littered pavements, dwarfed by the gray mushroom dome of St. Paul's.

Always courteous, he understood men very well. He told serious, capable Chief Officer Arthur Johnstone, who had come on from Westminster Abbey, to organize a shuttle service of lorries to the Regent's Canal, a mile north. The lorries could bring down only 1,000 gallons at a time to tip into the central 5,000-gallon dam, but it was a start. He grinned at District Officer Kirrage, who liked a joke. "We're in a hell of a mess, aren't we?"

On the phone to Home Office Fire Control he told Chief Superintendent Augustus May the grim truth, because he had to: "Mr. May, the fires around St. Paul's are out of control."

May never forgot the agitation in Jackson's voice. He urged him to hang on: relief engines were coming.

But Jackson's worst dilemma that night was known only to a few, and none of them were then on the spot. Just south of St. Paul's, fronting on Queen Victoria Street, stood Faraday Building, a nine-story concrete fortress dividing into four main blocks. Its northeastern block, known as The Citadel, was a top-secret emergency retreat for the British Cabinet. Winston Churchill had a suite there. Among those housed there on this night were Sir John Anderson, the lord president of the Council, and Minister of Labor Ernest Bevin—secure under a roof of reinforced concrete seven feet thick between walls of half that depth. This apart, the ten-acre site housed not only the City and Central telephone exchanges but the toll and trunk exchanges, the Continental exchange, and the Overseas Radio link with America and the Commonwealth.

If Faraday Building caught fire, Field Marshal Sperrle would have achieved the greatest triumph of that night's triumphantly successful raid. He would have disrupted London's link with the rest of Britain and curtailed vital telephone services on which so much of war production hinged to an extent never before achieved.

Already that night high-explosive bombs had grazed it. There had been fires which Superintendent George Robinson kept under control with a sweeping curtain of water down the front of the building.

But if the east wind grew stronger the building would stand no chance. The red-hot cinders driving from the east would pile six inches deep on gutters and window ledges. On the roof of Unilever House they had even fired the sandbags. And if that happened, there would be no holding Faraday Building.

At 5 A.M. on Sunday, May 11, this was one of London's most closely-guarded secrets. But rumor was in the air, made more disturbing by the fact that few knew the true facts. District Officer Edward Kirrage heard of a plan to send for the Royal Engineers, though it was abandoned for lack of time. Superintendent Joe Ansell had phoned Lambeth earlier for permission to cut off all electricity and gas to the City of London; he thought short circuits and gas mains were starting as much fire as anything. But the answer had been no.

In the lower echelons there was a strange unease. Along with dozens of others Fireman Harry Weinstock had spent the better part of two hours evacuating all the shelters around St. Paul's, bundling blankets over the women's heads so that they couldn't see the fires. Police Sergeant Reginald Goldsmith heard a senior fire officer—probably Jackson—say, "I'm thinking of evacuating the whole City." Goldsmith blenched; his wife Lily was in a shelter nearby. He thought, now which bloody bridge do *we* get out over.

Only Jackson and his immediate deputies knew that in the last resort the fires would be held off by a charge of dynamite large enough to blast both flames and buildings into a pile of ashes. The yardstick was whether the fires crossed Godliman Street, a narrow alley bordering Faraday Building on the east, running from St. Paul's Churchyard to Queen Victoria Street.

The street ran only 150 paces from the southwest corner of the cathedral.

At the Fire Service conference that had decided this the cathedral authorities had protested bitterly. A shock like this, following on the millions of gallons of water which the Fire Service had drained from under London through the blitz, would gravely jeopardize the cathedral's foundations.

Hence Jackson's despair. At 5.30 A.M. his anguish was as great as that of any man in London: to hang on in the hope of water and risk bringing London's communications to a virtual standstill or to risk endangering the cherished symbol of St. Paul's.

But the water just wasn't coming. At 5.30 A.M. there had been no pressure obtainable in the City of London at all for three and half hours—and the situation was as bad elsewhere. The river was now almost dead low, and, incredibly, the whole City locked in by a triangle of water was as dry as the Sahara.

Across the asphalt desert men took what action they could. Near the Elephant and Castle people ran after water lorries with buckets; each time the water slopped over the canvas dams they scooped it from the gutters. District Officer George Spurrett, finding a line of hose smoldering, stopped his car and kicked water from the puddles over it, looking guiltily around to see if anyone were laughing. Fireman Robert Coram and his mates had no water to make a fire break—just piled the entire contents of two shops on the pavements, leaving only the empty buildings. Off Fleet Street a dairyman saved his own premises, sluicing all the liquid he could find—milk, orange juice, soda water—over walls and ceilings.

But it was hard for anyone to comprehend. In Queen Victoria Street, by St. Paul's, Major Arthur Carr, Salvation Army, told a police sergeant: "If only we had some water we could save all this." The policeman gave him a long, pitying look. Under the railway arches at Bermondsey a young girl protested when First Aid Worker Alfred Bartlett used an astringent on a cut—"Wasn't he going to wash it first?" Bartlett explained patiently: "We have not got a cup of water to drink, let alone wash that." By Southwark Bridge a young sub officer sped up to a fire chief. "Sir, I want some more water." The fire chief was withering. "Son, I haven't got enough water to produce a good piss."

Farther east, into the City, the situation was as bad. In Hounsditch, behind Liverpool Street Station, District Officer Frederick Abbott couldn't stop the fires spreading north, try as he might; he had only one 5,000-gallon dam and four water lorries. The fire spread so fast there wasn't even time to reposition the branches; burning buildings kept burying the hose all the way from the river at London Bridge; sometimes the men had to lug the trailer pumps by hand out of the path of the fire. Superintendent George Robinson had taken up a last-ditch stand to prevent the fires leaping Aldgate High Street from the south and joining up with Abbott's fires around Hounsditch. Four hundred yards east Station Officer Cyril Tobias at last had that relay coming through from Tower Pier. He could stop his fires from spreading northeast to Hounsditch but even if the raid ended, the hose was still vulnerable. He, too, urgently awaited steel piping.

There was no longer much pretense at control. Where a fire chief was on the spot, the men worked doggedly on, filthy, exhausted, their eyes blood-red from the painful sparks. Elsewhere confusion reigned. Toward 5.30 A.M. Major Jackson sent District Officer Kirrage to sort out the chaos around Whitechapel; the station had been hit, the pink slips detailing the fire calls were piling up in the watch room. Most of the firemen had disappeared; without orders they had slumped exhausted into any shelter they could find. Often there was no need to shelter. The knowledge that scores of pumps and men stood idle at spent fires, unwilling to move on to a fresh fire ground, kept District Officer Thomas Goodman on the go for hours.

For all practical purposes the City was now a battlefield. With telephone lines out, streets blocked, it became every man for himself. At the Elephant water was just coming through from the Waterloo Bridge relay when the line again went limp. Simmering, Assistant Divisional Officer Geoffrey Blackstone drove to the scene to find another officer had plugged into the charged hose to tackle a fire of his own. The forceful Blackstone turned the air blue with curses, but the damage was done.

And the provincial pumps now trickling on to the scene were fair game for anyone. As a convoy jolted past the Cut street market by Waterloo Bridge, Fireman Leslie Horton calmly impressed the last three. He had no idea whether they were booked for more important work; his own fires took priority. The out-of-towners themselves were none the wiser.

A few had no intention of being taken prisoner. By Hounsditch District Officer Frederick Abbott saw a burning building about to totter; he ran into the road to warn a small convoy of two towing vehicles and a trailer pump. Evidently they suspected his motives, repaid his solicitude by trying to run him down.

There were flashes of the same ugly mood all over. When a top-ranking Fire Service officer gave what seemed a nonsensical order, Superintendent Harold Norman of Whitechapel couldn't hold himself in check. "For Christ's sake," he snarled, "take yourself off, will you? We can do without you when we're busy." The officer was completely abashed. He turned and walked away.

It was small wonder that tempers were frayed. The worst air attack in London's history, coming on top of nine intermittent months of blitz, had been too much. Many Fire Service officers—George Adams, Joe Ansell, Cyril Tobias—still swear that in all that time they never removed their clothes except to take a bath. They slept in their uniforms when and where they could, then carried on with the daytime job of running the station.

In the cold, acrid-smelling dawn men swayed on their feet, still going through the motions, in an agony of fatigue. From his

"You Will Never See Another Sunrise"

Control point by Smithfield Meat Market Superintendent Ted Overton sent for sardine-and-tomato sandwiches and a flask of coffee, then went to sleep as he ate, still standing. In Southwark Street District Officer George Spurrett found two firemen as drugged as men in shock still clinging to a branch. He had to punch them into wakefulness. Farther on, by London Bridge, two firemen lay asleep in the gutter, only a third sitting upright chanting "Rule Britannia."

At the last fatigue had anaesthetized the body against everything—fear, pain, even the sense of duty. Deptford Warden Harry Cable went to sleep on a stool, toppled face first into a brazier. As the others dragged him clear he didn't really seem to care. Station Officer Robert Stepney, summoned to a topstory fire in an Upper Thames Street warehouse, couldn't summon the energy to climb the stairs. He stood and watched the building burn down, ripe cheeses thundering like skittles from the upper floors. Along the street people stood staring, lost in thought.

There was much to think about. For some there was the irony of being in a strange place at a strange time. Basil P. Bothamley, bank manager, would normally have been asleep in respectable suburban Purley. Now, at dawn, he found himself in the Cock Tavern at Fleet Street. He had just quenched a small fire; now he was quenching his thirst with a tumbler of neat brandy.

Leutnant Martin Reiser should have been back in the mess, or, better, still asleep above the bar restaurant in Mitwitz, Bavaria. Today he had planned to visit the beehives, and post some color snaps back to Maria. Instead, for the first time in his life he was in a prison cell with only a hard plank bed, an enamel toilet, and a Bible he couldn't read. The policeman wouldn't tell him where he was; he guessed it was Tunbridge Wells because it was on the man's helmet, but that conveyed nothing either.

For Mr. Alvah Clatworthy, the silver-haired draper, there was a change in plans to consider. He had meant to spend the morning attending Baptist chapel, the afternoon teaching in Sunday school. Now he decided he must go to Friday Street, City of London, and see if his stock of Duchess sets and tapestry cushions had suffered.

Dairyman Edward Morris, on the spot in Upper Thames Street, thought it time to act. Some firemen had arrived from Witney, Oxfordshire, but had lost their rations on the way. Before they could tackle any fire they insisted they must eat. Morris saw there was nothing they could do to save the warehouses, but his own dairy restaurant was only just alight. "You save it, boys," he cried. "I'll feed you." The bargain was clinched.

A few recalled that this day had never spelled good luck. Diplomat Edward Penrose-Fitzgerald, awaiting hospital treatment, remembered May 10, 1940. Then he had been in a French train which the Germans machine-gunned. For the first time Hauptmann Albert Hufenreuter, lying painfully in a military hospital, remembered it, too. It was the anniversary of his being shot down for the first time and taken prisoner by the French.

Some perhaps wondered why they were in London at all. Lieutenant John Hodgkinson had come on a whim for a change of scene. Fireman John H. Good should have been on leave, had stayed to help. Now he was fighting a blazing inferno in a 14-acre Stepney timber dump. Dr. Barbara Morton was sick with neuritis, checked on duty when things got bad. Now she examined patient after patient with the black "M"—morphia needed—scrawled in skin pencil on their foreheads.

Some were thinking more of others. Gladys Henley had wandered up from Bermondsey Control room, awaiting the all-clear. It was four hours since she had last seen her husband; now she almost wished he had stayed below. Then she remembered how shocked Albert Henley had been at a recent Mansion House reception. He had heard one mayor say to another, "Where was I in the last raid? In the shelter, of course."

"You Will Never See Another Sunrise"

Henley had come home and told his wife: "If I ever sink to that and get trapped, I hope the rescue men won't dig me out."

She thought that Chauffeur Eddie Taylor, who was standing near, told her: "The guvnor's gone on a job round town." (On the other hand, Taylor remembered saying, "No, I've been looking for him.") He had just heard the news after his fruitless all-night hunt but he didn't want to be the first to tell her.

To some it had seemed time to abandon hope. At Post D2 Headquarters, St. Marylebone, Eileen Sloane was sunk in silent despair. For a long time now the area had been quiet. Since Stanley Barlow had been reported trapped in the blazing synagogue there had been no news at all. Presently Miss Donaldson, the telephonist, approached her. "I think we'd feel better if we had a cup of tea."

At that moment Stanley Barlow was scarcely thinking of Eileen Sloane or of anything at all except the need for sleep. It was a long time before he even realized that he had faced his own personal crisis squarely and passed the test. There was no longer any need to be fearful of fear.

Incredibly, he had not faltered as the sparks and timber swallowed him from view. He had even kept his grip on Mrs. Roth. He carried her to the street where her husband and the others awaited him, to be joined now by Warden Arthur Fayers. He sent Fayers in charge of the party to a nearby shelter.

Always thorough, Barlow now abided by his own training as scrupulously as any of those he had inspired that night. He remembered another maxim: a warden doesn't write off an incident until he has personally made certain there is no one else on the premises. He stumbled back into the synagogue to make sure. About 1.45 the whole roof fell in on him.

This time, strangely, it was easier. He was responsible for nobody's life but his own. Clawing and gasping for breath, retching the plaster almost from his bowels after every breath, he finally managed to grope his way out by a side entrance, emerging farther up the street. He saw wardens and ambulance workers milling around the synagogue entrance but it didn't occur to him they were looking for him. He had noticed something they hadn't. The roof and ground floor of No. 143/9, Great Portland Street, just opposite, were alight. His card-index brain told him that there were fire watchers here, too.

Next instant he had charged down the stairs. These men, too, were trapped in the basement; Barlow was becoming practiced at moving debris but here, unfortunately, debris was not the biggest problem. The three men were badly shocked, cut by flying glass, quivering with fear. Worse, both basement and ground floor were part of a motor company's showrooms. All the cars were alight, the metal ticking gently in the sultry shut-in space, soft, hot flames licking gently at the paintwork.

Barlow had just cleared some kind of passage through the rubble and got two of the men as far as the stairs when a whip-lash report seemed to split his head open. Another, then another. The air seemed to rain long, wicked daggers of glass, and walls were crumbling.

As Barlow got the first two men into the street and doubled back for the third, he was certain some anti-aircraft gunner had got the wrong range and was lobbing shells into the building next door. In fact, they were liquid-oxygen cylinders exploding in a dental company's premises, but it made them no less dangerous.

On his second trip to the basement more debris had blocked the way. Again Barlow used his tin hat to good advantage. The one thing really on his mind was the neat, methodical evacuation of all the buildings affected by fire. He could see that his rubber boots were badly cockled by the heat and he was vaguely aware as he scrabbled that his ankles felt sore. Only later he found that the heat had fused the woollen socks he wore into a sticky, frizzled mass.

By the time he had almost carried the third man from the

basement, weaving in and out of the burning cars, the concrete floor was thick with embers, the soles of his feet felt red-hot. The blood of the wounded man mingled with the sticky white paste of plaster dust coating his denims.

Barlow then buttonholed a passing warden and saw the three men hastened off to the nearest first-aid post. It had just occurred to him that Hallam House, an office block at right angles to the synagogue in Hallam Street, had looked pretty badly blasted by the same bomb. There were 15 people sheltering there, too—he knew the total without even checking.

This time luck was on his side: at least 13 of them had managed to claw their way over the rubble and escape by a back entrance. Only two remained numbed by shock, sprawled out behind a fallen wall. Once more Barlow doffed his steel helmet. Twenty minutes later they were free.

By now the fire in the synagogue showed every sign of spreading, the Fire Service hadn't arrived, but there was a 5,000-gallon dam brim full around the corner. For the next two hours Barlow was organizing a bucket chain of fire watchers to keep the walls of the buildings on either side cooled down.

At Post D2 Eileen Sloane was sitting on a window sill sipping tea. Sunk in grief, she heard the door open but didn't look up. The first thing she saw was Barlow, covered from head to foot in thick white dust; only his eyes, bloodshot with pain and fatigue, seemed alive. Near hysteria, she thought, "My God, it's his ghost."

Barlow was thinking, "I just could use a cup of tea." Then he became aware of the silence—both women staring at him, neither speaking. "What's the matter?" he asked. He sensed the tension now.

"I thought you were trapped in the synagogue," Eileen Sloane replied. "I thought you were dead." Suddenly she felt the tears coming, and even though she tried she couldn't stop them.

Barlow tried to comfort her. "It's all right now," he kept

227

saying. "Look, it's all over. It's all right now." He couldn't trust himself to say anything more, and Eileen could say nothing, nothing at all.

Stanley Barlow, of course, was only striving to bring comfort, but it *was* all over. The last bomb dropped at 5.37 A.M. precisely, plumb on the northwest turret of Scotland Yard, bringing the index cards of a million criminals plus the filing cabinets smack on to the desk of the commissioner, Sir Philip Game. Only half an hour later he would have been sitting there.

The raid ended as it had begun—with one of the longest silences ever endured by man. The sun came up over the Kentish fields, and overnight the weather had changed again; a warm west wind was blowing. Only the inky pall of smoke wreathing the horizon to the north witnessed that for seven hours all hell had been let loose over the City.

At the Royal Observer Corps Bromley, Kent, Controller Arthur Collins heard the last bombers departing—the slow, steady drone of the engines beating toward the Channel. It was 5.50 A.M. Then he wrote a very human comment in the official log: "Phew!"

Underground, in Fighter Command Ops room, they could see nothing. But as Squadron Leader Cyril Leman watched, the last red arrows were receding—over Kent; over Sussex; across the Channel waters. Captain Clifford Mollison had just one suggestion: "Coffee!" Flight Lieutenant Ronald Squire pressed a button among the battery before him.

London, 5.52 P.M., Sunday, May 11. The clarion call of the all-clear, like a liner nearing safe haven, ringing over the whole City.

"How Many Are You for, Mate?"
After 5.50 A.M.

"OH, Mummie, my birthday cake—my birthday cake's all gone," little John Simons sobbed bitterly as he clutched the hand of his mother, Mrs. Rose Simons, outside the ruins of No. 155, Lisson Grove, St. Marylebone.

At 6 A.M. on Sunday, May 11, Mrs. Simons did not, could not, answer. Together with the birthday cake had gone everything she and her husband possessed—their home, their furniture, their wedding presents, all ground to a clinging yellow powder. Beside her Private Arthur Simons stood like a man in a trance. Presently he muttered something like, "Everything a man owned . . . not even a toothbrush." Still, unable to imagine greater deprivation than that birthday cake, his little boy wept uncontrollably. Private Simons had no heart to scold him. He was crying for the world he knew.

There was excuse for tears on this May morning. Across the wounded acres of brick and stone a drifting shroud of choking brown smoke rolled like a sea mist. Burning embers from the fires eddied and spiraled above the wreckage. The sun was a dark-red disc in a near-invisible sky. In the warm, almost windless air the stench of the broken City seemed to catch the pit of the stomach—rubber, sulphur, leaking gas, the acrid tang of burning wood. By Marble Arch the smoke parted to reveal a tattered cinema poster—"So Ends Our Night."

The City That Would Not Die

In many streets a sharp, nerve-jarring clatter broke the silence; armed with brooms or dustpans and brushes, the house-wives were defying Field Marshal Sperrle, sweeping the jagged icicles of broken glass from their front doorsteps. But it was not a sight that went much remarked. The people who struggled past them, faces blackened like coal miners coming off shift, moved as unheedingly as the inhabitants of a dream world. Time and again, in the few roads still navigable, motorists jammed on their brakes to avoid mowing down men as blind as sleepwalkers. There was a strange sense of mass self-control being very near to snapping. In a crowded Battersea teashop a waitress let fall a tray of plates; for a moment terror showed, naked and animal, on every face.

Elsewhere an appalling stillness hung like a curtain—above the gray rooftops, their slates prickled and ridged like a hedge-hog's spines; above the countryside, where charred paper swirled and danced over quiet woods 30 miles away. On para-pets and bridges long lines of pigeons and sea gulls roosted, blinking at the unfathomable pea-souper of smoke, and they, too, were unnaturally still.

At first, understandably, it was personal suffering that made the deepest impact. It wasn't that people had no time for the heartbreak of others—that would come. It was merely that at first the devastation was too vast to comprehend save in per-sonal terms. Rich and poor, famous and unknown, in Mayfair and Stepney and Croydon, were crying for the world they knew.

Marguerita Stahli was in Dulwich Hospital. She was not crying yet; the fear and horror had lodged like a block of ice where her stomach should have been, and every muscle in her body had clenched tight in protest. In the hospital ward men and women were packed impartially together, bed nudging bed; the doctors moved mechanically, hollow-eyed with fatigue, and the sound of sobbing trembled in the graying light. Presently a woman cleaner in a ragged overall brought them all cups of tea, and later Marguerita's girl friend, Marjorie

Jacob, visited and brought some clean handkerchiefs. They talked of everything but the one thing that mattered until Marguerita cut quietly across Marjorie's sentence: "Is he dead?" When Marjorie nodded, Marguerita said, "I thought so." But that was all.

Later still they moved her, slung on a stretcher in a Green Line coach, to Epsom Hospital, Surrey. It was there that Eileen, her married sister, found her and brought Jim Norman with her. Somehow he was the last person Marguerita had expected to see today. He was really her brother Jack's friend, a young airman who lived nearby; he had been in and out of Aunt Maud's house as long as she could remember. They had all played tennis together and seen each other at All Saints' Church every Sunday for years. She had always rather taken Jim Norman for granted before, yet today she was especially glad to see him.

He had even managed to retrieve her bicycle from the ruins of Turney Road—and she has it still. Marguerita was worried as to what Aunt Maud would say when she returned from her weekend in the country to find her home in ruins, but Jim Norman reassured her. He would go right back on Monday and see if he couldn't at least salvage the aspidistras that were the old lady's special pride. He was so reassuring and so nice that day that now, illogically, Marguerita did want to cry.

Elsewhere the people conducted their own post-mortems and came to terms with grief. Winston Churchill was in the ruins of the House of Commons. He stood with Lord Beaverbrook and Lord Reith, the minister of works, and the tears rolled unchecked down his old cheeks. From early on, guessing something of what he would see, he had been unusually quiet, nursing grief. But perhaps he had no true picture of what lay ahead. The Bar no longer stood to check intruders. The green leather-padded benches were charred beyond recognition. The Debating Chamber, the Press Gallery, the Strangers' and Ladies' Galleries—all had gone. So Churchill wept—and then, because he was a fighter, he straightened up and his bodyguard, Detective Inspector Walter Thompson, saw him light a fresh cigar. "People will expect it of me, Thompson."

A minute later, when he emerged from the House, Quentin Reynolds noted that cigar—it had the angry jut of a man who meant business. As they passed, Beaverbrook said gravely: "It was a long night, Quentin." And Reynolds agreed that indeed it had been. But Churchill said nothing; his heart was too full for words.

Almost everywhere it was the same scene—the silent, staring crowds grouped before ruined landmarks, the sudden departure of someone who found all of it too poignant. In Oxford Street Ambulance Officer Eileen Young saw an old gentleman in a frock coat weeping alone outside a burning store. Pretty Marjorie Felton, driving past the gutted Queen's Hall in her father's car, felt the same. She didn't cry, but she could hardly bear to look. It was too much like intruding on private grief. And something of her youth had gone forever.

For some the association lay deeper—a life's work vanished with a puff of smoke. In the City of London Mr. Alvah Clatworthy arrived by St. Paul's Cathedral to find Friday Street gone—only twisted acres of masonry as if wreckers had been at work. The police wouldn't have let him through at all if he hadn't come straight from his South London post wearing warden's uniform. As it was they thought he belonged; they let him tread reluctantly up the street to find firemen cooling down the steaming ruins of his wholesale drapery.

Mr. Clatworthy was direct. "You're not going to save anything here, are you?"

"Not a thing."

But it was hard, at the age of sixty, to see twenty years' work gone in a night, to know that there would be compensation only for the £100 worth of stock stored on the premises— which were his on lease. Standing there, the little draper struggled not to cry, to seek strength from his Baptist teachings. At last, with a great sigh, the words were wrung out of him: "The Lord will provide."

"How Many Are You for, Mate?"

In the ruins of Clubland the Reverend Jimmy Butterworth mourned, too—nineteen years' work for the boys and girls of the South London streets, and now the church, the gymnasium, the theater, the workshops, gutted to black wet slime. One of his boys, scorched by the long night's fire fighting, saw him.

"Wotcha crying for, Jimmy?"

"Because this is the end."

"The end, me eye. You've still got us, aintcha?"

No doubting it was true. That night, in the ruins, several hundred teenagers came to worship, and one among them read the lesson, "I will lift up mine eyes unto the hills . . ." With their help Jimmy Butterworth worked on to build Clubland anew.

Some wounds were healed less easily. Outside Bermondsey Town Hall Gladys Henley still stood waiting, not anxious yet, just hoping her husband would soon appear. In a moment Controller W. E. Baker approached her. "Gladys, I'm afraid Albert has been injured. He's been taken to St. Olave's Hospital." As the car ground through the mean streets, Gladys Henley said impulsively, "I don't care if he's got two arms off as long as he's alive." Nobody answered. Still, until she reached the hospital, she knew nothing until a doctor, in gentle, halting phrases, broke the news.

A long time afterward, when she again met the Duke of Kent, he asked about the "lucky sweater." Then she remembered.

There wasn't always time for gentleness. Back home in Hammersmith Mrs. Edna Clarke was getting worried sick; her fireman husband's breakfast was ready but he was long overdue from Shoreditch. Another fireman was there, actually, steeling himself to tell her when a policeman arrived, announcing bluntly: "You're wanted to identify a body at Hackney Mortuary." Once she had willed herself to get there she realized the raid had been even worse than she had thought. Later she had to join a queue for a death certificate. Behind

233

her a Cockney with heavily bandaged hands asked flatly: "How many are you for, mate?"

It was so bizarre that Mrs. Clarke thought she must be in the wrong place. Then the man explained: his wife, sister, and two daughters had all been buried and killed.

Not everyone can have known with such certainty. In Angel Lane, West Ham, Publican Bill Barker had just opened up The Lion for the early shift workers when Inspector Reg Jones of the local C.I.D. came in. Barker knew Jones as a "half-of-bitters" man, but as he went to pull the measure the policeman stopped him short. "Bill, for God's sake give me a double scotch. I've just inspected half a ton of unidentified flesh."

And the sorrow was universal. At Hyde Park Corner, by the Alexandra Hotel, the policeman on point duty was weeping openly; he had heard that his "lovely lady," Mrs. Frances Morgan, was among the dead. In Shoreditch Chief Warden William Coyne saw rescue men carrying the bodies of children from the ruins. Some were former jailbirds, convicted for razor slashing, yet the tears rolled down their cheeks. In Soho Rescue Chief Leslie Lane saw his men cheer wildly, cry from sheer reaction, when a mother cat and her kittens were dug out alive.

Some thoughts lay too deep for tears. At Post D2, St. Marylebone, Stanley Barlow took time out to deal with neglected paper work, unearthed a brand-new warden's certificate. Now he remembered what he had forgotten to tell Tailoress Winnie Dorow as she set out on her first, and last, patrol. She had that day qualified as a fully-fledged warden: the news had been phoned through for him to tell her. The others gave him a wide berth; he was sitting too still, too quiet.

Many had nothing to grieve or celebrate, but the sheer joy of being alive was enough. Crossing the courtyard of the National Temperance Hospital, St. Pancras, Miss Frances Thirlby thought that the sunshine had never been so beautiful. At Westminster Control Center Message Supervisor Elsie Ferguson wanted to cheer, then found that after dealing with 3,000 messages she'd lost her voice. The New York *Times*' Bob Post thought that the phrase "Glad to see you" had a new meaning.

A few were lightheaded with bravery. A youngster arrived at R. B. Kingham's post near Paddington to explain exactly how he had extinguished his first incendiary bomb. He wanted to know: did this qualify him for a medal?

It was almost pathetic, yet many right on the spot never realized their peril. At Waterloo Stationmaster Harry Greenfield sat in gloomy solitude in his office. No trains could run; his station had no water, gas, electric light, or power. His one comfort: the ten-pump team who had eventually turned up to deal with the fire in the vaults had reported it out.

Suddenly, to his chagrin, District Officer Thomas Goodman burst into his office. Greenfield, whose father had been royal train guard to Queen Victoria, ruled his domain with a firm hand; he pointed out that a stationmaster's door was there to knock on. Goodman's reply, ungrammatical but to the point, became a classic in Fire Service circles: "If I don't get some assistance soon, you won't have any station to be stationmaster of." The hard-pressed crews hadn't stayed long enough; in the vaults beneath Waterloo was alight from end to end, a fire so consuming that the whole upper structure might collapse into the pit. Greenfield's face seemed suddenly to crumple. He could only whisper: "As bad as *that*, mate?"

Thereafter he worked alongside the firemen like a Trojan, even though the neglected fires, rampaging through 23 acres of catacombs, were by then white hot; 30 feet above, the asphalt on the platforms steamed like cooling toffee. It was Lieutenant Commander John Fordham and Geoffrey Blackstone who found the solution; plowing through the station taxi rank with a pneumatic drill, they vented the fire, allowing the almost-boiling air to rush like a geyser to the sky. But it was four anxious days before the fires were subdued.

Preoccupied with their own problems, nobody realized there were crises on every hand. Thomas Sinden, the bride groom-to-be, had been afraid all night that he would never marry Beatrice; this morning he was sure of it. He had trouble getting from the East End to Aldgate Pump; when he insisted he was hurrying to his wedding in Acton, all the taxi drivers shrugged him off as drunk. Finally he got a lift in a doctor's car, a nightmare detour to the north, with only the gray dome of St. Paul's as a familiar landmark on the skyline.

Sinden had no idea that the cathedral stood at that moment in grave peril. By midmorning the fires were creeping on toward Faraday Building. Superintendent Henry Davies, who had charge of operations, held his breath. If the flames crossed the narrow alley of Godliman Street he would have to send that call for dynamite.

To check the fire, Davies had only skeleton equipment—a fireboat on the Thames by Blackfriars Bridge, a water unit, a hose-laying unit, and six pumps. He, too, had nursed the same secret as Jackson for many months, although the relief officers drafted in to help him this Sunday morning knew nothing of the issues at stake. To Captain Herbert Eaton, chief officer of Chigwell, Essex, Fire Brigade, it was only another routine job— sorting out the vast snake pit of redundant hose by Blackfriars Bridge to get more water and quicker results.

But Davies' heart was sinking. The steel piping was coming, but with appalling slowness—few men had been trained in its elementary use—and the river was pitifully low. All the while the flames crept nearer. By noon the top stories of the houses on the east side of Godliman Street, nearest to St. Paul's, were burning. Worse, the pressure obtainable was nowhere near the 2,300 pounds per square inch that was needed.

A jet like that, Davies knew, could punch through the envelope of solid heat and knock out the fire at source.

The buildings were liable to go, the hose might disintegrate, but he took a risk. He ordered his men to snake their branches right into the upper stories and drench the fires from close at hand. That done, he drew them back.

Hour after hour Davies kept a drifting curtain of water saturating the crumbling buildings on the east side of the narrow alley until every brick was cold and wet to the touch. To the northeast, close to St. Paul's, Captain Eaton watched other fire-men doing the same for Walting Street corner.

By 6 P.M. Faraday Building and St. Paul's Cathedral were out of danger, but the fire had left its mark in more ways than one. Soon after Davies had a breakdown in health and retired from the Fire Service. The strain had been too great.

Yet the ordinary civilian could hardly have believed it pos-sible. When part-time Fireman Percy Madden staggered into his suburban home groaning, "Oh, what a night," his wife had a word of comfort: "Nothing to worry about, they went up over the Midlands." Out on Sydenham Hill, an untouched oasis between Lambeth and Croydon, old Mr. Reginald Harpur noted in his diary: "I hear casualties were very light—30 at the most." Even Journalist Charles Graves, on the doorstep of the great Druce's fire, grumbled: "These astrologers are very dis-appointing. They promised something sensational to happen last night."

In the remote suburbs the ignorance was total. In Wembley C. L. Miles couldn't understand why the Sunday papers were late. Euston's Arrivals Inspector John Atkinson, 17 miles away at Watford, thought the dark atom mushroom of smoke above London was a thunderstorm, cursed that he hadn't brought a raincoat.

Even the visiting firemen couldn't believe their eyes. As the convoy that had left Birmingham six hours back came into the City from the north, they were shocked into silence. From Hendon, eight miles north of the City's center, onward, house after house burst with a dry, intense roaring. Yet there wasn't a fire engine in sight, not a soul on the streets.

That same feeling that had struck Hauptmann Aschenbren-ner six hours earlier now struck them: this was a city of the dead. Sub Officer Charles H. Gibbs summed it up for all of them: "What the hell are we coming into?"

Above all, they were entering a city that had done some hard reappraisal. In six hours millions of people had learned, as never before, the meaning of total war. Overnight, through the medium of Field Marshal Sperrle, they had become, in the fullest sense, adult.

For twenty-one years—an ironic total—many people had convinced themselves that it could not happen here. To Guernica, to Shanghai, even to Rotterdam, but not to London. And in a sense, once and for all, their complacency died that night and they came of age. The symbols of a proud past lay in ashes.

District Officer Edward Baker, watching the fires leaping south of the Strand, thought there was every chance of a conflagration in that packed terraced property. Moving men and pumps rapidly from street to street, he forced himself to ignore historic St. Clement Danes. From a side street he heard but did not see the roof of Wren's church come smashing down.

It was in most ways a significant gesture. A new age was dawning. The grim system of priorities which the Fire Service had to enforce this night was in keeping with the new unremitting conception of war. If, in a nuclear battle, victory consists of atomizing only 22 per cent of an enemy's industrial potential, what chance would a church—even a Wren church—stand in the future?

By dawn on Sunday, May 11, the old Charterhouse was a brown stinking ruin. On the Old Bailey's dome the gilded blindfolded figure of Justice stared bleakly above the ruined northwest wing. The sixteenth-century hall of Gray's Inn was a mound of shimmering ash.

The destruction was really a tragic catalogue of what the well-traveled tourist should see—the Elizabeth Greycoat Hospital; the house where Catherine Parr lived before her marriage to Henry VIII; London's oldest house, at 10 Nevill's Court, Fetter Lane, which even the fire of 1666 had not razed; the halls of five great livery companies; Devonshire House; the Grand Priory Church of St. John of Jerusalem; St. Columba's (Church of Scotland) Pont Street; and the masterpieces of Wren; St. Mary-le-Bow; St. Mildred's, Bread Street, his "little St. Paul's"; St. Nicholas Cole Abbey, Queen Victoria Street; his finest of all St. Stephen's, Walbrook.

And insensibly out of this night a new spirit was to arise—tougher, more skeptical, more scientific materialistic. If seven hours' bombing could topple the symbols of centuries, was tradition really the inspiration it was accepted to be? And people have had less patience with tradition since that time.

In many ways, of course, the seeds of the Quiet Revolution were irrevocably sown. The beginnings of the blitz had seen to that. But May 10 marked the grand finale, and nothing could ever be the same again.

As with traditions, so with people. Rightly or wrongly, most people tended to blame the politicians for their suffering, although in the final analysis Neville Chamberlain's pathetic sortie to Berchtesgaden was only the inevitable outcome of a long tradition. Other governments than his had bent over backward to appease the dictators. Other governments than his had refused to sanction more than £100,000 a year on civil-defense expenditure.

But a people tends to get the government it deserves. The blitzes of the past nine months had been a warning—for the government but for the people, too. Yet on May 10 Flanagan and Allen's refrain about how completely the blitz had failed spotlighted the prevailing mood. The Cup Final and kindred distractions claimed priority. Fire watching, even the instinct to save one's life, came a long way down the list.

In both cases the lesson held good. People have looked to the politicians increasingly for quick results, not promises. And both government and people have lived under the shadow of war ever since.

Within weeks London's emergency water needs had undergone a drastic revision, and every major provincial city had received the same treatment. (In the Southern Division Lieutenant Commander John Fordham and his aide Geoffrey Blackstone didn't even wait for sanction: they cemented up forty-four sites, a total of more than one and a half million gallons, in two months). Steel piping, borehole pumps on bridges, became the order of the day. By August the National Fire Service, as a unified fighting force, was an established fact. And despite later denationalization the skeleton remained—standard ranks, above all standard training and equipment.

It marked the end, too, of Herbert Morrison's uneasy flirtation with *laisser-faire*. By Tuesday the minister had called on every London borough for detailed reports on how the fire-watching system had fallen down. Within days the regulations were being enforced more stringently by prosecution, even jail. A hard lesson had been learned: if a country is to survive total war no man can please himself—and in a nuclear war a strong central authority would have to grasp the reins even tighter. The people have been learning to live with controls from that time on.

It began a new era for the Press, too. *The Times* and *The Daily Telegraph* had fought vigorously for a National Fire Service. Now, despite wartime security, other newspapers became openly resentful that the government had revealed so much less than the truth. Alexander Werth, remembering a Ministry of Home Security press conference, commented, "Clearly something had gone seriously wrong . . . with this much-vaunted emergency water supply." *The Evening Standard* was brusque: "Let's face the facts—London has *not* learned the lesson of the fire raids . . . but Goering's fire raisers may be here tonight." *The Daily Mail* was cynical: "It must not happen again, but we said that last time!"

It was a pointer. The Press has been more thrusting, less ready to take things on trust—some would say less respectful—as the years have gone by.

The world of which the Alexandra Hotel was somehow a symbol didn't vanish that night, but it took a beating from which it can never now recover. Death duties and taxes were part of the answer, but the question goes deeper than that. If former chauffeur, Herbert Mills, the film stunt man, Albert Marotta, tobacconist Nat Williams were the kind of men needed to restore order from chaos, were the wealthy and educated really as omnipotent as they had always seemed? In any case, such men became increasingly conscious of their right to a place in the sun. May 10 marked a subtle turning point in Britain's drift toward a classless society.

The advantages of a good address were diminishing, too. Never again could Bartender Michael Gonley at the Ritz confidently serve dry martinis as the bombs were striking West Ham. The complaint received by one town clerk—that the scion of a noble house had been improperly sent to the mortuary in the Council's dust cart—would strike a sour note, too. The intercontinental ballistic missile, any more than the flying bomb or the V-1 rocket, is no respecter of persons or borough boundaries. Macaulay said "Moderation in war is imbecility," but the scientists had yet to make that supremely true.

The same would apply to those empty Belgravian mansions that Architect Arthur Butler and his fire party found so frustrating. A first-class ticket to a country retreat would seem a futile enough gesture in the nuclear age.

On the other hand, much that was good, if hopelessly chivalrous, vanished forever on May 10. Rescue Worker George Smith, lying for two hours in the ruins of a Battersea home to hold a woman's head; Police Constable Reginald Oakes walking the plank at the Alexandra; Mrs. Daley's pathetic vigil with the dying man; these were the gestures of the men and women who held the lives of others sacred, even when they themselves were under heavy bombardment. Today the same spirit of devotion could not, for obvious reasons, hold good, within the lethal 15-mile zone of nuclear attack.

What strikes one most forcibly in conjuring up that lost world is the loyalty that prevailed. The way Jimmie Sexton and his mates stuck doggedly to *their* factory; Alexandra Porter Frederick Willis coming back on duty to keep Andrew Verdie company; Yard Inspector Robert Bromley risking death by fire to find the correct channels for filing a damage report. The loyalties are there still, but somehow subtly confined; in a grimmer, more elemental world people would probably give pride of place to their families rather than their firms.

To one observer trudging the streets later that day it seemed that people had become newly possessed of an old emotion: cold, deadly anger. In Whitehall, walking north to Bloomsbury through Trafalgar Square, Quentin Reynolds saw it time and again—the tight-set lips, the glances of implacable hatred, men muttering over and over, "The dirty bastards." He recalled a line of Kipling's, "The English began to hate. . . ." and wondered what shape that hate would take if the bombers came back.

But they were not returning. Although no one then realized it, the all-clear crying through a sea of smoke this Sunday morning signaled more than the end of London's greatest air raid. On May 22 the whole of Feldmarschall Albert Kesselring's Air Fleet Two moved to Poznan. On June 22 the attack on Russia began from the Arctic to the Black Sea. There would be other raids on London but never one like this. The blitz was over.

But nobody knew this then or even later. A third of the Luftwaffe was left behind in France. Winston Churchill warned that the attacks might continue in force. The telecommunications branch of the General Post Office did some frantic costing: if they excavated tunnels 105 feet deep, below underground railway level, burying the telephone cables deeper, was it likely to break the banks?

And there was the problem set by Rudolf Hess. Many men, Winston Churchill among them, later showed a human tendency to be wise after the event: Hess was an obvious psychopath, no real store could be set by his visit. But there is no denying the electric excitement that was running through 10 Downing Street and Fighter Command in the days that followed.

Not that Hess's peace plans—a free hand for Britain in her own empire provided Germany had a free hand in Europe—were ever likely to have been accepted. The enigma boiled down to two questions: was Hess's self-portrait of a quixotic intermediary, a man sickened by the senseless slaughter of raids like May 10, a living likeness? Or was he the trusted emissary of a Hitler who felt secretly that Britain's war-waging potential stood higher than it really did? The answer to the riddle may never be known for certain, but the weight of opinion—Churchill's included—came down on the first score.

If so, the irony seems almost too bitter. The raid of May 10 had started as a whim. The methodical Sperrle planned it as well as a good tactician can when time is against him. Yet somehow on that night everything went against the City. If the moon hadn't been so bright; if the tide hadn't been so low; if the telephone cables and the water mains hadn't gone so fast; if the raid hadn't been so widespread as to defeat the Fire Service; if reinforcements had come quicker; if only more night fighters had been equipped with radar.

As it was, Sperrle had everything with him. In a reprisal raid to end all reprisal raids his bombers had wrought havoc. More than 50 per cent of all telephone trunk circuits, 60 per cent of all outgoing toll circuits were inoperative. Fourteen hospitals had been struck, a score of Fire Service and ambulance depots. The Port of London was already cut down to a quarter capacity; now four large docks and 24 river wharves were damaged, too.

Intelligence was slow to trickle in. For instance, the digest report presented to the Cabinet on May 21 cited only 147 water mains broken. The Metropolitan Water Board finally put the grand total at 605—the biggest of the entire blitz.

The picture of the air war also underwent some revisions. On Monday May 12 every newspaper, *The Times* included, announced 33 German bombers shot down: on the basis of this figure Quentin Reynolds gave it as his opinion that on this night Britain had won the war. As this news was going to press Fighter Command had already whittled the total to 28—19 to the day fighters, four to the night fighters, four to the anti-aircraft gunners, one to an intruder plane. Even so, there seemed grounds for optimism—almost one in ten shot down if 300 aircraft had been over.

It was a long time before anyone realized that Sperrle had launched more than five hundred bombers against the capital that night. Or the more disturbing fact that of this number he had lost few more than eight, with a further three damaged. For seven hours the Luftwaffe had hit London with everything they had, escaping virtually unmolested.

Certainly the RAF had made their claims in all good faith. But in the flaring excitement of combat it was often hard for the pilots to tell whether or not their hits were lethal. Or a pilot might report a bomber down at the precise moment that two independent Observer Corps posts were also reporting bombers down in slightly varying locations. It was thus all too easy for three bombers to be claimed where only one existed.

Nor could the damage be reckoned only in terms of lives lost and ancient monuments destroyed, the only yardstick that security would then permit. More relevantly, the raiders had knocked out 71 key points—at least half of them front-line factories like Peek Frean's (tank parts and ration packs), Siebe Gorman's (deep-sea breathing apparatus), Dean's Rag Books (Mae Wests for airmen), J. W. Shale of Stepney (Bailey Bridges). The railways had taken such a battering, as Winston Churchill announced later, that the through routes were not open again until June.

It was worse on the roads. Almost eight thousand streets—a third of greater London—were virtually impassable with rubble and coiled hose. At London Region Headquarters Deputy Administrator Officer Julian Simpson told a colleague who had just checked on: "If we get another like this tonight we shall have to call the troops in." His colleague was impressed and with reason: if troops were needed, the 44,000-strong civilian force who handled road repairs and debris clearance must be already swamped.

It was little wonder. In central London no east-west route lay open nearer than the Euston Road. South of the river every approach route was closed: a labor gang of 400 was working at the Elephant alone. Warden Arthur Moore, who despatched

200 homeless shelterers from the Guildhall to a nearby field kitchen, didn't see them again until dusk; the ten-minute walk and the lunch took them five hours to negotiate. It took Fire Watcher Claude Evans the same time to travel from Bishopsgate to Hove, Sussex—normally a ninety-minute journey. En route to Paddington Station the Reverend Cecil Curwen watched a taxi meter ticking up in silent dismay. A routine ten-minute journey had clocked up an hour's fare.

If the men at the top were slow to realize the implications, the men nearer to the people weren't. Late on the Sunday Southwark's Civil Defense chief, Alderman Leonard Styles, was one of many attending a top-level conference with Admiral Sir Edward Evans, joint regional commissioner, at the Imperial War Museum, South London. To the admiral's reassuring "Chin up, chaps," Styles had a short answer: "In my opinion, sir, two more nights of this and London will be at a standstill."

Styles was not talking emptily. The people of his own borough were among 155,000 families who on this Sunday were without water, gas, or electricity—and without water even the bakers were unable to work. As sixteen-year-old William Sherrington, grimy with his night's fire fighting, led his mother Sophie from the Elephant and Castle shelter she was one of many women who began suddenly to cry. There was a lovely joint of lamb at home and how she was going to cook it she didn't know....

Almost everywhere there was the same problem. People breakfasted how and where they could, thankful to be eating at all. In Diana Riviere's flat behind Westminster Abbey Diana and John Hodgkinson ate a pensive breakfast of bread and butter, honey, and cold milk. At Cloak Lane Police Station, City of London, Police Constable Thomas Farquharson and his mates settled for bread, cheese, and beer. If utensils were lacking, Londoners improvised. At St. Leonard's General Hospital, Shoreditch, Mrs. Rose Flaxman, the night cook, found all the teacups broken; she served up tea in kidney bowls from the operating theater. Temporary Fireman John French, in Upper

245

Thames Street, suddenly thought of that bonded warehouse where he had parleyed with the customs men. He went back, found some brandy intact, drank it from his tin hat.

But the greatest problem was not people but industry: even many factories that were totally unscathed lacked water, gas, and power to keep going. The Londoners weren't beaten in the same sense that they thought themselves defeated—but no city can survive long without the means of production. In December the Metropolitan Water Board had calculated that if the raids kept on at that peak the City would be waterless by February. On May 11 they revised their estimate: four more raids on this scale and the same crisis would be reached.

Taken with the slow attrition of the Battle of the Atlantic it makes a frightening picture. In that week only 92 colliers were signaled past Tilbury Dock; during the fortnight the totals dropped steadily. For all the public undertakings on which London depended—gas, transport, electricity, water—there was only six weeks' reserve of coal.

And out of this chaos a strange wickedness was arising. Heavy rescue men strolled into Edward Penrose-Fitzgerald's Kensington flat as he slept exhausted, stole a gold pencil and a torch. In Gracechurch Street, City of London, men calmly stepped through jagged plate glass and redressed themselves at a big outfitter's expense. Others looted a London County Council depot—there was a sudden strange rash of bogus park keepers and nurses. In Southwark looters stripped a public house of its entire stock, even stole the fittings from the firemen's hoses at the Elephant and sold those. In Wandsworth a blitzed school was shorn of planks and broken tables while the dust was still rising.

With many there seemed a strange, almost callous indifference to the sufferings of others. At the Elephant and Castle District Officer Thomas Goodman found a police inspector in despair; he could no longer control the vast crowds of ghouls swamping in from the suburbs. Near the Guildhall Miss Julie Boxhall was shocked to hear one woman hail another: "Oh,

come down here, there's nothing to see down there." By Hounsditch jokers ransacked an outfitters, carried off some wax
dummies of girls in one-piece bathing suits, arranged them in
the firemen's canvas dam. Many came dressed in their Sunday best, girls in gay cotton frocks and head scarves, youths in
natty blazers. In the City of London this holiday garb so in-
censed Warden Arthur Moore that he burst out, "The bastards
are wearing straw hats!"

In a locust swarm they descended on the cafés, demolishing
every bun and biscuit, draining the tea urns dry, chattering
nineteen to the dozen like picnickers. They choked the queues
for scarce busses and trams so effectively that many priority
workers found it impossible to get home. Others were luckier
with rationed petrol, and their car wheels cut the firemen's relay hoses to ribbons. Near the Elephant four young bucks hailed
a policeman from a car: "You're just the chap to tell us where
to see the sights." For three scorching minutes the policeman
let fly, then turned to Station Officer Ronald Thorn: "If that
takes the cape off my back, it was worth it."

The firemen had troubles enough of their own. At Lambeth
Headquarters Major Jackson was once more on the phone to
Chief Superintendent May. By 6.40 A.M. he had canceled all
officers' leave; now he wanted 1,000 relief firemen drafted in
by bus, five hundred pumps to stand by on the London borders.
Despite this he knew that if the Luftwaffe came again tonight,
the situation would be indescribable. The bulk of the fire fighting, with a ruptured water system, would fall on the relief
firemen's shoulders—yet few knew one street from another, let
alone the positioning of the hydrants.

Already they were taking over. At a blazing timber dump in
Stepney Fireman John H. Good had mixed feelings as the relief crew rolled up—scrupulously unrolling coils of scrubbed
white hose across the charred slime. Near St. Pancras Station a
fire engine turned up from Nottinghamshire with its brass
gleaming like a sunrise. Their chief explained the delay to

Warden Wilfred Avery: they had been up all night polishing the engine in honor of a London call.

There was much for them to do. Of the two thousand fires still charted, hundreds were out of control—a magnificent flare path for any bomber force that might come on the Sunday night. At 4.30 on the Sunday afternoon the Metropolitan Water Board reported the worst: in the Shoreditch and London Bridge areas more than a thousand acres of the City, they could provide no water at all. Later Jackson's deputy, Principal Officer Clement Kerr, admitted: "I shudder to think what would have happened if the Germans had returned."

For the men who had fought against such overwhelming odds were for the time being out of the fight. Station Officer James Ellis lay down on the floor fully clothed and slept. In Whitechapel Cyril Tobias chose a trestle table. Fireman Harry Weinstock reached his bunk but couldn't be bothered to shrug out of his sodden uniform.

As the German pilots' reports flooded in that Sunday morning Field Marshal Sperrle professed himself more than satisfied, and General Hans Jeschonnek concurred—"a brilliantly successful raid." The bulk of the national Press felt the same. The *12-Uhr Blatt* asked: "Do you want any more refreshments, Mr. Churchill?" *Volkischer Beobachter* was more to the point: "London is one single sea of flames."

But the final decision rested with Hitler—and Hitler's mind was on other things. The Russians had been a thorn in his flesh for too long, and to his aides it seemed that the defection of Hess rankled too deeply. In the Reich Chancellery at Berlin, whence he had returned in haste, Pilot Hans Bauer saw the Fuehrer accost Goering passionately: "He must have gone mad or he couldn't have done a thing like that to me . . . he's stabbed me in the back!" When Goering urged the continuance of the blitz rather than a Russian campaign for which neither troops nor planes might be adequate, Hitler broke in furiously. When Russia was beaten to her knees, then was the time to talk about England. . . .

Thus when the much-maligned Hans Schmidt's more detailed report arrived via Portugal six weeks later the die was already cast. The Luftwaffe were now irrevocably committed on the eastern front.

Again the irony is breathtaking. In one raid Sperrle had achieved almost everything that Hitler had always urged. He had wrought a havoc that followed by another week of such raids might have put London, the symbol of the civilized world's hopes, out for good and all. The fires his bombers lit were never conquered—rather did they smolder themselves out, so that not for eleven days were the last pumps withdrawn. Three weeks later many big mains were still unrepaired; the level of the vital Crouch Hill and Maiden Lane reservoirs had not reached normal.

And then—the bitterest irony of all—the Luftwaffe had to let the greatest opportunity of the blitz slide by. From start to finish the whole effort, the lives wasted on both sides, were in vain. Again Hitler's whim had prevailed. The raid had proved nothing at all.

All this still lay in the future. Meanwhile, there were no heroics, only an impassioned determination that Hitler should not interfere with the planned routine. The London Philharmonic's musicians turned up at the Queen's Hall, took a long look at the empty shell, and decided that the afternoon's concert must go on. They salvaged enough instruments from the still-dripping ruins to hold the concert at the Royal Academy of Music, with the doors left open for all those who could get pavement room only.

Thomas Sinden, the bridegroom-to-be, arrived at St. Helen's Church, Acton, to find things looking almost as unpromising. Beatrice, his bride, had had to send to Willesden, three miles away, for fresh carnations to make her pancake hat; next she had settled for toilet roll centers covered with silver paper to make tiers for the wedding cake; finally she had spent half an hour driving in a hired car round a church that was no longer there. But somehow, though the porch was all that remained, the vicar had managed to rig it up to look like a church in miniature. Despite Sinden's doubts and premonitions the wedding did take place.

Everywhere people were putting as brave a face on it as they could. Father George Coupe had been injured so badly at Poplar Hospital that his right leg would have to be amputated, but he consoled himself that now he would have more time for reading; from his bed in the London Hospital he ordered the complete works of Shakespeare. At the Royal Hospital, Chelsea, Captain Cecil Townsend, who looked after a section of the red-coated pensioners, found that flying metal from an incendiary had scored deep into his instep, took comfort that it had at least burned out a particularly vexing corn.

It seemed to be tacitly understood that no one must make a fuss. "What a game, eh?" the bus drivers shouted as they passed each other north of the city. "We're in a pretty pickle, aren't we?" Dr. Anthony Feiling, driving in from West Middlesex Hospital and anxious for his wife's safety, found Jane, the family maid of all work, faintly disapproving of his hasty arrival. She asked, "What have you come home for, sir? There haven't been any telephone messages."

Yet many had nothing left at all but the clothes they stood up in. In Lewisham the council could only fix up the bombed-out Patrick St. Aubyn with a woman's peach-colored pajama top with a green collar. Near Westminster Bridge the Chicago *Tribune's* Larry Rue saw a girl wearing only pajamas and a mink coat. Canon Roger Berry of Westminster Abbey went off to preach in a sports coat and dirty flannels—everything else had gone. To some appearances mattered more than to others. Assistant Matron Olive Sales left Poplar Hospital thick with mortar dust but a sister was adamant about making her up a fresh starched cap.

In fact, nobody was putting on an act; to them these were the natural things to do. City of London chemist, W. G. Harries, served lipsticks and aspirins ankle deep in a thick sludge of tooth powder, water, and zinc oxide. General Josepha Hallera left the ruins of the Alexandra for Mass at the Polish Church, marveled to see a totally-blitzed newspaper kiosk draped with a blanket labeled "Business as Usual." Nor were the usual courtesies neglected in this time of stress. Rear Admiral Bennett at the Stanhope Court Hotel had three baths to sluice away the plaster dust, then went straight to apologize for the state of the bathroom.

It was the same with Jimmie Sexton, trudging wearily through blasted streets with his small attaché case. He wasn't surprised to meet his father taking his morning walk near the Oval Underground Station. The old man had taken that morning walk every Sunday for fifty years; the strange thing would have been to find him missing. As his father asked casually, "Hullo, boy, what's happened?" the conversation seemed everyday, too.

"Fields' has gone, Dad."

"I thought it had. I said to the gels, 'That could be Fields,' that fire by Waterloo.' "

"It was and all."

"Then how have you lived, boy?" old Mr. Sexton asked, and Jimmie Sexton could only think to reply, "I don't know, Dad—but here I am."

For millions it was the sense of duty that prevailed above all else. Charles Mattock was back at the Alexandra Hotel, by Herbert Mills' side. He was still sick and shaken, plaster dust coated his royal-blue livery. But he even contrived a little joke when Chef Theo Kummer reported for duty. The bewildered man asked what had happened, and Mattock recalled a conversation a lifetime ago when he and Dearlove and Willis and Mr. Verdie had been drinking tea in the hall. He answered, "I don't know, but our dinners are still under the grill."

And where else could Mattock be at a time like this? He was the only man alive now who had known the habits of the guests—their little idiosyncrasies, in just which corner of the hotel the rescuers should search for them. A good servant to them while they lived, Mattock could still be of use to them in death, too.

Mills stayed on until it was plain that what remained of the Alexandra would rest precariously intact so long as the rescue work continued. And by midmorning it was plain that every living soul had been rescued from the hotel, even the woman who had cried so piteously though she died soon after. Only the twenty-four who had been killed outright still lay crushed among the rubble. But Mills worked patiently on—even persuaded the rescue men, at a woman's urgent request, to salvage a pair of corsets from an upper room. To his surprise she called back to present him with a bottle of whisky.

Others, the leaders or led, stayed patiently on, doing their best. A. J. Burgoyne's fire-watching squad sat patiently on the rubble in Fenchurch Street, City of London, waiting for the next squad to relieve them. The building had burned right down to the ground, but it seemed only proper to stay. Chief Warden William Coyne sat sleepily in the Jacob's Well public house, Shoreditch, a pint of beer in his right hand, his left hand jetting a stirrup pump on to a small fire outside the window. District Officer William Cesana was fighting the Waterloo vaults fire the same way—munching ham sandwiches with the hose propped on a branch holder. The heat was so intense that the melting fat trickled slowly down his wrists.

To most the pressing need was for sleep. Mrs. Margaret Daley had taken a bath, carefully cleansed the filth from her uniform and from her body. As she sank exhausted into bed she could not banish the memory of the dying man from her brain. It was momentarily hard to reconcile with her faith. Then, quite simply, it came to her. She had prayed to God to protect her and those at her depot. And God had not only protected them again but had guided her to where she had been most needed, as a man had been guided long ago on the road to Jericho. It was as simple as that.

Herbert Mills went back to the post in Belgrave Square. Reverently he uncorked the precious bottle of whisky and poured a tot for himself and Nat Williams. Only a small tot, but within twenty minutes he was as dead to the world as a youngster taking his first unwary nip. The whisky and the fatigue had done their work.

Pilot Officer Andrew Humphrey also slept—the blissful sleep of a young man after a healthy night's exercise. The interrogation had been a bore, but the beer and the bacon and eggs had gone down well. Miles away Hauptmann Albert Hufenreuter also slept, the uneasy sleep of the drugged. He dreamed that he was spreadeagled on a relief map of England and was trying to dive off it, to swim across the Channel to France. But something held his leg in chancery; a swarm of German fighters hovered, trying to rescue him, then British fighters swooped in and drove them away. He woke up, drenched with sweat, the pain in his broken leg stabbingly alive.

Marguerita Stahli lay drowsily in a clean white ward at Epsom Hospital. They had given her a sedative, and the first tearing pain of grief was dying away, leaving her numb and spent. She tried hard not to think of Windsor or Rex but of more pleasant things, and found herself remembering Jim Norman's smile as he sat beside the bed earlier on. There was a quiet strength in it that somehow reminded her of Windsor— kind, yet firm, a man who would not let you down. She wondered why she had never noticed it quite like this before.

Outside, the death pall of smoke still lay over London, motionless and threatening, but *here* there was only the warm air, the green lawns bright with daffodils, the liquid sound of bird song. The afternoon sunlight flooded the wide windows of the ward and Marguerita Stahli slept.

FACTS ABOUT MAY 10–11

THIS book is the story of a few people on the night when the fate of their city hung in the balance. Not the whole story, for that is beyond one man's power to tell; it does not present all of the facts or anywhere near all of the facts. Few of the 6,000,000 Londoners who lived through this fateful night noticed the peak points of the raid's intensity—between 12.30 and 1.15 A.M. and between 3.00 and 4.30—as phased by the Ministry of Home Security. They were too frightened, too angry, or too stunned by the cataclysm—or too busy to notice the passage of time. So such a night is not the best climate for pinning down what happened when—and since no other raid ever provoked such controversy, even the basic statistics must be accepted with caution.

Bearing those points in mind, here is an attempt to answer some fundamental questions:

> *How many bombers did the Germans send?* The original Home Security Appreciation of May 18 estimated 320 over the target—about 30 believed to have made a double sortie. T. H. O'Brien's *Civil Defence* (History of the Second World War, UK, Civil Series) shows 550 aircraft involved. But there seems no reason to doubt the official German records, which show that of 541 bombers slated to fly, 505 reached the target—358 on the first sortie, 147 on the second. Other planes developed technical faults, returned after fighter interceptions, or were shot down.

What was the tonnage of bombs dropped? O'Brien estimates 440 tons of high explosive plus many parachute mines and large numbers of incendiaries. German totals are far higher, showing 708 tons in all—498 tons of high explosive (including naval mines) dropped on the first sortie alone, 210 (again with mines) on the second. On both sorties they loosed, in all, 86 tons of incendiaries. Of the mines and high explosives, 167 failed to explode.

How many bombers were lost? Paradoxically, German figures show 14 lost—higher than the revised British estimate of 8 destroyed, 3 damaged. The German figure seems reasonable: 14 did not return to base and were presumably written off by British action. The RAF lost only one Beaufighter, which crashed on landing.

What were the casualties? Approximately 1,436 people were killed and 1,800 seriously injured—close to the total of fatalities in the San Francisco earthquake of 1906 and a greater total of fatal casualties than on any other London raid. And the first total, compiled from the Register of Civilian War Dead, does not include those seriously injured who later died as a result. Of those killed only 20 were under cover in an approved public shelter.

How many fires were started? A tally of London Fire Brigade records agrees with O'Brien's estimate—nearly 2,200. Of these 9 were eventually reclassified as conflagrations, 20 as major fires (rating over 30 pumps), 37 as serious (up to 30 pumps), 210 as medium (up to 10 pumps). Records show they consumed some 700 acres—one and a half times the area damaged by the Great Fire of 1666, though spread over a wider area.

What time did various incidents happen? Everybody agrees that the first bombs dropped, simultaneously to the sounding of the siren, on the barge *Fraser* at the Royal Albert Dock; the last bomb on Scotland Yard at 5.37 A.M. But in between there is much discrepancy. Every time given in the text follows an entry in an existing log, but in the midst of such strife an hour could elapse before an incident was definitely logged. For instance, many firemen who gallantly fought the Elephant blaze put the peak of the conflagration at about 9:30 P.M. on the Saturday night—ninety minutes before the siren had even sounded, two hours before the fire in question, a good five hours before some of them had arrived on the scene.

The time phases indicated at the head of each chapter should be taken as a rough guide only. Inevitably some incidents began earlier and finished later than the compass of that chapter.

What did people say? There are no imaginary conversations in this book. Such dialogue as is quoted is the genuine endeavor of one or more individuals to reconstruct the conversation as he or she remembers it. Here, too, there is margin for error: witness the unimpeachable but widely diverse accounts of what was said by whom at the time of Rudolf Hess's arrival.

What was the damage done? Aside from the mammoth-scale strategic damage referred to in the text, and the damage done by fires, high explosives and naval mines demolished some 5,500 houses, damaged another 5,500 beyond ordinary repair, rendered 12,000 people homeless. These figures are based on feeding and shelter station returns and necessarily cannot include those who found sanctuary with friends or relatives.

The sterling value of the total damage is almost incalculable, but a few random figures give pointers: the City of London, approximately £800,000; Westminster Abbey, £135,000; Waterloo Station, £30,000 worth of goods; Scotland Yard, £22,000. On the final figure, probably even £20,000,000, by 1941 values, is a modest estimate—double the damage caused by the Great Fire of 1666.

Like so much else concerning May 10 that final figure may never be known for certain. Some historians have agreed, some have disagreed violently, on almost every one of the points discussed above. While some are irreconcilable, a writer can only, to the best of his ability, try to weigh the evidence and give his own opinion on the others. In the end only one thing remains certain: no mortal man will ever know the full truth of all that happened on the incredible night when London burned.

ACKNOWLEDGMENTS

"THERE never was a raid like it," Reg Matthews reminisces. "Another one like that and they'd have had us on our backs." Mr. Matthews should know. As a General Post Office telecommunications engineer he fought back at the Luftwaffe through all of them: the docks raid of September 7; the City fire raid of December 29; the two great April raids.

But no—it is May 10, even at this distance of time, that remains branded forever on his mind. The Bride Street subway, with its eighty-three main cables gone and all the westward trunk routes; the Queen Victoria Street subway; all the cables in Westminster Bridge Road; the Great Dover Street cable, the one link with the Dover defenses. Long in retirement, Mr. Matthews had journeyed to London on a graying afternoon to share with me his memories of that night.

Everyone who had a part in it showed a similar spirit. Cabinet ministers, air chiefs, fire officers, wardens, dock laborers—596 people in all—gave their unstinted help toward the compiling of this narrative.

Many of them, in an effort to help me recapture how it felt, yielded much more than one still-lucid memory. For instance, young Mr. James Verdie relates how, weeks after the Alexandra Hotel tragedy, he salvaged his father's copy of the trade diary their firm produced. A sentimental souvenir, yet what sent a shiver of horror through him was that the page for May 10 stood blank, innocent not only of entries but of any print whatsoever, even the date. In time he called in every other copy of the diary he could lay hands on. And all were as the printer would have wished them. Only his father's copy contained that blank.

Acknowledgments

The raid seems to have gathered to it that same supernatural aura that surrounds all the great events of history. The strange incidence of the moon worshipers at York Terrace and Dr. Mawby Cole's prophecy; and the unidentified officers at the Alexandra; the belief among many people that the dead did walk that night; the almost unique configuration of all the planets and the uncanny part that coincidence played all through; the warnings which so many chose to ignore. Even the uncanny arrival of Rudolf Hess had figured in the dreams of a Yorkshire dairy farmer, Ernest Almond, on April 28, was broadcast to impartial witnesses. So this, too, was foreseen.

You feel the haunting quality of the time when Jimmie Sexton, now reunited with his family in London's dockland, tells how, on the Monday morning, crowds of men stood silent and weeping outside Fields' factory; when Stanley Barlow, today a fully-fledged accountant and married to Eileen Sloane, shows the livid scars that the fires of the synagogue imprinted on his flesh; when Mrs. James Norman (then Marguerita Stahli) speaks of the hour she became resigned to dying. Heard in the peace of a Kentish cottage, the story has a strange power to take you back to the horror of that night, to its glory and its agony.

Superficially, the raid seems to have touched these people hardly at all—neither their homes nor their way of life. Once more a chauffeur, Herbert Mills thumbs over his stained incident officer's notebook in a mews flat not a stone's throw from where the Alexandra Hotel frowned above the spring flowers in Hyde Park. Mrs. Margaret Daley, still working as a waitress in Croydon, has walked times without number on the street where she once gave succor to a man whose name she has never known. Yet the changes are there. In the first place, even the youngest of these people seem more vigorous, more alert than their contemporaries. In the second place, they have taken pains far beyond anything that I had a right to expect. After passing through the valley of the shadow, they seem to have emerged with a truly Christian desire to help others.

For without their aid the book could not have been written at all. Its planning, really a minor military operation, involved more than

Acknowledgments

fifteen thousand miles of travel, not only in London, the heart of the story, but to seventy towns in Great Britain and Germany. The testimony of 470 eyewitnesses—more than seven million notes of words and reports—was the raw material from which it was fashioned.

Many contributed more than a personal narrative; they freely loaned personal papers that proved invaluable. In this respect I particularly thank Chief Officer Geoffrey Blackstone, Hertfordshire Fire Brigade, for his contemporary reports on the Elephant and Waterloo fires; Sir Arthur Dixon for a summary of the night's fire situation; Claude Evans; John H. Good; Harry Greenfield, for the stationmaster's diary, Waterloo; John Hodgkinson, for a letter written to his father following the raid; Mass Observation, Ltd., especially Leonard England, for a host of contemporary diaries; Chief Officer Charles Tharby for the log of West Ham Fire Brigade.

The families of many no longer living have been equally helpful. To Peter Bathurst, Mrs. Gladys Henley, Stanley Murdoch, Wing Commander J. Darlay Pyne, Miss E. M. Tweed, James C. Verdie, and Mrs. Nora Willoughby go my heartfelt thanks for their cooperation in what must sometimes have been a painful task.

Nor can I easily express my gratitude to the officials of the twenty-nine Metropolitan boroughs of London and the outer London corporations. Many not only arranged for me to inspect original logs and incident messages, they themselves spent precious time tracking down survivors. The time and patience devoted to this end by Sam Shutt (Bermondsey), Colonel F. C. Lorden (Croydon), Arthur Moore (City of London), S. A. Hamilton (Poplar), E. J. Pitt (Southwark), and Sidney Bennett (Westminster) saved me more hours than I like to compute.

The other authorities have been equally cooperative. Among those who made available records of paramount importance I have to thank: Mr. E. C. Baker, chief archivist to the GPO; Chief Officer Frederick W. Delve and Miss Margaret Winsor for the records of the London Fire Brigade; Mr. E. R. Hambrook and Miss Irene Darlington, London County Council, for the London Civil Defense

Acknowledgments

Region Branch Intelligence Reports that form the hard core of this book; Mr. C. D. Shaw of the BBC Secretariat, for detailed summaries of every program then broadcast; Colonel Arthur Young and Superintendent Shannon for the records of the City of London police.

The RAF were invariably helpful not only in making records accessible, but in answering endless supplementary queries. My particular thanks go to Mr. L. A. Jackets, chief of the Air Historical Branch, Air Ministry; to Group Captain Tom Gleave; and, for helpful narrative accounts of the night in question, to His Grace the Duke of Hamilton, Lord Douglas of Kirtleside, Air Chief Marshal Sir Thomas Pike, Air Commodore Pat Jameson, Air Commodore Whitney Straight, and Group Captain Andrew Humphrey.

Many people went to untold trouble to suggest sources or to provide background material that would put the raid in better perspective. Some by degrees evolved into my experts on a given subject and found their kindness shamelessly abused. In particular I recall fruitful afternoons spent discussing London's gas supply with Sterling Everard; the kindness of Lieutenant Commander John Fordham, chief officer, Kent Fire Brigade, in relating the facts which sparked off the National Fire Service; an intriguing tour of the Palace of Westminster with Victor Goodman. Others to whom I shall always remain indebted are Mr. George Bennison; M. R. James of the Metropolitan Water Board; Observer Commander F. W. Mitchell and Observer Lieutenant A. J. Lardner for their help on the Royal Observer Corps; C. F. Tomlinson of the Port of London Authority; H. M. Turner, regional controller, London Telecommunications Region. Above all to Wing Commander Bob Wright and Squadron Leader "Jimmy" Rawnsley for more help on all aspects of the RAF than can ever be detailed here.

Some of my new-found friends arranged for me to have discussions with those who had studied the subject at firsthand; of inestimable value from this aspect were my meetings with the Right Honorable Herbert Morrison, the Honorable Sir Arthur Howard, Commander Sir Aylmer Firebrace, and Major T. H. O'Brien.

Acknowledgments

I must stress that none of the people acknowledged thus far necessarily agree with all—or in some cases with any—of my conclusions. For the views expressed or implicit in the course of the narrative, for any errors that may have crept in, I alone am responsible.

The various information and public-relations officers have worked like beavers to insure that the errors should be few. C. Conway-Gordon of London Telecommunications Region; Peter Coomb of the Savoy Hotel; Percy H. Fearnley of the Metropolitan Police Division, New Scotland Yard; F. D. Faulkner and M. B. James, respectively, of British Railways' Southern and Eastern divisions; A. Fowler Kearton and Christopher Moyle at the Home Office; Harold Wilson of Cable and Wireless; all helped the wheels of research to turn more smoothly. W. J. Coles proved that even in his eighties he can still locate every man who ever served with the London Fire Brigade.

In Germany I had not only matchless cooperation on all sides but full access to the little-explored records of the Luftwaffen-akademie, Hamburg. General Paul Deichmann, Colonel Greffrath, General the Baron von Falkenstein, General Alexander Holle, Major Fischer, Colonel von Grauert, Leutnant Colonel Hans von Ploetz, and Rolf Künkel—none of their kindness and hospitality has been forgotten. The former air crews, though facing no easy task in being interrogated by an inquisitive foreigner, weighed in handsomely with narrative accounts. Readers who followed their stories may be interested to know that Albert Hufenreuter is now a schoolmaster teaching English in Hamburg, while Martin Reiser is once more back in the bar restaurant business in Westphalia. And the Baron Von Siber now runs an electrical business in Salzburg, Austria.

Thanks to wartime security, printed contemporary accounts of the raid are harder to find—though this blitz, in large, has been written about more often than any other. On detailed anecdotal coverage the London *Times* far outstripped the others, although the American press had some telling points—notably Robert P. Post's account in the New York *Times*, Larry Rue's despatch in the

Acknowledgments

Chicago *Tribune*, Eddie Gilmore's report in the New York *Herald Tribune*.

Inevitably most published accounts saw the raid from local viewpoints. The best is unquestionably Quentin Reynolds' fine account in *Only the Stars Are Neutral* (Cassell/Random House, 1942), and I am grateful to him for answering more questions than any reporter should expect to answer after a job so thorough. Other accounts saw the raid from Hackney (Reginald Bell's *The Bulls-eye*, Cassell, 1943), the Temple (Alexander Werth's account in *The Saturday Book*, Hutchinson, 1943), the Strand (Ben Robertson's *I Saw England*, Jarrolds /Knopf, 1941). And many privately printed histories offered valuable clues. A. H. Pullin's *The History of Reporting Post 12, Southwark*, for the Elephant; E. H. Warmington's *History of Birkbeck College in the Second World War*; J. F. McCartney's typescript account in *Unilever House at War*; Dr. P. J. Watkin's Lambeth Hospital: *Fifty Years in Retrospect*; Volume XV of *The British Museum Quarterly*. Aside from William Sansom's *Westminster in War* (Faber and Faber, 1947), incomparably the best study, local histories are all too few. But there are useful hints for Stepney in F. R. Lewey's *Cockney Campaign* (Stanley Paul, 1947) and in W. H. Berwick-Sayers' *Croydon and the Second World War* (Croydon Corporation, 1947).

Many important clues came from specialist publications and periodicals. Charles Graves' *London Transport Carried On* (London Passenger Transport Board, 1947), the same author's *The Thin Red Lines* (Standard Art Book Co., 1946), and Bernard Darwin's *War on the Line* (Southern Railway, 1946) were all of much use. Geoffrey Blackstone's *History of the British Fire Service* (Routledge, 1957) reoriented most of my previous ideas on the subject. And there were rewarding gems to be found in John D. McLauchlan's article "Poplar Hospital in War-Time" (in the *Medical Press and Circular* for October 6, 1943); in E. C. Baker's contribution to the *Post Office Electrical Engineers' Journal* for October 1942; in John McGeorge's study of the last night of Electra House, Moorgate, in *The Zodiac* of June 1944; above all in the files of *Fire: The Official Journal of the British Fire Service*. My special thanks go

Acknowledgments

to Editor Harry Klopper for what resolved itself into a long-term loan of the back numbers for the period.

Readers seeking a final answer to the riddle of Rudolf Hess will find facts to tickle their fancy in Sir Winston Churchill's *The Second World War, Vol. III, The Grand Alliance* (Cassell, 1950), as well as in T. E. Winslow's *Forewarned Is Forearmed* (William Hodge, 1947), Hans Baur's *Hitler's Pilot* (Muller, 1958) and General Adolph Galland's *The First and the Last* (Methuen, 1955/ Holt, 1954).

Finally the loyalty and pertinacity of the research team who worked alongside throughout deserve special mention. Cynthia Walker did an unparalleled job of research across the length and breadth of the British Isles. Invaluable, too, was the persistent delving of Bryan and Joan Morgan, Diana Riviere, Caitriona Mac-Donald, Michael Brampton, and, above all, of my wife, who not only researched it and typed it but endured a two years' marital monologue on the subject with the serenity of temperament which enabled her, off-duty in the heart of London, to sleep undisturbed through the pandemonium of May 10.

THE EYEWITNESSES

The 470 men and women listed below contributed untold help in the preparation of this work—through furnishing specially written accounts, through the loan of contemporary letters and diaries, or by patiently submitting themselves to a detailed question-and-answer interview. To avoid confusion the ranks and in some cases the names given are those which then pertained, followed by the vantage point from which he or she saw the raid.

District Officer Frederick Abbott, LFS, *Hounsditch*.
Bernard Abrahams, *St. Marylebone*.
District Officer Bill Absalom, LFS, *Baker Street*.
Superintendent George Adams, LFS, *Elephant and Castle*.
Squadron Leader Russell Aitken, RAF. *No. 3 Squadron, Martlesham, Suffolk*.
M. Abel Alban, *Westminster: Savoy Hotel*.
John D. Allen, *Camberwell*.
Chief Superintendent Joe Ansell, LFS, *Holborn—City of London, Queen Victoria Street*.
Signalman Ernest Archer, *Liverpool Street Station*.
Miss Patricia Arden, *St. Marylebone*.
Denis Argent, *Tonbridge, Kent*.
Miss Doris Arnold, *Kensington*.
Miss Mabel Ash, *Ealing*.
Freddie Aspinall, *Westminster: Mayfair Hotel*.
Arrivals Inspector John Atkinson, *Euston Station*.
Miss E. J. Ausden, *Watford, Herts*.
Wilfred Avery, *St. Pancras*.
Nat Ayer, *Westminster, Pimlico*.
District Officer William Ayres, *LFS, Whitechapel*.

The Eyewitnesses

William Baddeley, *Cuddesdon, Oxford.*
Leonard Baer, *Paddington.*
Thomas W. Baillie, *Kensington.*
District Officer Edward Baker, LFS, *St. Pancras—Soho.*
Frederick R. Baker, *Deptford.*
Edward Ball, *Westminster, Palladium Theatre.*
Josh Barham, *Elephant and Castle.*
R. W. "Bill" Barker, *West Ham.*
Stanley M. Barlow, *St. Marylebone.*
Superintendent Sidney Barnes, LFS, *Whitechapel.*
Alfred Bartlett, *Bermondsey; Peek Frean's Factory.*
Booking Clerk Sidney Baulk, *King's Cross Station.*
Ralph Bayne, *Croydon.*
Ernest Bedford, *Stoke Newington.*
Station Officer Bernard Belderson, LFS, *Millwall Docks.*
Reginald Bell, *Hackney, HQ Group 3, London Region.*
Paymaster Dennis E. Belton, *East Ham.*
Rear Admiral Martin Bennett, *Westminster: Alexandra Hotel.*
Sidney Bennett, *Westminster: Alexandra Hotel.*
Superintendent George Bennison, LFS, *Baker St.—House of Commons—*
    Ebury St.
Dr. Richard Bentley, *Kennington, Kent.*
Thomas R. Berg, *Westminster.*
Jack Bickle, *Chelsea: St. Luke's Hospital.*
Reverend John G. Birch, *Stepney.*
Chief Superintendent Frank Bitten, LFS, *City of London: Mark Lane.*
Assistant Divisional Officer Geoffrey V. Blackstone. LFS, *Elephant*
    and Castle—Waterloo.
Jack Blaine, *St. Pancras.*
George Blake, *Bermondsey: Town Hall.*
Joe Blake, *Bermondsey: Town Hall.*
Charles T. Boothby, *Camberwell.*
Basil Parkinson Bothamley, *City of London: the Temple.*
District Officer Victor Botten, LFS, *Baker Street.*
Station Officer Sydney Boulter, *Elephant and Castle.*
Miss Julie Boxall, *City of London: Gresham Street.*
Chief Inspector Tom Breaks, Home Office Fire Inspectorate, *Tottenham*
    Court Road.
Stationmaster James Bridger, *Victoria Station.*
Frederick R. Bristow, *Bethnal Green.*
Harold Brockman, *St. Paul's Cathedral.*
Oberleutnant Max Brodemeier, Luftwaffe, *K.G. 41st Flying Corps.*

The Eyewitnesses

Yard Inspector Robert Bromley, *City of London: Bishopsgate Goods Depot.*

Peter F. Bromwich, *Maida Vale.*

Sidney P. Brook, *City of London: Electra House, Moorgate.*

Miss Kathleen Brooks, *Knightsbridge.*

Mr. Shirley Brooks, *Paddington.*

Miss Diana Brown, *Shoreditch.*

Oberleutnant Hugo Buchs, Luftwaffe, *HQ K.G.* 77, *Laon, France.*

Station Officer Walter Bunday, *LFS, Camberwell.*

A. J. Burgoyne, *City of London: Fenchurch Street.*

Thomas J. Burling, *City of London: Fenchurch Street.*

J. W. A. Burness, *Paddington.*

Arthur Stuart Butler, *Westminster: Belgravia.*

Mrs. Sakunthala Butler, *Kensington.*

T. Blake Butler, *Westminster: Alexandra Hotel.*

Reverend Jimmy Butterworth, *Camberwell: Clubland.*

Arthur Caldwell, *Bethnal Green.*

Mrs. Maisie Capel, *Lambeth: Brixton Hill.*

Major Arthur Carr, Salvation Army, *City of London: Queen Victoria Street.*

Mrs. Henrietta Cartwright, *Dulwich.*

Herbert Cartwright, *Dulwich.*

Mrs. Phyllis Catt, *Croydon.*

Arthur Chandler, *Stepney.*

Chief Superintendent Sidney Charters, LFS, *London Bridge—Queen Victoria Street.*

David Cherry, *Hammersmith.*

Mrs. Doris Chase, *Bethnal Green.*

Sub Officer Sam Cheveau, LFS, *Bethnal Green—City of London: London Wall.*

Ernest Christensen, *St. Marylebone: Queen's Hall.*

Auxiliary Fireman Charlie Chrysler, *City of London: the Temple.*

W. S. Churchill, *Baker Street.*

Albert Churchman, *Deptford.*

H. Dixon Clark, *Islington.*

Mrs. Edna Clarke, *Hammersmith.*

Godfrey Clarke, *Paddington.*

William Clarke, *West Ham.*

Alvah Clatworthy, *City of London: Friday Street.*

Walter Clayton, *Elephant and Castle.*

Mrs. Mary Cohen, *City of London: Old Bailey.*

The Eyewitnesses

H. A. Cole, *St. Pancras.*
Rob Connell, *Islington.*
John Connolly, *Stepney.*
Edward W. Cook, *Battersea.*
Yard Inspector Alf Cooke, *St. Pancras Station.*
Herbert Cookson, *Wandsworth.*
Douglas Copp, *Elephant and Castle.*
Auxiliary Fireman Robert Coram, *Elephant and Castle.*
Miss June Cory, *Hendon.*
Station Officer Norman Cottee, LFS, *Elephant and Castle.*
Joe Cotter, *Poplar.*
Leading Fireman Joe Cotterell, LFS, *City of London: Fleet Street.*
Third Officer George Cotton, *Letchworth, Herts, Fire Brigade.*
Father George Coupe, *Poplar Hospital.*
Chief Warden William Coyne, *Shoreditch.*
Station Officer George Cramp, LFS, *City of London: Faraday Building.*
Lieut. Frank G. Creswell, *London River, H.M.S. Tower.*
Major Charlie Creswick-Atkinson, *Stoke Newington.*
Miss Dorothie Crombie, *Camberwell.*
Rev. Cecil Curwen, *Southwark: Old Kent Road.*

Mrs. Margaret Daley, *South Croydon.*
Chief Superintendent Frank Dann, LFS, *Elephant and Castle.*
Superintendent Henry G. Davies, LFS, *Westminster Abbey / St. Paul's.*
Station Officer Charles Davis, LFS, *St. Thomas's Hospital.*
Jack Davis, *Westminster: Leicester Square.*
John Davis, *Deptford.*
General Paul Deichmann, Luftwaffe, *HQ II Flying Corps, Ghent.*
Auxiliary Fireman Paul Dessau, LFS, *Elephant and Castle.*
Squadron Leader Howson Devitt, RAF, *GCI Station, Durrington, Sussex.*
Miss Maisie Dickens, *Stoke Newington.*
Police Constable John Dickie, *Westminster: Hyde Park.*
Herbert Dines, *Deptford.*
Booking Clerk Aubrey Dodge, *Chadwell Heath Railway Station.*
Walter Donaldson, *Holborn.*
Miss Helen J. Donovan, *Islington: City Road.*
Air Marshal Sholto Douglas, RAF, AOC-in-C., *HQ Fighter Command.*
John Dovaston, *St. Marylebone.*

District Officer George Earl, LFS, *Lambeth: Fields' Factory.*

The Eyewitnesses

Chief Officer Herbert Eaton, Chigwell Fire Brigade, *City of London: St. Paul's.*

Miss Florence Edwards, *Royal Victoria Docks.*

Richard Edwards, *Southwark Control.*

Porter William Eggins, *Chelsea: St. Luke's Hospital.*

George Eiffel, *Finsbury: Holford Square.*

Station Officer James Ellis, LFS, *City of London: Mark Lane.*

Miss Angela Elliston, *Westminster Control.*

Alfred Elms, *Bermondsey: Peek Frean's Factory.*

Acting Arrivals Foreman Jack Emberton, *Euston Station.*

Dr. Edward M. Ensor, *Westminster: St. George's Hospital/Alexandra Hotel.*

Claude Evans, *City of London: Bishopsgate.*

George Evans, *Chelsea.*

Goods Guard William Everett, *West Ham, Temple Mills Sidings.*

Flight Lieutenant Jack Evers, *HQ Fighter Command: Filter Room.*

Police Constable Thomas Farquharson, *City of London: Old Jewry.*

Arthur Fayers, *St. Marylebone.*

Percy H. Fearnley, *Westminster: War Office.*

E. P. Featherstone, *Elephant and Castle.*

Mrs. Helga Feiling, *St. Marylebone.*

Miss Marjorie Felton, *St. Marylebone: Queen's Hall.*

Miss Elsie Ferguson, *Westminster Control.*

Albert Fey, *Lambeth: Fields' Factory.*

Feldwebel Josef Fischer, Luftwaffe: *No. 3 Wing, 53 Group.*

Eric John Fisher, *Bermondsey Town Hall.*

Sub Inspector R. A. Fisher, *City of London: Queen Victoria Street.*

Miss Ann Flax, *Golders Green.*

Mrs. Rose Flaxman, *Shoreditch: St. Leonard's Hospital.*

Miss Carissima Fontaine, *Hampstead.*

Police Sergeant Andrew Forbes, *Westminster: House of Commons.*

The Rev. Hubert Ford, *Stepney.*

Lieutenant Commander John H. Fordham, LFS, *Elephant and Castle/Waterloo Station.*

Sir John Forsdyke, *British Museum.*

Harry Frazer, *Hackney.*

Sydney J. Freeman, *Lewisham.*

Temporary Fireman John French, LFS, *City of London: Upper Thames Street.*

Unteroffizier Karl Frey, Luftwaffe, *No. 1 Wing, 28 Group.*

The Eyewitnesses

Terence Fuller, *Westminster, Pimlico.*

Bill Fulton, *Finsbury.*

Oberleutnant Adolph Galland, Luftwaffe: *No. 26 Fighter Group, St. Omer.*

Observer Stanley Gardner, Royal Observer Corps, *Orrington, Kent.*

Ben Garman, *Stepney.*

Station Officer Albert Garrod, LFS, *Clerkenwell.*

Sydney Garvey, *Chelsea.*

E. Willoughby Gee, *South Croydon.*

Sub Officer Charles Gibbs, LFS, *Birmingham/Holborn: Theobalds Road.*

Percy F. Gillam, *Camberwell.*

Joe Gilmore, *Westminster: Berkeley Hotel.*

Edward Glading, *Chelsea: St. Luke's Hospital.*

Edward J. Goddard, *Lewisham.*

Police Sergeant Reginald Goldsmith, *City of London: St. Paul's.*

Michael Gonley, *Westminster, Ritz Bar.*

Fireman John H. Good, LFS, *Stepney.*

Station Officer George Goodman, LFS, *Westminster, Knightsbridge.*

District Officer Thomas Goodman, *Elephant and Castle/Waterloo Station.*

Victor Goodman, Chief Civil Defense Officer, *Westminster: House of Commons.*

David Grant, *Shoreditch.*

Walter Greaves, *Goswell Road: Gordon's Gin Distillery.*

Stationmaster Harry Greenfield, *Waterloo Station.*

Jim Gray, *St. Marylebone.*

Auxiliary Fireman Bill Grisley, LFS, *City of London: the Temple.*

George Groom, *City of London, Cheapside.*

Dr. Calvert M. Gwillim, *Westminster: St. George's Hospital.*

District Officer Walter Hall, LFS, *Holborn/City of London: Queen Victoria Street.*

General Josepha Hallera, *Westminster: Alexandra Hotel.*

Superintendent George Halley, LFS, *Elephant and Castle.*

Miss K. Halpin, *Westminster: Tothill Street.*

Group Captain, the Duke of Hamilton, RAF, *No. 13 Group, Turnhouse Sector, Scotland.*

A. Bertie Hancock, *City of London: Unilever House.*

Ranald Handfield-Jones, *Paddington, St. Mary's Hospital.*

Fred Harding, *City of London: Paternoster Row.*

John Harper, *Battersea.*

The Eyewitnesses

Reginald Harpur, *Sydenham Hill.*
W. G. Harries, *City of London: Gracechurch Street.*
Ambulance Supt. William Harrison, *Camberwell.*
William Hawkey, *Camberwell.*
Police Constable Cecil Heaysman, *City of London: Southwark Bridge.*
Station Officer S. J. Hender, LFS, *Lambeth Control.*
Mrs. Gladys Henley, *Bermondsey Town Hall.*
Percy Henley, Bermondsey: *Town Hall/Peek Frean's Factory.*
Station Officer Walter Henson, LFS, *Shoreditch.*
District Officer Thomas Hesketh, LFS, *Baker Street.*
Charles Hicks, *Westminster: Dean Street, Soho.*
Len Higgs, *Camden Town.*
Miss Annie Hill, *St. Marylebone.*
Bob Hill, *Battersea.*
Lieutenant Commander Kenneth Hoare, LFS, *Holborn Viaduct/Upper Thames Street.*
Edward Hobbs, *Westminster: Mayfair Court.*
Mrs. Edward Hobbs, *Westminster: Mayfair Court.*
Miss Sheila Hobbs, *Westminster: Mayfair Court.*
Lieutenant John Hodgkinson, *Westminster: Millbank.*
Leonard Holmes, *East Ham.*
Fireman Leslie Horton, LFS, *Lambeth: Fields' Factory/The Cut.*
The Hon. Sir Arthur Howard, Principal Warden of London, *Westminster Control.*
Mrs. Edward Huckstepp, *Kennington, Kent.*
C. G. Huddy, *Lambeth Hospital.*
Hauptmann Albert Hufenreuter, Luftwaffe: *No. 5 Wing, 53 Group.*
Harry Hughes, *Southwark Town Hall.*
Pilot Officer Andrew Humphrey, RAF, *266 Squadron, Wittering, Lincs.*
Mrs. Eleanor Humphries, *Blackheath.*
Miss Florence Hunt, *St. Marylebone.*
Miss Beatrice Hynes, *Acton.*

James Ireland, *St. Marylebone.*
Driver George Irish, *St. Pancras Station.*

Horace "Jacko" Jackson, *Battersea.*
Mrs. Minnie Jackson, *Camden Town.*
William Jacobs, *Lewisham.*
Squadron Leader Pat Jameson, RAF, *266 Squadron, Wittering, Lincs.*
Station Officer Richard Jewson, LFS, *City of London: Old Street.*

The Eyewitnesses

Chief Officer Arthur Johnstone, *Enfield Fire Brigade, Westminster Abbey/Queen Victoria Street.*

Storekeeper Arthur Jones, *Chelsea: St. Luke's Hospital.*

Nurse Monica Jones, *Knightsbridge.*

M. Eugene Kaufeler, *Westminster: Dorchester Hotel.*

Robert Kennedy, *South Croydon.*

Mrs. Rose Kenny, *Wood Green.*

Principal Officer Clement M. Kerr, LFS, *Westminster: Buckingham Palace/House of Commons.*

Ticket Collector William Kidd, *Liverpool Street Station.*

Anne Kingham, *St. Marylebone.*

R. B. Kingham, *St. Marylebone.*

Mrs. Nora Kirby, *Lewisham.*

District Officer Edward Kirrage, LFS, *City of London: Queen Victoria Street/Whitechapel.*

Arthur Knight, *Elephant and Castle.*

Wally Knight, *St. Marylebone: Queen's Hall.*

George Lambert, *Deptford.*

Leslie W. Lane, *Westminster: Old Compton Street, Soho.*

Dan Lawrence, *Bermondsey: Peek Frean's Factory.*

William Laycock, *Elephant and Castle.*

Charlie Lee, *St. Marylebone.*

Squadron Leader Cyril Leman, RAF, *HQ Fighter Command: Ops Room.*

Porter William Lester, *Chelsea: St. Luke's Hospital.*

Victor Lewis, *Wandsworth.*

House Governor David Lindsay, *Poplar Hospital.*

S. D. Lindsay, *Wimbledon.*

C. A. Linge, Clerk of Works, *City of London: St. Paul's.*

Jack Lippold, *Barnes.*

C. E. "Bert" Livings, *Battersea.*

Harold Lock Kendell, *South Croydon.*

Bert Lockett, *Finsbury.*

Geoffrey Lonsdale, *Camberwell.*

Percy Lovett, *Camberwell.*

Police Sergeant Alfred Lucas, *City of London: London Wall.*

Auxiliary Fireman Percy Madden, *Bermondsey: Peek Frean's Factory.*

Ernest Maidwell, *Dagenham.*

Charles H. Major, *Kensington.*

The Eyewitnesses

A. R. Malcolm, *Camberwell*.

Cecil A. Manning, *Camberwell*.

Albert Marotta, *Westminster: Alexandra Hotel*.

Assistant Stationmaster Frank Marshall, *King's Cross Station*.

Ronnie Marshall, *St. Marylebone*.

Arthur "Tich" Massara, *Westminster: Savoy Hotel*.

Reg Matthews, GPO, *City of London: Queen Victoria Street*.

Charles Mattock, *Westminster: Alexandra Hotel*.

Geoffrey Maxwell, *Paddington*.

Chief Superintendent Augustus May, *Whitehall: Home Office Fire Control*.

Leonard McColvin, *Westminster Control*.

E. D. McDowall, *Brixton: HQ Group 5, London Region*.

Margaret McGrath, *Westminster: Windmill Theatre*.

Assistant Surgeon John McLauchlan, *Poplar Hospital*.

C. L. Miles, *Wembley*.

Herbert S. Mills, *Westminster: Alexandra Hotel*.

Eric Mirams, *Kensington, Elvaston Place*.

Cyril Mitchell, *Westminster: Scott's Bar*.

Herbert F. Mitchell, *Aldgate*.

Captain Clifford Mollison, *HQ Fighter Command: Ops Room*.

Sub Officer Frederick Moon, LFS, *St. Marylebone*.

Arthur Moore, *City of London: Guildhall*.

John Morgan, *Deptford*.

Sydney Morgan, *Deptford*.

Edward Morris, *City of London: Upper Thames Street*.

Mrs. Edward Morris, *City of London: Upper Thames Street*.

Sir Parker Morris, *Westminster Control*.

Right Hon. Herbert Morrison, minister of home security, *Home Office, Whitehall*.

Dr. Barbara Morton, *Bermondsey Medical Mission Hospital*.

Dr. Herbert Moss, *Wandsworth*.

John Murphy, *City of London Control: Lloyd's Building*.

Francis R. Mulliss, *Greenwich*.

Supt. Bernard Nicholls, Anglican Pacifist Unit, *Westminster: Hungerford Arches*.

Jim Norman, *West Dulwich*.

Supt. Bill Norwood, LFS, *Westminster: House of Commons*.

Police Constable Reginald Oakes, *Westminster: Alexandra Hotel*.

275

The Eyewitnesses

John O'Connell, *Bermondsey*.

The Rev. Hubert D. Oliver, *Southwark: Old Kent Road*.

Superintendent Edward W. Overton, LFS, *Holborn/City of London: Farringdon Street*.

Frederick Pace, *Elephant and Castle*.

Kenneth Parker, *Kensington: HQ London Region*.

Ticket Collector Alfred Payne, *Liverpool Street Station*.

Tom Peace, *City of London: Unilever House*.

Ernie Pearson, *Hackney*.

Edward Penrose-Fitzgerald, *Kensington: Elvaston Place*.

Mrs. Isabel Penrose-Fitzgerald, *Kensington: Elvaston Place*.

Miss Joan Peters, *Kennington, Kent*.

Thomas Pharoah, *South Croydon*.

Auxiliary Fireman T. E. Phillips, LFS, *Millwall Docks*.

Wing Commander Thomas Pike, RAF, *219 Squadron, Tangmere*.

Assistant Matron Margaret Pirie, *Lambeth Hospital*.

Mrs. Monica Pitman, *Hampstead*.

Cyril R. Platten, *Edgware/Southwark Control*.

M. Campbell Pook, *Paddington*.

Mrs. Esther Prisant, *Stepney*.

Major William Pritchard, Salvation Army, *Southwark: St. George's Circus*.

Mrs. Florence Pritchard, *Southwark: St. George's Circus*.

Thomas H. Probert, *Westminster: Pimlico*.

Miss Rowena Quelch, *Kensington*.

Porter Walter Rainberg, *St. Pancras Station*.

Mrs. Ellen Raines, *Lewisham*.

Kennedy Reid, *Kensington*.

Leutnant Martin Reiser, Luftwaffe: *No. 9 Wing, 55 Group*.

Quentin Reynolds, *Westminster: Savoy Hotel*.

Squadron Leader "Dickie" Richardson, RAF, *HQ Fighter Command: Filter Room*.

Mrs. Alice Rickett, *Plaistow*.

Miss Diana Riviere, *Westminster: Millbank*.

Miss Denise Robins, *Westminster: Alexandra Hotel*.

Superintendent George Robinson, LFS, *Hammersmith/City of London: Queen Victoria Street—Aldgate*.

George Ronus, *Westminster: Dorchester Hotel*.

Yardmaster Dudley Rose, *West Ham: Temple Mills Sidings*.

The Eyewitnesses

Station Officer Frederick Rose, LFS, *Hammersmith.*
Mrs. Bertha Roston, *Stepney.*
Sub Officer Herbert Rous, LFS, *Westminster: House of Commons.*
Eric Rumsey, *Streatham.*
Mrs. Anne Russell, *Hampstead.*
Miss Patricia Russell, *Hampstead.*
Thomas Russell, *St. Marylebone: Queen's Hall.*
Police Constable Horace Rutter, *Leytonstone.*

Mrs. Disa Safey-Eldin, *Westminster: Soho.*
Mrs. Ettie St. Aubyn, *Lewisham.*
Miss Sheila St. Aubyn, *Lewisham.*
Mrs. Kathleen Sales, *Streatham.*
Assistant Matron Olive Sales, *Poplar Hospital.*
Temporary Fireman Conrad Sanders, LFS, *Westminster: Westminster Hall.*
Police Sergeant Fred Scaife, *City of London: Cannon Street.*
John K. Scott, *Camberwell.*
Mrs. Phyllis Scott, *St. Columbas (Church of Scotland) Pont Street.*
Ernest Seabrook, *Paddington Control.*
Jack Searle, *Battersea.*
Jimmie Sexton, *Lambeth: Fields' Factory.*
Nat Sharpe, *Islington.*
Miss Mary Shearburn, *Ditchley Park, Oxfordshire.*
Walter Sherrington, *St. Marylebone.*
William Sherrington, *Elephant and Castle.*
Police Sergeant Aubrey Shiers, *City of London: Fleet Street.*
Ticket Collector William Sibthorpe, *Liverpool Street Station.*
Miss Olga Silva, *Casa Prada Restaurant, St. Pancras.*
Private Arthur Simons, *St. Marylebone.*
Mrs. Rose Simons, *St. Marylebone.*
Station Officer Leslie Sinden, LFS, *Baker Street.*
Thomas Sinden, *Plaistow/Acton.*
Eileen Sloane, *St. Marylebone.*
Station Officer Arthur Smith, LFS, *Lambeth: Canterbury Music Hall.*
Chief Warden Edward Smith, *Poplar.*
Jack Smith, *Westminster: Alexandra Hotel.*
Mrs. Olive Smith, *Bayswater.*
Sidney H. Smith, *City of London: Martin's Bank, Lombard Street.*
Sidney Smith, *Paddington.*
Booking Clerk Jack Southgate, *King's Cross Station.*
John Spencer, *Paddington.*

The Eyewitnesses

District Officer George Spurrett, LFS, *Elephant and Castle.*
Louis Squersky, *Stepney.*
John Squires, *Westminster: Alexandra Hotel.*
Miss Marguerita Stahli, *West Dulwich.*
Driver Leslie Stainer, *Cannon Street Station.*
Station Officer Robert Stepney, LFS, *City of London: Upper Thames Street.*
Passenger Yard Inspector Jabez Stevens, *King's Cross Station.*
Mrs. Winifred Stockman, *St. Marylebone: Queen's Hall.*
Squadron Leader Whitney Straight, RAF, *242 Squadron, Martlesham, Suffolk.*
Percy Straus, *Westminster: Alexandra Hotel.*
Arrivals Foreman Ted Streeter, *Euston Station.*
Alderman Leonard J. Styles, *Elephant and Castle.*
John Sutton, *Westminster: Public Health Control.*
Station Officer William Sutton, LFS, *Goswell Road: Gordon's Gin Distillery.*
District Officer Bill Swanton, LFS, *Millwall Docks.*
Station Officer Terence Syrett, LFS, *Lambeth Palace.*

Albert Tagg, *Bermondsey: Peek Frean's Factory.*
Station Officer Harry Tanner, LFS, *Lambeth: Albert Embankment.*
Bob Taylor, *Westminster: Dolphin Square.*
Driver Charles Taylor, LPTB, *Baker Street/Elephant and Castle.*
Eddie Taylor, *Bermondsey Town Hall.*
Sub Officer Charles Tharby, West Ham Fire Brigade, *West Ham.*
Miss Frances Thirlby, *St. Pancras: National Temperance Hospital.*
District Officer Ernest Thomas, LFS, *Lambeth Control.*
Jack Thomas, *Stoke Newington.*
"Tommie Thompson," *City of London: St. Martin's-le-Grand.*
Detective Inspector Walter Thompson, *Ditchley Park, Oxon.*
Superintendent William Henry Thompson, LFS, *Lambeth: Fields' Factory/Waterloo.*
Station Officer Ronald Thorn, LFS, *Elephant and Castle.*
Police Constable Frederick Tibbs, *City of London: Queen Victoria Street Station.*
George Titcombe, *Hampstead.*
District Officer Cyril Tobias, LFS, *Whitechapel.*
C. F. Tomlinson, *HQ Port of London Authority.*
William Tompkins, *Croydon.*
Captain Cecil Townsend, *Chelsea: Royal Hospital.*
Charles C. Toye, *Westminster: Savoy Hotel.*

The Eyewitnesses

Mrs. Mabel Truncheon, *South Croydon.*
Major E. M. Turnbull, *Silverthorne Goods Yard, Wandsworth.*
Police Constable Abe Turner, *City of London: Cloak Lane.*
H. M. Turner, G.P.O., *City of London: Provincial House.*
Ernest Uphill, *Paddington.*

John N. Vautier, *City of London: Electra House, Moorgate.*
James C. Verdie, *Westminster: Alexandra Hotel.*
Theater Sister Margery Vickers, *Mile End Hospital, Stepney.*
Leutnant the Baron Walther Von Siber, Luftwaffe: *No. 3 Wing, 53 Group.*
Sub Officer John Waddingham, LFS, *Westminster: Pimlico.*
Gilbert Wadham, *Paddington.*
William Whaley, *Hampstead.*
Assistant District Railway Controller William Walton, *Kentish Town Control.*
Ann Ward, *Kennington, Kent.*
Edward Ward, *Kennington, Kent.*
Charles Warner, *Bermondsey.*
Dr. Philip Watkin, *Lambeth Hospital.*
Joan Watson, *St. Marylebone.*
Ruby Watson, *Bermondsey Medical Mission Hospital.*
Alec Watt, *Surrey Commercial Docks.*
Tommy Watts, *Lewisham.*
Miss Phyllis Wayne, *Harrow.*
Miss Violet Webb, *Hammersmith.*
Fred Webster, *Holborn.*
Signalman Stanley Weekes, *Kings Cross Station.*
Auxiliary Fireman Harry Weinstock, LFS, *City of London: Queen Victoria Street/St. Paul's.*
Norman Wells, *City of London: Unilever House.*
Colonel W. Thomas Wells, Salvation Army, *City of London: Queen Victoria Street.*
H. M. Westgate, *Battersea.*
The Reverend John Westlake, *Stepney.*
Police Constable George Wharton, *City of London: King Street.*
Edwin Wheeler, *East Ham.*
Harold Whetstone, *Blackheath.*
Dr. Charles White, *City of London Control: Lloyd's Building.*
Nat Williams, *Westminster: Alexandra Hotel.*
Eric Wills, *St. Marylebone.*

The Eyewitnesses

Lieutenant John Woodburne, RNVR, *London River: HMS Tower.*
Superintendent Alfred Wooder, LFS, *Southwark Bridge Road.*
Alec Woolfe, *Battersea.*
Victor Wootten, *Westminster: Lincoln's Inn.*
Mrs. Betty Wright, *Deptford.*
Harry Wright, *Finsbury.*
Flying Officer Robert Wright, RAF, *HQ Fighter Command.*

Mrs. Eileen Young, *St. Marylebone.*
Miss Nancy Young, *Lewisham.*
Section Officer Sadie Younger, *WAAF, HQ Fighter Command:
    Filter Room.*

Leading Fireman Morrie Zwaig, LFS, *Holborn: Theobalds Road.*